CONGRATULATIONS
—— ON YOUR ——
RETIREMENT

TED HEYBRIDGE

CONGRATULATIONS ON YOUR RETIREMENT

Summersdale Publishers Ltd
46 West Street
Chichester
West Sussex
PO19 1RP
UK

www.summersdale.com

Printed and bound in the Czech Republic

ISBN: 978-1-84953-624-0

Substantial discounts on bulk quantities of Summersdale books are available to corporations, professional associations and other organisations. For details contact Nicky Douglas by telephone: +44 (0) 1243 756902, fax: +44 (0) 1243 786300 or email: nicky@summersdale.com.

To......................................

From..................................

Whatever with the
past has gone,
The best is always
yet to come.

Lucy Larcom

Retirement is wonderful.
It's doing nothing without
worrying about getting
caught at it.

Gene Perret

There's never enough time to do all the nothing you want.

Bill Watterson

If you obey all the rules,
you miss all the fun.

Katharine Hepburn

A comfortable old
age is the reward of a
well-spent youth.

Maurice Chevalier

I am getting to an
age when I can only
enjoy the last sport left.
It is called hunting for
your spectacles.

Edward Grey

WEEKDAYS
ARE THE NEW
WEEKENDS!

How pleasant is the day
when we give up striving
to be young or slender.

William James

My only regret in life
is that I didn't drink
more champagne.

John Maynard Keynes

Youthfulness is about
how you live not when
you were born.

Karl Lagerfeld

Retire from work,
but not from life.

M. K. Soni

Age is not a particularly interesting subject. Anyone can get old. All you have to do is live long enough.

Groucho Marx

If you want a thing done well, get a couple of old broads to do it.

Bette Davis

GOODBYE TENSION –
HELLO PENSION!

To me, old age is always
15 years older than I am.

Bernard M. Baruch

The key to successful
ageing is to pay as little
attention to it as possible.

Judith Regan

Retirement at 65
is ridiculous. When I was
65 I still had pimples.

George Burns

When they tell me I'm
too old to do something,
I attempt it immediately.

Pablo Picasso

May your pockets be heavy
and your heart be light,
May good luck pursue you
each morning and night.

Irish blessing

The golden age is before us, not behind us.

William Shakespeare

WELCOME

TO YOUR ANNUAL

52-WEEK
HOLIDAY!

Youth is the gift of nature,
but age is a work of art.

Garson Kanin

You only live once,
but if you do it right,
once is enough.

Mae West

To succeed in life, you
need three things: a
wishbone, a backbone
and a funny bone.

Reba McEntire

First say to yourself
what you would be;
and then do what
you have to do.

Epictetus

I have found that if you love life, life will love you back.

Arthur Rubinstein

The trouble with retirement is that you never get a day off.

Abe Lemons

LET THE RELAXATION
BEGIN!

May you live all the
days of your life.

Jonathan Swift

You are only young once, but you can stay immature indefinitely.

Ogden Nash

Man's life is a progress,
and not a station.

Ralph Waldo Emerson

A wise man will make
more opportunities
than he finds.

Francis Bacon

Nobody can go back and
start a new beginning, but
anyone can start today
and make a new ending.

Maria Robinson

Don't simply retire
from something; have
something to retire to.

Harry Emerson Fosdick

HERE'S TO YOUR NEXT BIG ADVENTURE!

Learn from yesterday, live for today, hope for tomorrow. The important thing is not to stop questioning.

Albert Einstein

Live each day as if it were your last, and garden as though you will live forever.

Anonymous

A little nonsense now
and then
Is relished by the
wisest men.

English proverb

You can't help getting older, but you don't have to get old.

George Burns

To get back my youth
I would do anything in
the world, except take
exercise, get up early,
or be respectable.

Oscar Wilde

When you get to
retirement, you switch
bosses – from the one who
hired you to the one
who married you.

Gene Perret

IT'S TIME TO PUT YOUR FEET UP!

May you live as long
as you want,
And never want as long
as you live.

Irish blessing

The more side roads
you stop to explore, the
less likely that life will
pass you by.

Robert Brault

The past is a guidepost,
not a hitching post.

L. Thomas Holdcroft

You can't turn back
the clock but you can
wind it up again.

Bonnie Prudden

We're fools whether
we dance or not, so we
might as well dance.

Japanese proverb

Age is strictly a case
of mind over matter;
if you don't mind, it
doesn't matter.

Mark Twain

TIME TO
BREAK OUT THAT
WISH LIST!

The older we get, the better we used to be.

John McEnroe

If you enjoy living, it is not difficult to keep the sense of wonder.

Ray Bradbury

People are always asking
about the good old days. I
say, why don't you say the
good now days?

Robert M. Young

Let us celebrate the occasion with wine and sweet words.

Plautus

We do not stop playing because we grow old, we grow old because we stop playing.

Benjamin Franklin

There's one thing I always wanted to do before I quit: retire!

Groucho Marx

LIVING 'LA VIDA LOAFER'!

Growing old is compulsory,
growing up is optional.

Bob Monkhouse

I'm not interested in age.
People who tell me their
age are silly. You're as
old as you feel.

Elizabeth Arden

The more you praise
and celebrate your life,
the more there is in
life to celebrate.

Oprah Winfrey

They say that age is all in your mind. The trick is keeping it from creeping down into your body.

Anonymous

When a man retires, his wife gets twice the husband but only half the income.

Chi Chi Rodriguez

How old would you be
if you didn't know how
old you were?

Satchel Paige

HAKUNA MATATA
MEANS – NO MORE
WORRIES!

Tell me, what is it you
plan to do with your one
wild and precious life?

Mary Oliver

Beautiful young people
are accidents of nature,
but beautiful old people
are works of art.

Eleanor Roosevelt

If people concentrated
on the really important
things in life, there'd be a
shortage of fishing poles.

Doug Larson

How beautiful it is
to do nothing, and then
to rest afterward.

Spanish proverb

Every man is the architect of his own fortune.

Appius Claudius Caecus

Age is only a number,
a cipher for the records.
A man can't retire his
experience. He must use it.

Bernard M. Baruch

SET YOUR ALARM CLOCK TO 'WHO CARES?'

How blest is he
who crowns,
in shades like these,
A youth of labour
with an age of ease!

Oliver Goldsmith

Take rest; a field that
has rested gives a
bountiful crop.

Ovid

Age is a matter of feeling, not of years.

George William Curtis

Is the glass half-full,
or half-empty? It depends
on whether you're pouring,
or drinking.

Bill Cosby

I've been attending lots of seminars in my retirement. They're called naps.

Merri Brownworth

Eventually you will reach a point when you stop lying about your age and start bragging about it.

Will Rogers

I DON'T WANT TO –
I DON'T HAVE TO –
YOU CAN'T MAKE ME!
I'M RETIRED.

Here's to the corkscrew
– a useful key to unlock
the storehouse of wit, the
treasury of laughter, the
front door of fellowship, and
the gate of pleasant folly.

W. E. P. French

The three ages of man:
youth, middle age, and
'My word you do look well.'

June Whitfield

If wrinkles must be
written upon our brows,
let them not be written
upon the heart.

James A. Garfield

There is a whole
new kind of life ahead...
Some call it retirement.
I call it bliss.

Betty Sullivan

When it comes to old age we're all in the same boat, only some of us have been aboard a little longer.

Leo Probst

It's 4.58 on Friday afternoon. Do you know where your margarita is?

Amy Neftzger

OLD ENOUGH TO
RETIRE – BUT
NOT OLD ENOUGH
TO KNOW
BETTER.

One of the good things about getting older is you find you're more interesting than most of the people you meet.

Lee Marvin

I don't feel old. I don't feel anything till noon. That's when it's time for my nap.

Bob Hope

The key to retirement is to find joy in the little things.

Susan Miller

A bottle of wine contains
more philosophy than all
the books in the world.

Louis Pasteur

I used to think I'd like less grey hair. Now I'd like more of it.

Richie Benaud

I'll keep swivelling my hips
until they need replacing.

Tom Jones

RETIREMENT:
WHEN YOU STOP
LIVING AT WORK
AND START WORKING
AT LIFE.

A great pleasure in life
is doing what people
say you cannot do.

Walter Bagehot

Retirement is like...
Las Vegas. Enjoy it to
the fullest, but not so
fully that you run out
of money.

Jonathan Clements

Just remember, when you're over the hill, you begin to pick up speed.

Charles M. Schulz

Now that I'm over 60,
I'm veering toward
respectability.

Shelley Winters

Age is just a number. It's totally irrelevant unless, of course, you happen to be a bottle of wine.

Joan Collins

I'm not sure that old age
isn't the best part of life.

C. S. Lewis

YOUNG AT HEART –

SLIGHTLY OLDER IN OTHER PLACES!

Retirement means no pressure, no stress, no heartache... unless you play golf.

Gene Perret

As we grow older, our bodies get shorter and our anecdotes longer.

Robert Quillen

Happiness grows at our own firesides, and is not to be picked in strangers' gardens.

Douglas William Jerrold

When grace is joined with wrinkles, it is adorable. There is an unspeakable dawn in happy old age.

Victor Hugo

There is no pleasure worth forgoing just for an extra three years in the geriatric ward.

John Mortimer

Just the simple act of
tasting a glass of wine
is its own event.

David Hyde Pierce

SCRIMP, SAVE, INDULGE OR RAVE – THE CHOICE IS YOURS!

One ought, every day at least, to hear a little song, read a good poem, see a fine picture, and, if it were possible, to speak a few reasonable words.

Johann Wolfgang von Goethe

The ageing process has you firmly in its grasp if you never get the urge to throw a snowball.

Doug Larson

There is no physician
in your retirement years
like a true friend.

Anonymous

Fun is like
life insurance; the
older you get, the
more it costs.

Kin Hubbard

I'm happy to report
that my inner child is
still ageless.

James Broughton

The key to a happy retirement is to have enough money to live on, but not enough to worry about.

Anonymous

TAKE NEXT LEFT FOR EASY STREET.

Anyone who keeps
the ability to see beauty
never grows old.

Franz Kafka

I still find each day too short for all the thoughts I want to think, all the walks I want to take... and all the friends I want to see.

John Burroughs

Laughter doesn't
require teeth.

Bill Newton

Older people shouldn't
eat health food, they need
all the preservatives
they can get.

Robert Orben

If I am doing nothing, I like to be doing nothing to some purpose. That is what leisure means.

Alan Bennett

In your retirement years never drink coffee at lunch; it will keep you awake in the afternoon.

Anonymous

RETIRED,
HAPPY, WILD AND FREE!

Men chase golf balls
when they're too old to
chase anything else.

Groucho Marx

No man loves life like him that's growing old.

Sophocles

Wisdom doesn't necessarily come with age. Sometimes age just shows up all by itself.

Tom Wilson

Wish not so much to live
long as to live well.

Benjamin Franklin

Plans are nothing;
planning is everything.

Dwight D. Eisenhower

When men reach their sixties and retire, they go to pieces. Women go right on cooking.

Gail Sheehy

CARPE EMERITUS!

(SEIZE RETIREMENT!)

The problem with a
treadmill is that the ice
falls out of your glass.

Martin Mull

I still have a full deck;
I just shuffle slower now.

Anonymous

No man is ever old
enough to know better.

Holbrook Jackson

The future belongs to
those who believe in the
beauty of their dreams.

Eleanor Roosevelt

Whenever the talk
turns to age, I say I am
49 plus VAT.

Lionel Blair

Fan the sinking flame
of hilarity with the wing
of friendship; and pass
the rosy wine.

Charles Dickens

OFFICIALLY RETIRED.

Three o'clock is always
too late or too early for
anything you want to do.

Jean-Paul Sartre

It's sad to grow old,
but nice to ripen.

Brigitte Bardot

Not a shred of evidence
exists in favour of the idea
that life is serious.

Brendan Gill

There is life
after retirement,
and it is better.

Catherine Pulsifer

If you're interested in finding out more about our books, find us on Facebook at **Summersdale Publishers** and follow us on Twitter at **@Summersdale**.

www.summersdale.com

W9-ANA-210

I Remember, I Remember

Other Books by André Maurois

I Remember,
I Remember

By

André Maurois

Translated from the French by
DENVER and JANE LINDLEY

HARPER & BROTHERS *Publishers*

New York *and* London

I REMEMBER, I REMEMBER

CONTENTS

NOTE: Minor changes, additions and omissions have been made in the text of this book since its translation. The present text, therefore, does not agree in all particulars with the French, but there has been no alteration in meaning.

ANDRÉ MAUROIS

I Remember, I Remember

CHAPTER I

The Earthly Paradise

L AST night I made up my mind to write the story of my life. For
several days my wife and I have been living at a college in California. From my window I see a Spanish patio planted with palms and
cypresses where, books in hand, pretty American college girls stroll;
beyond the roofs of the college, giant eucalyptus trees with long gashes
in their trunks like martyrs' backs slashed by the executioner; and in
the background, above the pale foliage, the sharp contours of the
California hills, resembling in their clean lines the mountains of
Greece. The sky has been blue ever since we arrived; it will remain
clear all summer. How different this trustworthy climate is from the
capricious valley of the Seine where I spent my childhood; and
what strange events have been needed to transform that provincial
child, heir to Norman spinning and weaving mills, into a quinqua-
genarian professor on the Pacific coast!

In the next room someone is playing one of Bach's *Toccatas.* I recognize Miss Wang, a dainty, graceful and exquisite Chinese, who hands
me such charming compositions whenever she can write about music.
Two nuns enter the patio. One of them, Sister Agnes-Rita, teaches
French in a nearby convent; yesterday she gave me a brilliant and
sound appraisal of François Mauriac; her waxen face framed in a
white coif gave her the appearance of a portrait by Philippe de
Champaigne; her solid discourse seemed founded upon centuries of
theology and wisdom. The pretty blonde who greets the nuns with a
smile is Marion Morris of Salt Lake City, daughter and grand-daughter
of Mormons; she spent some years in Paris and speaks lovingly of the

Rue Jacob with its ancient courts and wrought-iron balconies. The soft-eyed brunette is Bettina Schuster, an exile from Vienna, who learned in Geneva the elegant and classic French of Rousseau and Amiel. It would not surprise me if she had genius; but I am a professor who is passionately in love with his calling and is always tempted to believe he has discovered a masterpiece the instant he recognizes the accents of sincerity.

Yesterday was my fifty-sixth birthday. I am approaching the sixties, that is, old age; and I feel, alas, that my heart is as young, my mind as new, as in the days when our master Alain in Rouen first threw open to us the world of ideas. Last night the girls of Mills College presented a sketch they had composed in honor of my birthday. The setting was a library. Midnight sounded. On the stroke, the heroes and heroines of my books—Colonel Bramble, Shelley, Byron, Philippe Marcenat, Odile, Lyautey, Denise Herpain, Bernard Quesnay—suddenly came to life and spoke. "There," I thought, listening to them with emotion, "there you have what is left of a life and a life's work."

A little later, when I had returned to my room, it occurred to me that a legend sometimes survives as well as a surprising, unreal being, whom I have called the Personage. The Personage is the man others believe we are or have been. He may be multiple. Two different personages, contradictory and even hostile to each other, may survive us in the minds of our friends and our enemies, to continue after our death a struggle in which our posthumous reputation is the stake. If we have been complex, reticent, mysterious, or simply honest, a whole army of Personages may carry on endless battles to gain the right of representing us, and the combat continues up to the moment when impartial oblivion puts these bellicose marionettes to bed together in the same box and locks it up forever. "In my case," I thought, "oblivion will come quickly. But today the clash of feelings is so violent that before eternal silence descends there may spring from me several very astonishing Personages. Some will be better than I, others worse. If I am to be loved or hated, at least I should like the hatred or sympathy to be for the real man. Why don't I try to depict him as I think I have known him?"

In that instant, on the night of my fifty-sixth birthday, while the breeze from the Pacific swayed the eucalyptus leaves beneath the stars, I decided to write the story of my difficult life in a direct, unromanticized form. Naturally, like every biographer, I shall make mistakes, some through fault of memory, others through fault of judgment. I hope, however, that if some leisured man of learning or some student in search of a thesis should ever attempt to disentangle the truth and poetry in this book, he will find few serious omissions or culpable complacencies. I shall not mask any of my faults. If I am conscious in all humility of my mistakes and weaknesses, I remember too, with pleasure, those moments, of which there have been not a few in my life, when I have deliberately sacrificed my own interests for what I deemed to be my duty. In choosing that duty I may have been mistaken. But that is not a mortal sin in the eyes of God, nor in those of the honest reader. The man I am going to portray for you is the man I was or the one I believe myself to have been. Forgive him his trespasses, good people, as he himself forgives all those who have trespassed against him.

My earliest memory is that of Sunday mornings in Elbeuf when I was four or five years old. The town used to be awakened by the bugles of the fire department. They would come down our street once a week, wearing antiquated helmets and hauling a hand pump, in order to test the hydrant. They always played the same tune: "As-tu vu, la casquette, la casquette . . . As-tu vu la casquette au Pèr' Bugeaud? . . ."[1] but this martial reveille never failed to delight me. My father would come in, pick me up in his arms, wrapping my long nightgown around my bare feet, and find a place for me beside him at the window. The fire chief, recognizable by his red plume, would shout to us, "Good morning, gentlemen!" To see the hose being unrolled, the powerful jet of water that rose higher than the house, the frail ladder that was hoisted, section by section, to the roofs, seemed to me the finest spectacle in the world. Then the ladder would be

[1] Have you seen the cap, have you seen the cap. . . . Have you seen the cap of Pèr' Bugeaud?

slid back into place, the hose would be rolled up again on its drum, the chief with the copper helmet would order: "Fall in!" the firemen would form a column of two's, the bugler would play *La Casquette*, and the company would set off in time to the music toward the next hydrant.

"They march like conscripts," my father would say, tucking the shivering little boy back into his still-warm bed.

That was the comment of an old soldier.

He had a passion for things military. A native of Alsace, he had seen the war of 1870, and at the age of seventeen had tended the French wounded on the battlefield of Froeschwiller. Later he had done his service in the infantry at Limoges, and had then become a scrupulous non-commissioned officer whose fine handwriting was the pride and joy of the sergeant major. As soon as my sisters and I could walk, he began drilling us and would make us keep step by singing marching songs. "My tunic has one button, march, march!" he would commence, and we had to reply "My tunic has one button, march, march!" . . . "March briskly, march briskly, together we march briskly," my father would go on, and we would thus get up to fifty or a hundred buttons. The first book I learned to read was a history of the war of 1870: *Frenchmen and Germans* by Dick de Lonlay. The names of Borny, of Rezonville, of Saint-Privat, of Gravelotte used to evoke in my mind confused, sanguinary and tragic pictures; those of Chanzy and Gambetta ideas of revenge and pride.

It is often said that those persons who remain optimists all their lives and, despite trials and tribulations, maintain their confidence in life, are the ones who have had the good fortune to enjoy a happy childhood. My case would support this theory. Few men have felt a keener and more lasting admiration for their parents than I. Even today when I think about them and compare them with the thousands of persons I have known, I can clearly see that they were superior in point of moral worth to almost all the others. My father, an unselfish man, brave, discreet, and appealingly modest, had four passions: France, Alsace, his mill and his family. As far as he was concerned the rest of the universe hardly existed.

Scrupulous to a fault, he used to tire out the local tax commission and the customs authorities by the meticulous detail of his declarations. One of the lessons he taught me, as soon as I was able to understand, was respect for laws and regulations. Later, when the income tax had been enacted and he would hear rich friends talk complacently about their ingenious and culpable frauds, he would become violently angry. His timidity, which was great and which made his conversation abrupt, nervous and difficult, would immediately vanish the moment his convictions were threatened. He had formed the most exacting conception of his duties and held himself responsible both for the quality of the products of the mill and the well-being of the workmen. If all captains of industry had lived and thought as he did the *bourgeoisie* would have become a respected aristocracy.

· · · · · · ·

My father, Ernest Herzog, was born in the Alsatian village of Ringendorf. He did well in his classes at the College of Bouxwiller and then, at the age of sixteen, entered the mill owned by his mother's brothers, the Uncles Fraenckel, at Bischwiller. This prosperous and well managed woolen mill employed at that time four hundred workmen. The defeat of 1871 created a difficult situation for my family as for so many others in Alsace. They had to make a choice. My great uncles and my father of course chose France. A short exploration convinced them that Elbeuf, a small industrial town near Rouen, was the closest French equivalent to Bischwiller in character and in products; they determined to move their mills there. It was an adventurous undertaking. My father, though still quite young, remained behind for a year in the Alsatian mill to complete its liquidation and at that time gave evidence of his great capacity for work and management. He arranged, despite immense difficulties, for the departure and journey of the four hundred workmen. Then he too came to live in Normandy. But nothing ever consoled him for having had to leave Alsace. Our house was full of engravings showing the cathedral of Strasbourg, storks nesting on gabled roofs, and girls with straw-colored hair tied with immense black ribbons. Every year the Alsatians in Elbeuf gathered for a big celebration at which they would sing their native songs and dance Alsatian dances. At such times I would see tears in my parents' eyes.

On Christmas eve we would always go to the Protestant church—whose pastor, Monsieur Roerich, was an Alsatian—to join in a Christmas tree party. The little white, red and blue candles, the tinsel, the gilded walnuts, the imitation snow thrilled me. Everyone there would sing: "Oh beautiful pine tree, king of the forest," and on the way home my father would describe the pine forests of Alsace in their mantles of snow. It was at one of these Christmas parties, when I was five or six years old, that I learned from another child, who was beside me in the church, that my parents were Jews and that this was an astonishing fact.

For a long time I had recited every evening, before going to sleep, a prayer that began with unfamiliar and incomprehensible words and ended: "God bless papa, mama, my grandmother at Elbeuf, my grandmother in Paris, my little sisters, my aunts, my cousins, my friends, Marie and Emily (these were the cook and the chambermaid) and everyone I love . . ." I thought the other children prayed in the same way. For a year my mother had given me Bible lessons, but I had never dreamed that there could be any connection between me, a little French boy born in Elbeuf, and a people who crossed the Red Sea in the midst of the waters, saw their food in the desert descend from Heaven, and conversed with God on the fiery summits of mountains. On Christmas night when I asked my father about my friend's comments, he told me that we were indeed Jews, but that Pastor Roerich's Christianity was a beautiful religion, too, the close relative and daughter of ours. The subject seemed to me to be exhausted and I thought no more about it for a long time.

My mother brought us up entirely herself and at the age of four taught me to read. Member of an Alsatian family like my father, she had gone to school in Paris. Prize books with gilt edges proved that she had been a good scholar. She wrote and spoke a pure classic French. While I was still a child one of my keenest pleasures was to hear Maman read poetry aloud, especially when the poem was sentimental, heroic and sad. I asked again and again for *Les Pauvres Gens* by Victor Hugo and two poems by Déroulède which must be in *The Soldier's Songs.* One was the *Death of the Bugler* in which each couplet terminated after the refrain: "The bugle call still sounds," by a bugle sounding the charge, each time more breathless and abrupt; of the other I remember only the beginning: "He was a lad, seventeen at most,—With long blond hair and clear blue eyes . . ." Perhaps these poems were very bad; I do not want to know and I have never reread them; they gave me my first literary emotions. I could not hear them without weeping. But these tears bore no resemblance to my tears of rage or fear; they were sweet and comforting and I think they made me better.

One remarkable characteristic of my mother was her exclusive and absorbing affection for her family. Her parents, her four sisters who lived in Paris, her husband, her children sufficed to fill her universe. She was inclined to be unsociable, not through disdain, but through indifference. My father, at the time of his arrival in Elbeuf, had made a great many friends in the industrial world of Normandy through the esteem which his character immediately inspired. In his youth he had been very gay. Because he had a good singing voice he had been received into the small local society of amateurs that staged popular operettas: *The Bells of Corneville, The Musketeers in the Convent, The Daughter of Madame Angot.* He knew them by heart and I can still see that dear form upright beside the piano whenever I hear songs from those operettas: "When you conspire . . ." or "Three times around the world I've gone . . ." After his marriage he had little by little ceased to see his friends, and Maman never invited anyone to dine at our home except "the Family." The latter, however, were numerous.

My father had two brothers. My Uncle Edmond was a short, thick-set, powerful and energetic man with walrus mustaches. He had been in the light infantry and always countered my father's military airs with the chasseur's marching song, *Sidi Brahim.* Like my father he had entered the Uncles' mill and, as will be seen, played a role of the first importance there. My Uncle Henry, who had a brilliant and paradoxical mind, had graduated with honors from the Polytechnique, and during the time of my childhood was State Civil Engineer at Guéret. From time to time he appeared like a brilliant meteor and was pointed out to me as an example. About 1895 he was named engineer at Dieppe quite close to us, and built there an ocean break-water, pounded by the waves, of which his brothers and nephews were very proud. Later he became Inspector General of Roads and Bridges and constructed for the Navy part of the Port of Toulon. He was, like my father, an enthusiast for things military but in a quite different manner. It was he who first said to me: "There's a man of genius in the French army, Lieutenant Colonel Foch," and who gave me *The Principles of War* the instant the book was published.

Uncle Henry loved to tell stories. His favorite was an Alsatian tale in which the Bad Wolf gains admittance to a house full of children in their mother's absence and devours them all save the one to whom the story happens to be told on that particular day. Toward the end of his life, after I had already published several books, my uncle timidly showed me the manuscripts of detective novels which he had been writing all his life. He had invented—before Conan Doyle but after Gaboriau—a character called Anthime Bonnardel who might have been the French Sherlock Holmes. I recall one of his ingenious inventions was a door latch held in place by a cake of ice. When the cake had melted it appeared that the door had been opened from the inside, a circumstance which misplaced by several hours the time of the crime and completely misled the police, but not the inspired Bonnardel.

My father and my uncles all three had an exacting and lofty moral code. I have rarely encountered characters like theirs except among the Unitarians and the Quakers. They had had, as my father later told me, a Protestant grandmother, and perhaps they inherited from her the puritanism of which they were so proud. In their eyes the families which became allied to ours remained unworthy aliens. They called their brothers- and sisters-in-law "imported goods," or "ducks' eggs," and treated them with affectionate and disdainful con-descension. Of their two sisters only one, Caroline, shared their cult;

the other, my Aunt Marie, was an ancient and inhuman spinster whose house fascinated and terrified me at the same time. She lived there with one of the Uncles Fraenckel, Uncle Adolphe, who had had a stroke at about the age of fifty, had recovered, but had spent his time since then stretched out on a sofa from morning till night reading the *History of France* by Henri Martin and the *Consulate and the Empire* by Monsieur Thiers.

Aunt Marie was disfigured by a hare-lip which made her a kind of monster; she was so conscious of this fact that the shades in her house were always drawn. Lithe forms glided about in the twilight, her cats. She raised whole litters of them. Every floor was covered with saucers of milk and skeletons of fish; all the rooms smelled of cat. That odor made my gorge rise as soon as I entered the house. At the same time I was frightened because I knew I would be led up to Uncle Adolphe's couch and that he would pinch my cheek, put down his volume of Henri Martin and question me about the kings of France. For this examination, which the darkness, the smell, and the disabled old man rendered terrifying, my mother had prepared me as best she could. Despite these many causes of fear, I liked to go to Aunt Marie's house because of a certain inkwell in the form of a doghouse. If one pressed on the dog's head the roof of the house flew open, revealing the ink. This bit of magic filled me with admiration. I could press the dog's head twenty times and always get the same pleasure. Later on, when Uncle Adolphe died, an elderly cousin named Albert, with whom the family did not know what to do, was given orders to go and live with Aunt Marie. They detested each other, but dared not rebel against a decision of "the Uncles" and lived together for twenty years with refinements of hatred that would have delighted Balzac.

But these visits were brief and infrequent. We spent most of our time, my sister Marguerite and I, alone with Maman or left to our own devices in the garden, which for me was the scene of varied and stirring adventures. At the end of the garden was a lilac with a forked trunk on whose branches I read the tales of Perrault and Andersen, all of the *Pink Library*, all of Jules Vernes and *The War of Tomorrow* by Captain Danrit. In one corner there was a rabbit hutch out of which I made a fort and there I dug trenches and played war games by myself. I was thinking of our garden in Elbeuf when I wrote in *Climats* about the childhood of Philippe Marcenat. Once a week the laundress, an old Alsatian woman, would come to boil the linen in a hot and mysterious wash house, whose very name *buanderie* sounded evil to me. I loved to see the deposits of soap that formed at the bottom of the wooden wash tub and to touch its soft and slippery sides. Sometimes, too, I would work with the gardener who planted our flower beds, as was customary at Elbeuf, with a center of begonias or geraniums and a border in forget-me-nots or heliotrope. Toward the end of summer the sawyer would come to prepare our winter supply of wood. His work fascinated me. The noise of the saw, the clean country smell of the wood, the sawdust which formed a thick soft mattress on the ground, the exciting instant when the log, completely cut through, parted and fell into two pieces, all this constituted a spectacle of which I never tired.

The events that broke the monotony of our days were petty. When there was to be "company for dinner" we would lie in wait for the arrival of the pastry man who always brought the same vanilla and strawberry *bombe glacé* in the shape of a truncated cone surmounted by a rose-colored ball, and the same plates of *petits fours*: glazed walnuts with pistachios, candied chestnuts, stuffed dates and tiny chocolate *éclairs*. When my parents went to the theater, which happened two or three times a year when a traveling company stopped at Elbeuf, they would bring us home a bag of candy bearing, as long as they lasted, the name of the play:

"The *Malade imaginaires* are good," we used to say, "but the *Demi-Mondes* were better . . ."

One day my parents went to see *The Surprises of Divorce*, and the same evening the hairdresser of Elbeuf in an access of jealousy shot his wife with a revolver. The two events became confused in my mind and for a long time I believed that a divorce was a pistol duel fought on the stage of the Municipal Theater. In a child's mind words are not well defined; they designate zones of emotion more or less extensive and not clearly bounded; in this respect many adults remain children all their lives.

On Twelfth Night in Normandy crowds of children with lighted lanterns used to come to all the doors and sing:

> Bon Dieu, allumez du feu,
> Donnez-nous la part à Dieu!
> Il fait si froid dehors
> Que mon camarade en tremble,
> Bon Dieu, allumez du feu,
> Donnez-nous la part à Dieu![2]

We would open the windows and hand them *sous* and presents. I can still see those boys shivering and happy in the lantern light against the blackness of the streets which gave the scene the chiaroscuro of a Rembrandt. I envied them and would have liked to go about with them begging alms "for the Lord's sake," but we weren't allowed to do it.

Once a year in September there would be the opening of the Elbeuf Fair. How magnificent it seemed to me! We lived close by the Fair Grounds, and in the evening a symphony of carnival sounds would pour into my bedroom. The calliope of the merry-go-round would blend with the clicking of the lottery wheels, the bells of the cake vendors, the reports from the rifle gallery, the cries of the barkers and the roars of the wild animals. Each year it was a question of vital interest to know "*who* was coming to the Fair." Two large menageries, Bidel and Pezon, used to alternate, and we would talk about the great animal trainers the way music lovers discuss the merits of famous singers. We knew the names of Monsieur Bidel's children and followed, from September to September, their progress in the dangerous art of exhibiting lions and tigers. The circus brought with it its healthy stable smell, the girl horseback riders—and tightrope dancers who

[2] In the Lord's name light a fire,
For the Lord's sake give us alms.
Here my friend must stand and shiver
Unprotected in the cold.
In the Lord's name light a fire,
For the Lord's sake give us alms.

were my first loves. From the booths where gingerbread and nougat were sold we would get unexpected presents and glorious cases of indigestion, especially when, stuffed with sweetmeats, we would clamber onto the giant wooden horses which careened forward at a slow and unnatural gallop. When later on I derived such keen pleasure from *Petrushka* and from the *ritournelles* which, in Stravinsky's music, dominate the noises of the festival, it was because I remembered the Elbeuf Fair.

The Cattle Fair, also, was held below our windows in the same square, bordered by chestnut trees. On the morning of that day we would be wakened by the mooing of cows, the whinnying of horses and the bleating of sheep. We would run to the window. Peasants with sticks or whips in their hands would be bustling among the animals. It was one of our rare contacts with country life. We knew scarcely anything of the fields, the farm's activity, or the tilling of the soil. Our walks as children were limited to the roads that led from Elbeuf toward the uplands and to the woods that bordered those roads. These short walks were enlivened by flower picking. In the spring the forests of Normandy were full of primroses, anemones, cowslips, and periwinkles. We would make bright delicate bunches of them which we clutched so tightly that they withered in our hands before we got home.

"Throw away your flowers," Maman would say to me as we came into town. "Don't you see they are dead? . . ."

I was to discover in the course of my life that the most coveted joys of life die as soon as they are gathered, like the anemones of my childhood. But at that time my hopes were irrepressible and the fate of my flowers never kept me next day from picking another bunch. When I try to recall the long-haired child that used to climb the banks and look for blackberries among the bushes, I find nothing but happy memories. What a peaceful life had been arranged for us, and how little we knew of the world and its ways!

The Tree of Knowledge

WHENEVER, in the course of our walks, we would catch sight from the hilltops of the town of Elbeuf, stretching along the bank of the Seine, I used to experience a sudden shock of joy. A line of chalk cliffs, topped by fields and woods, outlined the gentle and graceful curve of the river which was framed, on the other bank, by poplars and willows. From the town rose innumerable thin chimneys, slender pagan minarets of industry, from which ascended columns of smoke. Reservoirs of green water sparkled between the roofs of orange tile or bluish slate. We made a game of searching among all these houses and factories for *the* mill, my father's. Before long we would recognize it by its long courtyard between two parallel buildings, one for spinning, the other for finishing, and by the huge weaving mill six stories high. It made us proud to see how big it was. At noon and at seven o'clock when the workers left, we would stand amazed at these floods of men and women that suddenly filled Elbeuf's usually placid streets. Another thing we loved to look at was the torrential streams of blue, yellow and red that flowed from the dye works.

Transplanted to the soil of Normandy, the Alsatian mill had not wasted away. Quite the contrary, it had grown with surprising rapidity. About 1890 it employed more than a thousand workers. When I used to spell out the gold letters engraved on a plaque of black marble in front of the main entrance, I was surprised and hurt not to find my father's name. The firm name was FRAENCKEL-BLIN, and the other large mill in Elbeuf, which had also come from Bischwiller, was named BLIN & BLIN. "F-B and B-B" is what the people of Elbeuf called them. In *Bernard Quesnay* I have depicted the fierce rivalry between the two firms. Nevertheless the Fraenckels and the Blins were cousins and outwardly kept up friendly relations. Actually they fought each other for trade with vigor and bitterness. The firm of Blin was the older by twenty years, having been founded under the First Empire, and considered itself superior in the industrial aristocracy to the firm of Fraenckel. On the other hand, the latter was growing faster. Once when I was looking at this plaque I asked my father:

"But, Papa, why not FRAENCKEL & HERZOG?"

From the look of suffering which came over his face I realized that I had blundered upon a forbidden subject. Here is the story, which I did not learn until much later. My father and his brother Edmond were by unanimous consent the two most competent technicians in the mill. My father managed the weaving with his characteristic thoroughness; he knew each of the workmen, the performance of each loom; he was constantly searching for ways of improving the product and reducing the cost. My Uncle Edmond was the salesman; he went to Paris every week and brought back the orders that enabled the mills to run. But actual heads though they were of this large business, these two men were neither the founders nor the legal heads, and they submitted, my father with resignation and despair, his brother with indignation and impatience, to a patriarchal tyranny—that of the "Uncles."

In our eyes the Uncles were awe-inspiring, mysterious and sinister divinities. There had been five Fraenckel brothers: Emil, Wilhelm, Adolphe, Louis and Henry. Emil and Wilhelm had died before I was born and the family inflicted their names on me. I have mentioned Adolphe reading Henri Martin on his couch. "Monsieur Louis," as he was called by the personnel, was, during my childhood, absolute sovereign. He lived beside the mill and had his house so constructed that his own apartment communicated by an interior staircase with the offices. This architectural device was a symbol. "Monsieur Louis" had no private life apart from that of the mill. Clothed perpetually in a black alpaca jacket and wearing a black silk cap, his chin framed in a little collar of bristly beard, he spent his life in the Warehouse where the finished lengths of cloth were stored. Nothing in the world existed for him except wool and cloth and machinery. When my mother used to take me timidly to the mill, he would stare at the material in which she was dressed, would finger it and say: "This comes (or does not come) from us." Then he would pay no further attention to her. "Monsieur Henry" was scarcely more human. He had married one of my mother's aunts, Aunt Eulalie, a fact that made him doubly related to us. This Aunt Eulalie was my grandmother's sister and had acquired the same delightful culture, but in the end she had accustomed herself to being regarded by the Uncles (her own husband included) as an accessory not essential to manufacturing and therefore without interest, and led a completely vegetative existence.

The Uncles knew their business too well not to realize that the Herzog brothers were the heart and soul of the firm. Accordingly they had kept promising them since 1880 that they would both be made partners as soon as the deed of partnership was redrawn. But "Madame Louis," who had a jealous and exclusive love for her direct descendants, had vowed that her own son should become a partner before her nephews Ernest and Edmond. This son, Paul Fraenckel, was a brilliant fellow and had made an excellent record at the Lycée of Rouen; he was several years younger than my father. By making scenes she had succeeded in forcing her husband to agree to this injustice. In order to effectuate it without open conflict with his nephews, whom he needed and of whom he was fond in his rough way, he had had a new deed of partnership drawn up in secret by a lawyer from out of town; in this deed he had inserted the name of his eldest son, and to conceal the maneuver he had had the deed published in a distant agricultural county in an obscure paper which nobody read. For several years he had succeeded in keeping his nephews in ignorance of this trick. Then one day, quite by accident, my father discovered the disgrace.

The customs of the family were so completely patriarchal that the mill at this time did not even have a cashier. The Uncles, my father and his brother, each had a key to the safe and took out of it the money for their personal or business needs, writing down in a ledger what they had taken. They all left in the business the rest of what they earned and they took no interest whatever on their capital. It was the tacit agreement that the expenses of each should represent approximately the interest on his own current account. But such calculations were by no means exact. My father, because such was his nature, always took out less than the others and lived more modestly. Unlike his uncles and cousins, he had neither a carriage nor a male servant. My mother possessed no furs or expensive jewelry. But she directed and supported innumerable charities, and this was the one extravagance of which my father approved.

It happened one day when the Uncles had gone off to some family funeral that their nephew, who had remained behind alone, needed a ledger that was at the bottom of the safe. As my father bent over and lifted the big books, an old newspaper came to light with the ledger. Absent-mindedly turning its pages, he discovered, with the force of a sudden crushing blow, the deed in which he had been excluded. It was a shock that made him ill for a long time. At home, for the first time, my parents' conversation was cut short when I entered the room. I still remember the tone of bitter censure with which my mother pronounced the words: *"Those gentlemen"* in speaking of the Uncles. She told me only a few years ago that she had advised my father at that time to resign from the firm. Such was also the counsel of my Uncle Edmond:

"Let's start a little mill together," he said to my father when the latter told him of his discovery. "In ten years we'll have more business than F-B."

So proud and reserved was my father by nature that not only did he stay on but he said nothing. Nevertheless an essential mechanism, that of confidence and affection, had been damaged. And from that day forward he was never completely well. When he told me the story himself, twenty years had passed, the injustice had been rectified and he had long since granted his forgiveness, but he still trembled in thinking of it:

"When I saw that deed with Paul's name and without ours," he told me, "I thought I should go mad . . ."

Too many bonds attached him to the mill for him to leave it. Many of the workmen were those very Alsatians for whom he had arranged transportation to France. In the morning when he made his tour of inspection, he would stop in front of each loom and exchange a few words, often in Alsatian dialect, with the weaver or spinner. He knew all their families, was consulted about their marriages and was present at their funerals. His workmen loved him. "Monsieur Ernest isn't easy, but he's fair," they used to say, and they respected his extraordinary application to work. My father would never admit that an employer should arrive at the mill after the workmen or leave before them. When I was a child work began at six thirty; he would get up at six o'clock. He had learned how to perform himself each one of the complex operations that were under his charge, and without a moment's notice he could take the place of a weaver or spinner who complained of his task.

"This warp can't be woven, Monsieur Ernest. The thread's bad."

"We'll see about that."

And if the man was right, my father would acknowledge it. To be taken with him on his inspection was a reward that I eagerly sought. The din of the looms frightened me a little, but I loved the odor of the oily wool in the sorting room, the long twisted skeins turning in the vats of dye, the amazing silence in the drawing sheds, and the great steam engine with its brightly polished nickel work whose connecting rods my father would touch with a friendly hand as a trainer pats a favorite beast.

"What's new?" he would ask the engine-driver.

"Not a thing, Monsieur Ernest . . ."

. . . .

When I was six years old it was decided that I should take "courses" in preparation for the Lycée. I should have preferred to continue working with Maman, but she arranged with an elderly spinster from Alsace, Mademoiselle Paulus, for her to give instruction to me and three other boys, including my cousin, André Blin, and Christian Roerich, son of the pastor. She also had me begin piano lessons, at first with Madame Retling, an aged woman whose face was ornamented with long hairs which fascinated me, later with Monsieur Dupré, organist at the Immaculate Conception and father of the great organist Marcel Dupré. Monsieur Dupré was an excellent musician; he recognized very soon that I was not gifted.

"You understand music," he said to me, "but you haven't the hands for it."

Usually he spent the lesson period playing Chopin, Schumann, and Bach for me. If he did not make a pianist of me he did teach me to love good music, for which I am grateful to him. Each year when the pupils' recital was held, I had to take part in order to reassure my parents. I always played a certain *Oriental Serenade* for four hands with Monsieur Dupré himself:

"Don't worry about anything," he would tell me, "just simply go: *la*, and then at the octave: *la, la, la,* and I'll elaborate it."

He elaborated so ingeniously that I used to be complimented afterward.

My parents also had me begin English and German. My first German instructor was Bertha Bussmann, a bulky and virtuous Catholic spinster. She had been governess for a young lady in Elbeuf, the "Kleine Elisabeth," and had ended by staying on in town, where she was respected for her great piety. Fräulein Bertha talked to me constantly about one of her nephews, Heinrich Brüning, whose intelligence and abilities she used to praise. When Herr Brüning became Chancellor of the Reich, I wondered if by any chance this Brüning could be the "Kleiner Heinrich" whose praises I had so often heard sung. But Bertha was dead. Whom could I ask? The day came when in the home of Colonel Roosevelt in America I was able to put the question to the ex-Chancellor. It was indeed he, the nephew of Fräulein Bertha. Like his aunt, he was serious and pious. She hardly succeeded in teaching me German. Nevertheless with her I translated a play: *Thank God, the Table's Set*; and she made me sing:

> Ich hatt' einen Kameraden,
> Einen bessern find'st du nit . . .

As for English, which was to play such a large role in my life, I studied it most negligently with a young and pretty Irish girl, Miss Lizzy MacAnulty, whose maiden beauty was fading away in Elbeuf in melancholy loneliness because of some youthful indiscretion for which she had been exiled. She made me read *Little Lord Fauntleroy*, which I didn't much like, and *Treasure Island*, which frightened me. I used to dream about that iron hook which served the pirate in place of a hand. I remember that Miss Lizzy advised me for years to read a novel entitled *Thelma*. At the beginning of each lesson she would ask:

"Have you read *Thelma*?"

"No, Miss Lizzy."

Almost half a century has rolled by and I still have not read *Thelma*.

My father wanted me to learn to ride horseback.

"You will be a reserve officer," he said to me. "Riding will be useful."

There was a riding academy in Elbeuf run by a remarkable horseman, a former non-commissioned officer named Charpentier. He took a liking to me. My lack of aptitude for the piano was equaled by my natural aptitude for horsemanship. Charpentier handled me very roughly. He would start me at a trot without stirrups and keep me bouncing around for a quarter of an hour. Then he would give me stirrups, take up his long whip, and send me off at a gallop:

"Your toes, Cossack! You could hang three hats on them! Sit! Sit! Glide in the saddle! Get your body back! Watch your toes!"

At first the smell of the stables, the cries of Charpentier, the long whip which frightened my horse and the rapid-fire orders bewildered me. But very soon I became a good rider. One of the horses had been high-schooled. I would do the Spanish gait, the trot and change of feet in time to the music.

"Right knee, left rein! Left knee, right rein!" Charpentier would cry.

Then one day he said to me:

"That's all right. You're a horseman."

.   .   .   .

At eight I was entered in the Junior Lycée at Elbeuf. This was a miniature college, an annex of the Lycée of Rouen. The classes were small in number, ten or twelve pupils at most, but for that very reason the pupils did excellent work. Our masters had time to give individual attention to each one of us; and they had, like so many French teachers, a passion for their profession. My master in the sixth form, Monsieur Kittel, was a tall, thin, bald, emotional man who had married a rich woman and taught by vocation and not from necessity. He loved to correct exercises, and he insisted that we fold our papers lengthwise and write on only one half the page. The other half he himself would cover in a long sloping hand that looked like him. Thursdays he would take his pupils out bicycling and would treat them to strawberries and cream at one of the neighboring farms and would quote verses from Virgil or La Fontaine in description of the country through which we passed.

It was Kittel who first said to me that I might some day write books. I was not more than ten years old; he had given us as an exercise: *The Story of a Cane.* This cane, cut in the woods of St. Pierre, was supposed to write its own Memoirs. I no longer remember what sort of life I invented for it, but I do recall having composed with facility a long account which he read aloud to the class.

Another "narrative" whose subject has remained with me all my life as a memory and a kind of warning was *The Ring of Polycrates.* Polycrates, tyrant of Samos, having succeeded in all his projects and fearing that the gods may become jealous of him, decides to sacrifice a ring of which he is very fond and throw it into the sea. Next day a fisherman, cutting open a fish he has just caught, finds the ring and returns it to the tyrant. The latter, terrified, believes that the time of misfortune is upon him, and presently indeed he is vanquished, ruined, banished and dies. This edifying story troubled me.

"But," I said to Kittel, "since he sacrificed the ring, the gods should have allowed him to continue in his happiness . . ."

"Ah!" Kittel said, "he sacrificed *nothing but* the ring."

The parable was rich in meaning, but disturbing to a child.

Kittel also had me make my first speech. He made us (at the age of ten) talk for a quarter of an hour in front of our classmates. The subject of my maiden speech was: *A Comparison of the Esther of Racine with that of the Bible*. I prepared myself conscientiously, but a tragedy of vocabulary darkened my debut. In telling the story of Esther I used, apropos of "the proud Vashti," the word *concubine*. I did not know what it meant, but I loved its length and strangeness. Monsieur Kittel asked me to stay after class and was very severe with me:

"Why corrupt your classmates?" he asked. "If you have been reading the wrong sort of books, at least have the decency to keep it to yourself."

I burst into tears. Somewhat confused, he comforted me, but repeated that *concubine* was a terrible word which no boy of my age ought to use. This episode left me disturbed and curious, and my teacher's emotion excited in me much more dangerous thoughts than the proud Vashti could ever have done.

But I owe a great debt of gratitude to Kittel. He gave me a taste for literature; he taught me respect for language; he instructed me so thoroughly in the rudiments of Latin that everything that came afterward seemed easy. Today having traveled in many countries and observed many colleges, I can better realize the extraordinary good fortune we French students enjoyed in having as masters, when we were ten years old, men qualified to teach in any university in the world. These masters of secondary education were without ambition. They had no further wish than to mold to the best of their ability successive generations of young Frenchmen. To this task they devoted themselves with such passion that they suffered at the end of each academic year in losing their pupils. Kittel on the day before the distribution of prizes read us *The Last Class* by Alphonse Daudet. He had great difficulty in getting to the end of it; he wept and his voice shook. We were touched, surprised, and embarrassed. As a remembrance he gave me a book called *The Russian Soul* containing stories by Pushkin, Gogol and Tolstoy; in the front he put an inscription in which he asked me not to forget him when I became a writer. I have never forgotten him.

It was in the book I received from him that I first read *The Queen of Spades,* a story that made a great impression and inspired in me the desire some day to compose similar fantastic tales. For I had begun to write. After attending a lecture given by Monsieur Brunetière at the Elbeuf theater on the comedies of Corneille, I decided to hold a series of lectures myself, for which my sisters should be impressed as audience. On several successive days I took my seat behind a table on which I had placed a glass of water, and these two unfortunates had to hear me talk about the *Misanthrope* and about *Athalie.* They yawned, they wept, but I was merciless.

When I was twelve years old and in the Fourth Form I composed with great effort a tragedy in five acts in verse. It was called *Odette de Champdivers,* and its heroine was mistress of Charles the Mad. Why was I interested in this woman? I no longer know, and the play is lost. It must have been very bad. However, a new master, Monsieur Leroy, provided us with other models. Leroy, quite different from Kittel, was as much of a bohemian as the latter was upper middle class; he wore an immense, wide-brimmed felt hat, whereas Kittel dressed in a cutaway and high hat; he was as untidily long-haired as Kittel was neatly bald, as easy going in his ideas and vocabulary as Kittel was prim; but he was a great reader of Flaubert, Huysmans, Maupassant, and in the long run a useful influence for me. I learned some years later that he had left the University to become a doctor, and then I heard nothing more of him for forty years. One day about 1935 when I was at home in Paris, I was called upon by a white-haired old man whose eyes were too bright, whose clothes were threadbare, and who saluted me by sweeping off a wide-brimmed hat.

"You remember your old master of the Fourth Form?" he said to me.

I was filled with delight until he explained the object of his visit:

"It's necessary," he said to me in a low voice, "that you should put your influence at my disposal in order to defend the electrons. . . .

The electrons are being persecuted. . . . And I alone know that the electron is the secret of life. . . ."

My poor old master had gone mad.

· · · · · · ·

Another of my professors at that time had a great influence on me. This was Mouchel, teacher of mathematics. This little man with moist and drooping mustache, his vest always covered with chalk, was the son of a manufacturer in Elbeuf. At the outset of his career he had manufactured cloth like everyone else in town, but he was a theorist. He had developed some very subtle ideas about the weaving of wool, which was dangerous, had put them into practice, which was culpable, and had thus ruined his father and himself. Declared bankrupt, he had studied for a fellowship in mathematics, had passed the examination, and was teaching geometry and elementary algebra at Elbeuf. My father, who had a high regard for my other professors, showed hostility and distrust whenever I talked to him about Mouchel. A business failure seemed to him a poor preparation for the high calling of teacher. A man who did not know how to make cloth couldn't be expected to know how to teach.

But my father and all Elbeuf were mistaken. Mouchel explained the first books of geometry to us with admirable clarity.

"*Hein?* Do you understand? Do you understand?" he would ask us, his piece of chalk in his hand, and he wouldn't let us go until we did understand. Thanks to him I still know most of the definitions and demonstrations in Euclid. More important still, he gave us a method of procedure. He who goes steadily, step by step, finds everything easy; he who suddenly attempts, after squandering years, to make up lost time by frantic effort, finds everything impossible. The mind, like the heart, is formed early and many of us remain all our lives what our childhood made us. "*Hein?* Do you understand? Do you understand?" Thanks to little Mouchel of the moist mustache and the chalk-covered vest, we learned to reason.

What he was incapable of teaching us was to challenge reason. But another and greater was to see to that.

CHAPTER III

Paradise Lost

AT TWELVE I had finished the course at the Junior College of Elbeuf, which went only through the Fourth Form. I was to continue my studies at the Lycée Corneille in Rouen. For me this was like entering a new dimension. I left the industrial town for the provincial capital. Before speaking of this new world I should like to take my bearings by describing, in so far as I am still able, the sort of child I was as I emerged from the Fourth Form.

For my age I had done an immense amount of reading. My parents' library was limited but carefully chosen. It occupied the shelves of a huge, carved and gilded cabinet in Maman's drawing room, a room of state with shutters always closed, filled with furniture in white dust covers. Once a week on Wednesdays my mother, like all the ladies of Elbeuf, had "her day" and received callers. The other women contended bitterly for the six possible days and considered it a mortal insult that a newcomer should dare to choose *their* day. But my mother was indifferent to these small worldly vanities and was delighted when calls were infrequent. No man ever called, and it would have been a scandal in Elbeuf to be seen outside the mills or offices before seven in the evening. At four o'clock the maid served China tea in rose-colored porcelain cups. Even today the taste of China tea evokes for me Maman's day and the gilt bookcase.

On the other days of the week I was allowed to enter the darkened drawing room where I collided with the phantoms of chairs enveloped in their white shrouds. I used to open the shutters a crack—for to open them wide would have been a sacrilege—and I would "rummage"

24

among the books. I first came upon all the classics (those of the 17th Century, the 18th Century horrified my parents); then the great romantics, a complete set of Hugo, of Lamartine, of Vigny, of Musset; the *Memorial of St. Helena,* my father's favorite book, in a de luxe edition illustrated with engravings; the plays of Augier, those of Labiche and those of Dumas *fils*. One shelf was occupied by the literary texts that had been used by my mother in her girlhood; Villemain, bound in brown; Nisard, bound in blue. My parents used to give me as New Year's or birthday presents, in groups of six or eight volumes, Sainte-Beuve's *Causerie de Lundi,* the works of Taine, Reclus' *Geography,* and Michelet's *History of France.* But most important of all, with furtive enthusiasm I used to select from the books in the drawing room the innumerable bound volumes of *Lectures Retrospectives.* This was a magazine, now defunct, which reprinted all the masterpieces of the French novel. Thanks to the *Lectures* I read at that time, when perhaps I was too young, all of Flaubert, all of Maupassant, the early novels of Paul Bourget, of Anatole France, of Marcel Prévost, and of Maurice Barrès. I mixed the good and the bad, the serious and the frivolous, history and fiction. From good and bad alike I derived incredibly keen pleasure, literary delight and sensual emotion.

My sensuality awoke early and in ignorance and confusion. My parents' prudishness permitted no request for explanations of those delicious and terrifying subjects. My father, who used to blush if his friends talked about a scandal or repeated a coarse joke in his presence, was far from imagining the seraglio where I kept for the delectation of my daydreams Mademoiselle de Maupin and Madame Bovary. A small book, probably forgotten by now, *Monsieur, Madame and Baby* by Gustav Droz, did me a good deal of harm by its sentimental salacity. The word *breast* encountered in some classic text was enough to excite me. Wholly unprovided with instruction, I had to construct for myself by the aid of novels a picture of the relations between men and women. At school some of my fellow students, who were bolder and had been less strictly brought up, had bizarre adventures. One of them, a doctor's son, told me that a young courtesan of Elbeuf, whom we used to meet on the street and devour with our eyes, was ready to undress in front of us for twenty-five francs. He was looking for five contributors at five francs each to make up the necessary capital. I was terribly tempted but, disgusted by the vulgarity of the scene as I imagined it, I refused.

My true nature was romantic. I have described elsewhere how I read in one of my prize books the story of a band of students who decided to form an army and selected a girl student to be their queen. "The Queen was called Ania Sokoloff. She was a girl of remarkable beauty, slender, elegant and graceful." I loved the oath the soldiers swore to their Queen, the feats they performed to please her and the smile that was their reward. I do not know why this tale pleased me so, but thus it was, I loved it and, seated on the branches of the lilacs, smelling the perfume of the flowers as though it were that of a woman, I read and reread *The Young Russian Soldiers* and dreamed of a love that would be at once suffering, discipline and devotion.

To sustain me in this premature crisis of adolescence I had no religious faith whatever. I did not know (and even today do not know exactly) the doctrine of the religion which by birth should be mine. An aged weaver from the mill, a Russian Jew named Forster, used to come to teach me to read Hebrew, but he read it without understanding it, and when he talked French his accent made my sister and me laugh. "Do not laugh, do not laugh," Forster would say, smoothing his moujik beard, and we would go on laughing for all we were worth. This was my sole preparation for an initiation into religion which consisted in reading aloud in Hebrew one chapter of the Scriptures. There was never any talk of dogma. My father had a solid faith, but it was moral rather than metaphysical. In the domain of morals he agreed splendidly not only with Pastor Roerich but also with the Abbé Alleaume, superior of the Fénelon School and gifted priest, who was our neighbor and with whom he often went walking. My father respected the traditions of his family and abided by them, but fasts and unleavened bread were in his eyes archaic curiosities rather than divine regulations. I believe if at that time I had met a cultivated rabbi to make me read the Bible and explain it to me, I should have appreciated its sublime poetry, the wisdom of the Kings and the Prophets, the solemn nihilism of Ecclesiastes. But I did not come to know the Old Testament until much later and then through the English poets. It was Kipling and Milton who brought me in contact with the Bible, so that my real religious instruction was at first Protestant and literary. Later on, as I shall relate, with Alain it was Catholic and philosophical.

Like many children (and particularly Edmund Gosse who has told about it in *Father and Son*) I had unfortunate experiences with the efficacy of prayer. One day when there was to be an examination in geography I prayed that our master would choose as subject the *Tributaries of the Seine* which I knew, rather than those of the Loire which I could never remember. He gave us the Loire, and my faith was shaken. For some time my sister and I had recourse to the practice of magic. We had invented a very powerful devil called Monsieur Fate, whose temple was in one corner of the hall. If one went to this corner and cried aloud: "Monsieur Fate, grant that we be taken to the circus on Thursday!" the prayer was sometimes answered. It may have been because Maman heard it.

.   .   .   .

Without much effort I was first in my class at Elbeuf. The presentation of prizes which marked the end of the academic year was a pleasant occasion for me. The Elbeuf orchestra played the Marseillaise, and I still cannot hear it after all these years without seeing again the professors, in their yellow or red robes with the narrow strips of white fur on their shoulders, the black and white robes of the judges, in short the whole procession which approached at a pace heavy with honor and importance to take their places on the platform. We would listen patiently to the heavily humorous discourse of some university Polonius, and then the Censor would read the names of the prize-winners. I knew that I would leave there laden with green paper crowns and a gilded crown representing the Prize for Excellence, and with my hands full of books bound in red; but I understood quite well that in such small classes there was no great merit in standing first. The following year at the Lycée of Rouen would be an entirely different matter, and I looked forward to it with trepidation.

There were two possible ways by which I could continue my studies, and between these my parents had to choose. They could put me in the Lycée at Rouen as a boarder—it was thus that my Uncle Henry had prepared for the Polytechnique—or they could send me there each morning and have me return each evening. The daily trip would be tiring, for it would be necessary to take a train at 6.49 in the morning which meant getting up at a quarter to six and at least two hours a day would be wasted on the two trips. But my mother had an instinctive horror of my living away from home; and so, despite the fact that my health was not of the best, it was decided that I should return each evening to Elbeuf. There were, however, other young people, among them André Blin and one of Pastor Roerich's sons, to accompany me. We were soon known at the Lycée of Rouen as "the gang from the Elbeuf train."

Each day at dawn, with my schoolbag under my arm, I would walk through Elbeuf amid the laborers going to work. One could hear the machines in the factories slowly starting to turn. The great glass windows would suddenly light up on the stroke of six thirty. Presently in the smoky light of a railroad compartment, seated on dirty brown cushions, I would be trying to review my lessons. How many verses I have recited between Elbeuf and Rouen! Even today I cannot think of those hideous stations, that charming countryside, those rivers and forests without seeming to hear the stanzas of *Polyeucte, la Jeune Captive, la Nuit de Mai,* or perhaps: "Sing, goddess, the wrath of Peleus' son Achilles . . ."

The order of the stations, their distance from one another, their odd, dissimilar names formed a kind of musical phrase in my mind with a complex rhythm that I loved. First came Elbeuf-Rouvalets, a brief stop, a semi-quaver barely separated by a sigh from the point of departure. Then as far as La Bouille-Moulineaux was the longest run of the trip, an interminable pause, punctuated by a noisy tunnel in the course of which one could shout without disturbing the other passengers: "Eighteen eleven! O year when the numberless nations . . ." or: "Sad plain of Waterloo . . ." Then came in quick, regular succession Grand-Couronne, Petit-Couronne, Grand-Quevilly, Petit-Quevilly, and finally Rouen. *Tac-tac . . . Tac-tac-tac-tac.* That was the rhythm of my childish thoughts on this daily morning trip, and when the exigent maneuvers of a deputy resulted in establishing a station at Hêtre-à-l'Image in the middle of a woods, and thus interrupting my longest pause by a short and wholly useless stop, it seemed to me that a strange and alarming dissonance had been brought into my life.

·   ·   ·   ·   ·   ·   ·

The first day that I spent at the Lycée of Rouen was marred by a small but distressing incident that made so deep an impression that I should not consider it honest to omit it from this narrative. At that time it was the custom to begin the academic year by a mass called the Mass of the Holy Ghost, celebrated in the beautiful chapel of the Lycée, which had once been a Jesuit College; the purpose of this mass was to invoke the benediction of the Holy Spirit upon the labors of the students. A few minutes before the ceremony the Head Usher called us together in the grand courtyard and said:

"Let the dissenters withdraw!"

The dissenters were the Protestants and the Israelites. About twenty Protestants and three or four Jews stepped out of ranks.

"The others," the Head Usher went on, "will form in a column of twos and follow me into the chapel . . ."

There was the prolonged sound of tramping feet and the student body disappeared into a vaulted passageway. Our little group remained alone beneath the trees, disconsolate and with nothing to say. From the nearby chapel rose the music of the organ magnificently played by my master Dupré, and the murmured responses. We strolled in melancholy beneath the chestnut trees of the courtyard. We felt ourselves separated for an hour's time, on a solemn occasion, from a community which was, after all, our community, and we were unhappy, very unhappy, without knowing why.

Except for that one painful hour I fell in love at once with my new school. The beautiful Court of Honor, framed by symmetrical gray buildings constructed by the Jesuits in the 17th Century, the Latin inscriptions which ornamented the front of the sun dial and the pedestal of the statue of Corneille, the drum that rolled out from the head of the stairs at five minutes of eight, the ranks which immediately formed two by two, this rigor, this discipline gave me a joy which I was to recapture later on with my regiment, when we marched past the flag to the music of a military band. The consciousness of belonging to a well-ordered group is an aesthetic pleasure which I believe the musicians in an orchestra experience, as well as students and soldiers.

At the end of a week our professor, Monsieur Robineau, had us write a Latin composition. Thanks to Kittel, I knew how a Latin composition was made, and the text did not seem hard. Naturally I had no idea how I should rank in this class of forty students, none of whom I knew. A week later the Headmaster, Monsieur Desfours, appeared to read the marks. It was a solemn moment. The Headmaster, corpulent, bearded, executive, entered with his high hat in his hand, followed by the Censor, who held a large sheet of paper. The whole class rose.

"Greetings, Monsieur Robineau," the Headmaster said, rolling his r's. "Sit down, gentlemen. Your standing is as follows . . ."

And the Censor read:

"Latin Composition . . . First: HERZOG, Emile, . . ."

The Headmaster stopped him:

"Ah! I take this occasion to congratulate Monsieur Herzog. This is a triumph for the Junior College of Elbeuf . . . Gentlemen of Rouen, this is a challenge to you to do your best."

The young men of Rouen looked at me without benevolence. My heart pounded. I was filled with joy and I was very much surprised. That evening when I returned to Elbeuf and reported my success, my father who disliked pride said:

"That's all very well, but it may have been an accident."

This accident became, alas, the rule. I was first in French, in Greek, in Mathematics, in History. I was upset and troubled because those who had been at the head of the class the preceding year began to regard me with exasperation. A curvature of the spine forced me to wear an iron brace which made my movements slow and awkward. This object of ridicule, my unfortunate scholastic triumphs, the renewed interest in the *Affaire Dreyfus* combined, for a number of weeks, to make me the victim of certain conscienceless and cruel boys. I suffered frightfully, not having met, up to that time, anything but tenderness at home and friendship at school. Life at the Lycée, which I admired so much, would have become insufferable if I had not found support from certain potent avengers of wrongs.

These were a group of athletic students, dirty and high spirited, with buttonless vests tied together by pieces of string, who called themselves the Morin Family. Blot, a star forward in Rugby, was Father Morin; Fouchet, Mother Morin; Loustaunau, Bouchard, Godet, Pagny and Patau (whom the Morins called Pascaline) completed the family. We used to have our meals in a refectory, eight at a table. The Head Usher would say grace or, to be more accurate, he would mutter: "Sancti amen . . . Sancti amen . . ." Then we would sit down. The seven Morins, as soon as they saw that I seemed unhappy, requested the Usher to put me at their table; and since they were the best fighters in the Middle Form their friendship, joined to that of Abbé Vacandard, Chaplain of the Lycée, who enjoyed translating Virgil or Tacitus with me, quieted the brawlers.

From the beginning of the Second Form I could devote myself completely to the joy of studying. The discovery of the Latin and French poets was an intoxication. My professor in the Second, Nebout, called himself a romantic. He fitted the part, with his flowing hair, his cape, and his vocabulary. Two plays written by him had been performed in the local theater. He taught us to love the 16th Century, Rabelais, Montaigne, and to translate Lucretius. To him I owe the fact that I know by heart hundreds of verses of Ronsard, Victor Hugo, Baudelaire. On the other hand, Texcier, professor of rhetoric, a little man with a precise, delicate voice and a malicious smile, was a classicist. Through him I learned to love Virgil, Racine, Mérimée, Anatole France. Every week he gave us the subject for a French composition: "*Letter from one of Racine's admirers to Racine after the stir over Phèdre . . . Letter of Monsieur de Gourville to the Prince de Condé asking him not to lead an army against France . . . Letter of Conrart, Permanent Secretary of the Académie Française to Saint-Evremonde in defense of the Académie against the latter's satire . . .*" The research work, the arrangement of the material I collected, the imitation of the language of the time, gave me a delightful foretaste of the joys of authorship. From these years of study I have retained the memory of a long enchantment.

During my year of Rhetoric I conceived an odd ambition. Each year the Minister of War gave a medal at the Lycée to the best of the whole school in gymnastics. I had just been relieved of my iron corset and I passionately coveted that medal. I asked Pichon, the athletic instructor, a former non-commissioned officer, lean and muscular with wiry hair, to give me private lessons; and I worked on the parallel bars, the high bar and the trapeze during all the recreation periods. As I had hoped, perseverance finally overcame my awkwardness and Pichon taught me by being limber to accomplish a thousand feats which I could never have done through strength alone. When I was master of my movements I applied myself to improvement of form. With my body extended, toes pointed, muscles relaxed, I would swing about the bar in the sunlight, I would leap from trapeze to trapeze and I would mount the parallels at a bound. Success in gymnastics, as in politics and in war, depends on precise timing. A release of the knees, which gravitation will carry through for you if it is begun at the right instant, becomes dangerous a split second later. Pichon knew the value of timing. When at the end of the year the contest took place before the officers of the garrison, I got my medal. It gave me more pleasure than my successful baccalaureate.

This baccalaureate was my first examination. It was given to the students of Rouen by the faculty at Caen, the ancient capital of Normandy, whose massive and beautiful churches are constructed like the tragedies of Corneille. The subject for the French composition was a sentence from Renan: *"To have had common glories in the past, to possess a common will in the present, to have achieved great things together, to be determined upon further achievement, these are the essential conditions for being a people;"* it pleased me so much that I forgot where I was and why I was writing in the delight of composition. The oral examination seemed easy. I was questioned about Descartes and his influence on literature; about Livy (and I had just read Taine's book) and about a book of Homer which I knew by heart. Everything went smoothly except geography. An ill-tempered old man asked me the depth of the Rhone at Pont-Saint-Esprit. I never knew any figures, and this one least of all. But despite this culpable ignorance I passed.

For several years I had spent my vacations in Paris with my mother's family, and there I found an atmosphere that was not very different from that of the Lycée. My four aunts loved the theater and poetry. Every Thursday one of them would take me to the classical matinée of the Comédie Française. Before long I was commenting like a connoisseur upon the Mascarille of Georges Beer, the Pourceaugnac of Coquelin the younger or the Berenice of Julia Bartet. To see Mounet-Sully in *Œdipus Rex*, Coquelin in *Cyrano*, and later Sarah Bernhardt in *L'Aiglon* was for me a solemn, almost sacred, pleasure. When the exposition of 1900 opened, the Comédie Française organized a series of afternoon poetry readings at the Trocadéro and my favorite actors and actresses took part, uncostumed, in reciting the poems of Chénier, La Fontaine, Hugo, Baudelaire, Verlaine. I could imagine in advance the intonations and rejoice in the happy inspirations of the actors. I lived in a wholly unreal world of poetry and passion.

These days in Paris intoxicated me all the more inasmuch as I was in love. I did not know with whom. I longed to die for a beautiful and unhappy mistress. I loved to read in Sophocles or Euripides the story of Perseus rescuing Andromeda. I repeated with delight the beautiful sonnet of Ronsard:

> "Il ne faut s'étonner," disaient ces bons vieillards,
> Dessus le mur troyen voyant passer Hélène,
> "Si pour telle beauté nous souffrons tant de peine.
> Notre mal ne vaut pas un seul de ses regards . . ."[1]

My Helen for several months was the youngest of my aunts, after that the sister of one of my schoolmates whom I had glimpsed at the gateway of the Lycée, and then the popular actresses on the stage of

[1] "No cause for wonder," those venerable elders said upon the walls of Troy, seeing Helen pass, "if for such beauty we have suffered so much woe. Our ills are overbalanced by a single glance from her . . ."

the Française to whom I sent letters in verse which were never answered. But did I even expect answers? My love was not of this world, and whether they wished it or not these fair persons belonged to me in my dreams.

One day one of our masters at Rouen gave us as an exercise *The Palinode of Stesichorus.* "The poet Stesichorus, having reviled Helen in his verses for the woes brought by her upon the Greeks, is struck blind by Venus and, recognizing his error, composes a recantation in which he expresses his regret for having blasphemed against beauty." Never have I written an exercise with more sincere enthusiasm. The theme of sacrifice for beauty awakened in me such profound echoes that despite my extreme youth I felt shaken and I worked for two hours with an almost painful ardor, as though I had a premonition of how often in the course of my difficult life on this earth I should have cause myself to write the Palinode of Stesichorus.

CHAPTER IV

The River of the Arrow

THE Year of Philosophy in the life of a young Frenchman was, in my time, the year of intellectual puberty. One can see in Barrès' *Déracinés* the significance for him and his friends of their encounter with the philosopher Burdeau, and in the biographies of Proust the role played by the philosopher Darlu in the formation of Proustian doctrine. For ten years all our attention, first as boys, then as young men had been concentrated upon questions of form, grammar, style. Suddenly the depths were lighted up. Epictetus and Epicurus, Plato and Aristotle, Descartes and Spinoza, Locke and Kant, Hegel and Bergson, contended for mastery in our minds. The metaphysicians dissolved the universe into transparent clouds or dilated the individual until he became coterminous with the world. The moralists proposed contradictory doctrines to justify unvarying virtues. Dizzy and intoxicated, blind and drunk with power, the young man would allow himself to be deliciously borne away in the whirlwind of ideas.

My classmates and I at the Lycée of Rouen in 1901 awaited our Year of Philosophy with all the more impatience because our philosopher was a man who had already attained fame. He was named Chartier, but he signed the name Alain to the daily *Comments* which appeared in the *Rouen Dispatch* and which were written in the style of a poet and conceived with a vigor of thought that was unrestrained by prudence. At the People's University in Rouen (these groups for mutual education had sprung up all over France after the *Affaire Dreyfus*) he spoke every week, and even his political adversaries admitted that his lectures were original and eloquent. As for his pupils, our older schoolmates, they behaved like members of an esoteric religious cult, at once enthusiastic and secretive. Canet, a close friend of mine, who later became Director of Religious Affairs at the Quai d'Orsay, had received the Honor Prize in Philosophy the year before.

"You'll see," he told me mysteriously, "his class is not like anything you've ever heard before."

We were not disappointed. The assembly drum rolled out. The ranks defiled in front of Corneille and we proceeded to take our seats on the benches of the philosophy classroom. Suddenly the door burst open and in came a big fellow with a youthful manner and a fine Norman head marked by strong, regular features. He sat down at his desk on the platform, looked at us smilingly for an instant, then went to the blackboard and wrote: "Σὺν ὅλῃ τῇ ψυχῇ εἰs τὴν ἀλήθειαν ἰτέον."

He looked at me:

"Translate," he said.

I translated:

"One must go to the truth with all one's soul."

He let us meditate for some moments on Plato's sentence, then began his lecture on perception:

"Consider this inkwell on my desk," he said. "When I say *this inkwell* what am I designating? First of all, a black and white splotch of a certain shape that my eyes see; then a sensation of smooth resistance which my hand feels" (he extended his hand and touched the inkwell). "But how do I know that the sensation of smooth resistance and the black and white spot are the same object? What is it in me that can discover an identity? My eye? Certainly not, since my eye cannot touch . . . My hand? Certainly not, since my hand cannot see . . . From this we perceive at once that when certain philosophers tell us that there can be nothing in the mind that was not first known by the senses, we must be on our guard. . . ."

We had not been in class five minutes and already we felt ourselves shaken, provoked, stimulated. For ten months we were going to live in this atmosphere of passionate investigation. Chartier was a great admirer of Socrates and, like him, thought the best way of inducing men to exercise their judgment was not to offer them predigested doctrines, but to stimulate their appetite and their curiosity by constant surprises. Socrates liked to be called The Numbfish from the fish that gives an electric shock to all those who touch it. Chartier loved to shock us with paradoxical theses which he would support with all the trappings of specious logic. He would then sometimes demolish them himself, and sometimes let us find our own way out.

Like Socrates, too, he loved examples and apologues. Some of his stories recurred constantly and they were famous among us. There was one about a rabbi's maid who, when she was dying and delirious, began for the first time in her life to talk Hebrew; there was one about a sergeant, a veteran of the Colonial Wars, on whose legs a nurse put leeches, and he dreamed that he was amid the cactus in Africa; there was one about the Labrador duck which, when it is shut up, strikes the cement floor of its cage with its webbed feet in the naïve hope of making worms come out. The duck illustrated the lecture on instinct and habit, the maid illustrated the theory of memory and the old sergeant that of dreams.

Chartier had narrow and strong political convictions which he admitted. He was a radical, with some of the traits of Julien Sorel. But his radicalism was less a desire for reform than the perpetual vigilance of the citizen directed against the authorities. He held more strongly to freedom than to equality, and he believed that if freedom of the spirit remained complete it would suffice to maintain equality before the law, the only form of equality to which he attached importance. And so he was not a socialist, but this did not keep him from expounding the doctrines of that party to us with so much intelligence that he made me a socialist, as I shall recount, for several years. He was well pleased. "Anyone who is not an anarchist at sixteen," he said, "will not have enough energy at thirty to be a fire chief." But his political thought had another and quite different aspect. Devoted reader as he was of Auguste Comte and Balzac, he believed in the necessity of ceremonials and in respect for customs. Alain may have been anti-clerical, but he was certainly religious. Few men could talk better about Christianity. In fact, it was he who first revealed to me the grandeur of the Christian doctrine and led to my adopting so large a part of it.

Alain often quoted a maxim from the *Imitation of Christ*:

"Intelligence must follow faith, never precede it and never destroy it." Faced with a doctrine like that of the Incarnation, he never said: "Is it true?" but: "It is true for faith; what does it mean for reason?" And this is his reply: "Jupiter, the god of the Greeks and Romans, was neither god enough nor man enough. Jehovah, the god of the Jews, was no longer man at all. He was cut off from man, as the authorities are cut off from the people, and did not manifest himself to man except through external miracles: columns of fire, celestial manna and the tables of stone on Sinai. It was necessary for God to come closer to man again. And so religion incarnated him. To believe in the Father without believing in the Son is to give up knowing God. From this altar, the cradle, a religion arises and, examining this marvel, one finds the key. Look at the Child. This helplessness is God. This helplessness that needs everything is God. Such is the hope, by comparison with which even truth is an idol." These intentionally obscure statements gave us glimpses into vertiginous depths. Listening to Alain, the Voltairianism of Voltaire seemed to me almost as vapid as the Voltairianism of Homais. "Every proof," our master would go on to say, "is clearly discredited in my eyes." Which put understanding back in its place.

He made us read the Gospels and loved to comment on the most obscure of the parables. I remember he often talked to us about the fig tree cursed by Christ because it was not bearing figs.

"And yet," Alain said, "it was not the season for figs. Is it then a crime for a tree to be sterile in the season of sterility? No, of course not, but Jesus' thought becomes clear as soon as we consider that this sterile fig tree is man. For each of us, when acts of courage, charity or humility are demanded of him, replies that he would gladly perform them but that it is not the season, that he is ill, tired out, harassed, that he has other obligations, that he will see to it later on. To these vain excuses the parable of the sterile fig tree replies sternly that the Master will condemn us if we do not bear fruit at every season."

Alain's influence on my taste in literature was as strong as his influence on my ideas. In the preceding year, in the reign of the delightful Texcier, I had learned to love Anacreon and Catullus, the poets of the Anthology and the prose of Paul-Louis Courier and Anatole France. Alain's diet was stronger meat. He admired *Candide*, but considered France no more than a good minor writer. He revealed Stendhal and Balzac to me. With the former he had natural affinities since, like him, he had a love of liberty, a contempt for self-important people, and a passion for naturalness. When he praised the description of the passions in the *Chartreuse* or the *Rouge* we divined, despite our inexperience, that he had known violent ones himself. His almost unqualified admiration for *The Lily in the Valley*, a much discussed Balzac novel in which our taste as rhetoricians found matter for ridicule, throws light on his secret life.

Chartier was one of the most ardent Balzacians that I have ever encountered in my life. Not only had he read and reread the *Human Comedy* a hundred times, but he cited it constantly and often used the characters of Balzac as examples in his lectures. It may seem surprising that this radical, who was so bitter about reactionaries, should choose as his favorite reading a novelist who was a Catholic and a Royalist. But this is one of those miracles of France. Alain's passions made him distrustful and rebellious. His instincts of a Norman peasant brought him back to the wisdom of Balzac. I remember that he especially admired the *Country Doctor*, which should become the political Bible of all French conservatives. Thanks to him, the work of Balzac has become a part of my life, and since my Year of Philosophy I have never lived without having the *Human Comedy* within reach.

I have known few better readers than Alain. He would get at the details of a text and savor their beauty. He also wanted to remain a man of few authors. He believed that an ardent reader ought to have a limited library and reread the same books every year. If I remember rightly his consisted of Homer, Balzac, Stendhal, Saint-Simon, Tacitus, Plato, Descartes, Spinoza and Hegel. He also used to read, like my father, the *Memorial of Saint Helena*. Later on I made him add to his favorites Chateaubriand's *Memoires d'Outre-Tombe*,

Cardinal de Retz and Rudyard Kipling. Nothing was harder than to
get him to read a contemporary author.

"It's better to wait," he would say . . . "If in ten years you still
admire him perhaps I'll see."

Nevertheless, he himself adopted Claudel and Valéry between the
two wars and talked about them better than anyone else.

In our exercises he paid more attention to style than to content.
"This isn't *written*," in his mouth was a sentence from which there
was no appeal. The first thesis that he gave me was a thought from
Plato: Μακρότεραν περιτέον. "One must take the longer road." I still have
one of my compositions, at the top of which he has written in blue
crayon: "Compress, condense and end with a bang." He often put me
on my guard against measured prose and against phrase making:

"If you aren't careful," he told me, "you may become a distinguished
writer of flowery prose. That's not desirable. Read the *Civil Code* and
Henri Brulard. They'll save you from phrases."

The subjects he gave us were designed to discourage rhetoric: "A
young woman is about to jump off the parapet of the Boïeldieu Bridge.
A philosopher holds her back by the skirt. The ensuing dialogue." Or
again: "Dialogue between a sacristan and a fire chief on the existence
of God."

If I try now to reconstruct a picture of the world which our master
drew, this is approximately what I find. His course began with a long
discussion of the theory of perception. He showed us that to perceive
even the simplest object requires very complex reasoning and that this
reasoning may go wrong, hence the illusions of the senses. How often
he talked to us of the stereoscope and of the straight stick which appears broken under water, facts which reveal the weakness of the mind.
Then came the illusions of memory, of instinct and of reason. All of
this made apparent the difficulties that beset the search for truth.
Socrates and Descartes helped us at least to find a provisory method.
Spinoza taught us to make our emotions serve us in our search. Kant
kept us from pursuing the blind alley of metaphysics by showing us
that we would find nothing in that direction except the laws of our
own mind. Auguste Comte taught us to respect institutions and cere-

monies. One of Alain's striking characteristics was that when he was expounding the doctrine of some philosopher he would never criticize it, but would give us whatever truth was in it. Refutation seemed to him a miserable game. "It's a great mark of mediocrity to admire mediocrely." He admired generously, and he admired even some of the writers whom at that time it was smart to ridicule, such as Victor Hugo and George Sand. He considered (rightly) *Les Miserables* and *Consuelo* to be great books. Furthermore, in class he permitted hardly any discussion, holding it to be a waste of time. "The master teaches, the students work," he would say.

What I cannot convey by words is the enthusiasm inspired in us by this search, boldly pursued with such a guide; the excitement of those classes which one entered with the persistent hope of discovering, that very morning, the secret of life, and from which one departed with the joy of having understood that perhaps there was no such secret but that nevertheless it was possible to be a human being and to be so with dignity and nobility. When I read in *Kim* the story of the Lama who sought so piously for the River of the Arrow, I thought of *our* search. Alain gave us not so much a doctrine (he would gladly have said with Gide: "Wean yourself from me!"), not so much a system, as a method and a faith. "One must go to the truth with all one's soul." From his lessons I have retained a horror of hypocrisy, a desire to understand and a respect for my adversaries. Like all human beings I have, in the course of my life, committed many faults; if I have occasionally acted well I owe it to the example of my father and to the teaching of Alain.

At the end of the year he entered me in the *Concours Général* which was a very serious sort of competitive examination in which all the Lycées and Colleges of France took part, each represented by three or four of its students. The examinations were given, with every precaution, at the Prefecture. The papers arrived from Paris in sealed envelopes. The Lycée gave the contestants elegant lunches to take with them—lobster and cold chicken. The mayonnaise was in a bottle and had turned. The preceding year I had won a prize for Latin composition and another for Greek in the *Concours*; this had given the Lycée of Rouen a good standing and had filled the Headmaster with pride. The subject in Philosophy was: *"The Role of Habit in the Life of the Individual and in Society."* For a pupil of Alain it was an easy theme. All we had to do was to follow his method; a number of examples: the boxer, the gymnast . . . citation of authorities: "Just as one swallow does not make a summer, so a single virtuous action does not constitute virtue." *Ὥσπερ ἤδη ἡ φύσις ἦθος . . .* Auguste Comte on social habits . . . Habit and instinct: the Labrador duck . . . We were allowed eight hours; I had finished in four.

A month later I was in Elbeuf sick in bed with a sore throat when I received a telegram from the Headmaster: "Heartiest congratulations on receiving first prize in the *Concours Général.*" I had great difficulty in believing it, but it was true, and soon a superb pile of books arrived from Paris. When the prizes were awarded after a solemn rendition of the Marseillaise the Prefect handed me my diploma. My comrades gave me an ovation which was much sweeter to me than the prize. I found refuge on the platform beside Alain, whose athletic body bulged his academic gown.

"This is fine," he said to me, "provided you also understand that it is nothing . . . Now you must live . . . What are you going to do?"

That was a question I had been asking myself. I was passionately devoted to the life of the Lycée. It was delightful to attend classes conducted by a man of genius, to study, to pass examinations which appeared uniformly easy to me. Couldn't my whole life be one long examination in which I always received the notation *very good* and the congratulations of the examiners? This seemed not impossible. Why not enter the Ecole Normale? On two successive years the opportunity had been given in the *Concours Général* to pit myself against the best students of my generation. The result had been encouraging. Moreover the life of a professor would suit me. I did not hope ever to have in the eyes of my students the prestige of an Alain, but I might be a creditable professor, conscientious and perhaps beloved. In addition, I wished to write, and in some peaceful post in the provinces I should have leisure. I explained these plans to Chartier while the Censor was calling out:

"Class in Elementary Mathematics: LEFEVRE (Henri) . . ."

"I don't believe you are right," he said to me. "Not but that you would be sure to succeed in such a career. I can see you being admitted to the Normale without any trouble at all. But afterward? . . . There would be great danger for you. You have a dangerous facility. I am afraid you would write before you were mature enough to write. As a professor you would see almost nothing of the world that as a novelist you would have to recreate. While you were still too young you would be taken up by little literary cliques. It was not thus that Balzac began, nor Dickens. The one was a notary's clerk and printer; the other a journalist Those are professions that teach you about life. Isn't your father a manufacturer? I should much rather see you go into his factory. There you will see men at work. You will be David Sechard, César Birotteau, and perhaps Dr. Bénassis. In the evening you will copy out by hand the *Chartreuse* or the *Rouge* in order to learn the technique of writing, as young painters copy the pictures of their masters. There's a fine start in life."

That evening when I had returned to Elbeuf by the usual train, laden down with books, I repeated this conversation to my father. His kind face lighted up:

"I should never have wanted to use pressure," he said, "but since Monsieur Chartier has given you his advice, I am happy to be in agreement with him . . . I also believe that you ought to come into the mill with us or at least begin that way . . . If you continue to wish to write, your evenings will be free and, if you really have talent, no doubt in the end it will show itself . . . We must take into consideration that the workmen are attached to our family, that later on they would accept you as their head more willingly than a stranger, and that we have obligations toward all these Alsatians . . . In the mill you will have a very brilliant future . . . As for me I have suffered under the Uncles, but now they are old and the generation of young Fraenckels will be like brothers to you as they have been to me."

I was not tempted. What would I be doing, a reader of Plato and Descartes, amid these piles of cloth, these oily machines, this greasy wool? Why should I accept this arduous life, with practically no vacation, away from my beloved books, when it was within my power to lead the existence for which I felt myself fitted? Nevertheless, when I heard the two men I admired most in the world, Alain and my father, giving me the same advice though for quite different reasons I could not remain indifferent.

In the end I got a reprieve. This is how it happened: At that time a young man could agree to take a single year of military service at eighteen in a special platoon called "the exempt," provided he had gone through certain schools or had completed certain work at the University, that is, held a Master's degree. And so it was very much to my advantage to take my degree in Humane Letters (philosophy) when I was between seventeen and eighteen, to discharge my military service between eighteen and nineteen, and to find myself at the age of nineteen free of all obligations and master of my actions. My family approved this idea, and I returned to the Lycée of Rouen the following year.

The dear old Lycée, on the day of my return, was no longer an austere and rather terrifying edifice but a familiar building which I found pleasure in entering. I had decided to take my degree there, rather than go to the University of Caen or to the Sorbonne, so that I might remain near Alain. At the same time I wanted to attend classes in elementary mathematics since the preparation for my degree required little study. Unfortunately Alain was snatched away almost at once. In the *Concours Général* of the year before, in addition to my first prize Rouen had received two other high awards in philosophy. It was a brilliant triumph for Chartier, and the Lycées of Paris called him. One day in October Rabier, Director of Secondary Education, who was himself a philosopher, came unexpectedly to Rouen to see at first hand this amazing teacher who, despite his youth, seemed ready for rapid promotion.

I have retained a very vivid memory of that visit of inspection because it gave me another occasion to admire my master's character. That morning, as it happened, Chartier was delivering a lecture on morals and had commenced to talk to us about our "obligations towards prostitutes." It was a useful subject to discuss before young men of our age many of whom had had or were going to have relations

with women of this sort. Alain's thesis (which I do not dispute) was
that the worst immorality is not the prostitution of the body but that
of the emotions.

"That these women should render you a physical service," he said,
"is perhaps natural, and I do not think they suffer from it, but they
have their pride. It is distressing for them to prostitute their hearts.
So take good care not to ask them to counterfeit passions they cannot
feel toward you. You can in a large measure preserve for them the
dignity of human personality . . ."

He was at this point when the door opened and the janitor appeared
carrying two chairs. We knew that this stage setting betokened a general inspection. And indeed, a few seconds later the Headmaster in
cutaway and high hat brought in a thin man with a black goatee.

"Good day, Monsieur Chartier," said the Headmaster in his rum-
bling voice. "Monsieur the Director of Secondary Education has made
the trip from Paris in order to hear you. . . . Take your seats, gentlemen . . ."

Chartier said to Rabier:

"What do you wish us to talk about, Monsieur the Director? . . ."

"I wish you to continue the class," Rabier said, "from the point you
had reached, without paying any attention to me."

We looked at one another. What would Chartier do? Perhaps at this
moment his whole career was at stake. There was a moment of silence,
then Alain went on:

"I was in the process of explaining to these gentlemen their obligations toward prostitutes . . ."

The Headmaster gave a start; the Director remained unmoved. Our
eyes lighted with a look of pride. Our hero remained unscathed.

It must be recorded to the credit of the Administration that it did
not hold the liberalism of Chartier's lectures against him. Two weeks
later he was summoned to the Lycée Condorcet in Paris and we lost
him. I was inconsolable. I had sacrificed a year at the Sorbonne, which
would have been invaluable to me, in order to work with him. His
successor, a philosopher given to rhetoric, bored me. At that time one
could substitute a short thesis for certain parts of the examination.

I wrote one on: *Mathematical Demonstration According to Kant, Leibniz, and the Modern Mathematicians.* Recently I happened to reread it. Since that time I have learned a great deal, especially to be less sure of myself and to suffer, but I should like to recover the vigor and precision which the study of mathematics had given me at that time.

The examination for the Master's degree, like that for the Bachelor's degree, was child's play; because the foundations had been solidly laid long ago at the Junior College of Elbeuf by Kittel and Mouchel, the edifice stood firm. There was on the faculty of Caen an aged professor of Latin literature, Père Lehanneur, who had the reputation of being the most surly of the examiners. He received me with ill temper.

"Monsieur," he said to me, "I do not much like to have children in swaddling clothes applying for the Master's degree."

Thereupon he grumblingly handed me a text of Tacitus. I did not acquit myself too badly and little by little his face brightened.

"You know some Latin," he said.

It was he who read the results at the end of the examination. In announcing that I had passed he smiled grudgingly and added:

". . . with the excellent citation *Very Good.*"

His love of Tacitus had triumphed over his dislike of youth.

.   .   .   .

As a reward my parents sent me during my vacation on a long trip with my Uncle Henry Herzog, the engineer. Afflicted with an insufferably boring wife, he was one of those Frenchmen who love war and bars "because they can go there without their wives" and he profited by every occasion to flee the conjugal domicile. So he had agreed to be one of a commission sent to study the progress of work on the Simplon tunnel, then under construction; he took me with him. I have a happy recollection of those days. Some of the young engineers brought their wives along. We went into Switzerland and Italy. In the evening at the hotels there were little pastimes. The young women used to hide. I was the *Chérubin* of the party and I gleaned here and there a kiss, a ribbon, a caress.

My uncle's conversation, full of mockery and poetic melancholy, delighted me. He understood better than anyone else the strange boy I was at that time, because he had gone through the same phases. My academic successes had, despite the wise advice of Alain, given me a dangerous self assurance. Supported by the philosophers, historians and scientists, I believed I was always right. I gave the impression of being a pedant, a prig, a scoffer. With women I affected a high-handed manner; I behaved as though I were in a play by Marivaux or Musset, by Dumas *fils* or Becque. My true character was that of my father, timid and affectionate, but youth and my little triumphs inspired me with a heady exuberance which was destined to be of short duration. In the course of this trip, in the shadow of an Italian station or hidden by a cypress tree on one of the Borromée Islands, I would succeed in slipping my arm around a waist for an instant, holding a hand, or brushing the nape of a neck with my lips. My boldness went no further.

What mattered real women to me? At the bottom of my heart I still loved, as in my childhood, the Queen of the *Russian Soldiers* who had become the Natasha of *War and Peace* and the Irene of *Smoke*. I loved a being who was capricious and charming, spiritual and tender, heroic and pure, who had no part in any of the miseries from which the real women around us suffer. I loved a being made not of flesh and blood but of moonlight and crystal, of courage and passion. At the instant that I was attracted by a young woman's beauty I would lend her all the charms of my ideal, all the wit of Sanseverina, all the virginal fearlessness of Clelia Conti. Because her hair was the color of ripe wheat, because her eyes were like the cornflowers of my childhood, I could not believe that she was not, like me, mad with poetry and famished for knowledge, and at a time when she probably expected pretty speeches from a young man, I would talk to her about Spinoza.

CHAPTER V

Company School

I HAVE seen plenty of fellows work hard to keep out of the army,"
said the surgeon-major, "but this is the first time I have seen
anyone go to such lengths to get in."

He was talking to me. I was standing naked and thin as a rail under
the measuring rod. All the regulations were unanimous in ruling me
out. I had neither the required weight nor chest measurement. My
spine was not very straight. My heart produced an abnormal murmur.
But on the table lay ten letters from doctors who were friends of my
parents requesting that he accept me. I wanted to be accepted more
than anything else at that moment. Brought up by my father and my
two uncles on army stories, an enthusiastic reader through all my childhood of the warlike books of Danrit and later of Vigny, Stendhal,
Napoleon and Foch, I should have considered it a horrible disgrace
not to be a soldier.

"*Monsieur le Major,*" I implored, "take me. You'll see, I won't cause
you any trouble. I know very well I don't look vigorous, but I am. At
the Lycée of Rouen I won the Minister of War's medal for gymnastics . . ."

This last fact was decisive, and I was authorized to join the 74th
infantry regiment or, as it was called in Rouen, Seven-Four.

Through the barracks I came in contact with a new Rouen. For a
barracks extends far beyond itself. A whole military quarter surrounds
it: cafés, bars, lunch rooms, furnished rooms, girls in kerchiefs, the
small low dwellings of adjutants; the brick houses, three windows wide,
of the captains; the four window houses of the commandants; bazaars

where equipment is sold; restaurants almost like those of other quarters but nevertheless unmistakably soldiers' restaurants; just as soldiers' rooms are unmistakable. Rooms of young men harassed and pressed for time between supper and roll call; tired bodies, sleepy minds that no longer judge or see but simply accept. Rouen contains several of these military zones. In 1903 we infantry men only knew two: Zone of the Seven-Four, the Pelissier Barracks, and zone of the Three-Nine, Jeanne D'Arc Barracks.

An active rivalry existed between the two regiments. For me, a man of the Seven-Four, all men of Three-Nine were badly groomed, all officers ignorant of tactics, all regimental customs ridiculous. It was a different world, almost unintelligible. They buttoned their capes to the right; their about-face was slow, their drill absurd and their regimental singing frightful. In the evening our adjutants and theirs would meet at the Folies-Bergère. The room smelt of cigars and absinthe. A revue that we knew by heart was being played. The female lead was called Jeanne Paradis and she had fine legs. But we had spent the day on maneuvers out beyond Saint-Sever, farther out than the last trolleys, among the first fir trees on the road to Elbeuf, and we went to sleep in our seats.

How far away the Lycée seemed! Although it was just across the river on the high point of the other shore, I had no time to visit it. Nothing existed in the world except the barracks, the canteen, and hulking fellows drunk on cider brandy.

"Sing, goddess, the wrath of Peleus' son . . ." When sadness overcame me I used to try to evoke that happy life: reveries in the study, Chartier's classes, philosophers' walks beneath the chestnut trees in the Grand Courtyard. But I was surrounded by men I did not know— who talked an unfamiliar dialect and vomited between our beds. Voices off key and dripping sentimentality, the strong odor of twenty bodies in the steamy heat of a red stove—oh, how sad that singing was! . . .

"One year," I would say to myself, "still nearly a year. Three hundred days tomorrow morning."

Suddenly the superb notes of a bugle would sound taps beneath our windows. It seemed as if an arabesque of sound were drawn against the unsullied night. I imagined it dancing above the houses of Saint-Sever, crossing the Seine and reaching (a hardly perceptible refrain, distant, martial music) the students in their dormitories. I would wait enchanted for it to come again, a little attenuated by distance, for the second and third battalions. Then the uninterrupted silence . . .

"Douse that candle!" the corporal would say.

.   .   .   .

At the end of a month the platoon called "the exempt" was assembled and we left for Eu. It was a small Norman town that re-echoed with names out of history; one of the seats of the House of Orléans, the scene of an interview between Louis Philippe and Queen Victoria, it was surrounded by hills and woods well adapted for maneuvers. We were quartered in a country barracks, once a royal edifice, on the bank of the Bresle, a charming trout stream, overhung by willow trees and lined by poplars. We were a strangely assorted crowd. Many of "the exempt" were graduates of law schools, M.A.'s in literature or science, among whom was Etienne Gilson, who has since become the great authority on medieval philosophy, but who was then a bearded, good-natured, hairy and facetious soldier. There were numerous Normal students but they chose to keep to themselves. Finally there were the "journeymen of art," almost all sons of manufacturers, who had taken this easy examination for no other purpose than to be admitted to the platoon; such was the case with my friends from Elbeuf: Legrix, Bernheim and Boulé.

Just as I had loved the life of the Lycée I loved that of the regiment. To be well treated there all one had to do was to work hard, and I had the habit of work. A large part of our existence was still that of college boys. Various officers gave us courses. One of them, Lieutenant Breynat, whom we called "Chochotte" because of his pretty, womanish face, lectured us on military history and in particular on the war of 1870. Poor Breynat! He himself was not destined to survive the war of 1914. Lieutenant Isler taught us topography: thirty years later I found him a colonel of firemen in Paris. Lieutenant Giraudeau taught us the duties of a section commander in the open field. It soon became both a sporting and an intellectual pleasure for me to take part in company maneuvers. Each of us in turn had to take command of a section. "Company, left front into line!" Giraudeau would cry. It took quick reflexes to command immediately: "Left by fours!" If one of those responsible made a mistake, two sections would be back to back or tangled up together. This human geometry amused me.

This military service in the country was, in our sight, mainly an excuse for agreeable walks. What could be more delightful than to find oneself in the spring on double sentry duty with a sympathetic friend at the edge of the forest of Eu. The anemones, the primroses, the periwinkles reminded me of the Sundays of my childhood. One lay in the grass watching the life of the insects. At the end of an hour the hoofbeats of a horse would resound from the distance along the road. It would be Captain Moulin, our commander, an excellent man, altogether lacking in eloquence, who had said to us on the day of our arrival:

"You have all . . . euh . . . but a single heart . . . euh . . . which beats under the same tunic . . . euh . . ."

We used to say that the reason the platoon was in Eu was that the Colonel had asked Captain Moulin where we should be sent.

"Euh . . ." the Captain had begun.

"Fine, the very place," the Colonel had said briskly, "they shall go to Eu."

The Captain approached our thicket:

"Euh," he said to the two sentries. "Have you seen the enemy?"

"No, *mon Capitaine.*"

"Euh . . . Who is the enemy? Do you happen to know?"

"Sergeant Philippe with Gilson and Boulé, *mon Capitaine.*"

"Euh, good. Have they got on their white arm bands?"

"Yes, *mon Capitaine.*"

He would go on. Once a week he would have us capture by assault a little chapel situated at the summit of the hill which dominated the Bresle. Our one bugler would sound the charge. *"The bugle call still sounds,"* I would think as I ran. I was a long way from imagining that ten years later the Seven-Four would be rushing to attack real trenches. This training seemed to us at that time just one long, happy game. Soon the forced marches began, twenty kilometers with knapsacks on our backs; twenty-four kilometers; twenty-eight kilometers. All the marching songs were sung. We had an immense repertory, less delicate than my father's. *The Artillery Men of Metz* followed *The Louse and the Spider, Haton de la Goupillière* the *Père Dupanloup*. During the hourly rest period Gilson would tell stories:

"The setting is an immense desert . . . To the right, nothing. To the left, nothing . . . In the center a solitary date palm bows its head in melancholy. Seated beneath this palm there are three Bedouins . . ."

Captain Moulin rode up on his horse and addressed me:

"Euh," he said. "Why are you making this march? . . . euh . . . You are down on the sick list. Euh . . . I gave orders you were to be left in the barracks."

I got up and stood at attention:

"The Sergeant did tell me to stay in the barracks, *mon Capitaine,* but I asked permission to come on the march . . . I can stand it perfectly."

"Euh . . . But you are on the sick list . . . It's very irregular."

This insistence annoyed me:

"It was the Major who said I was sick, *mon Capitaine.* I don't feel sick."

"Euh . . ." he said. "I see. You are the *Malade-malgré-lui.*"

And he went on, pleased with his wit.

I have always thought with Disraeli: "Either perfect solitude or perfect sympathy." In the platoon I found this perfect sympathy. Jean Legrix, a native of Elbeuf like me and one of the noblest souls I have ever known, became a close friend at that time and remained so until the time of his death which, alas, occurred during the war of 1914. My other inseparable companions were Demanche, son of a Paris lawyer, and Harlé, whose father was a manufacturer of electrical supplies in Paris. Elective affinities are inexplicable. I could not say what it was that drew us three together, for we were markedly different, but we used to find in one another's company a pleasure that was constantly renewed. For dinner, which we took away from the barracks, about thirty of us had formed a club which was presided over with authority by Jean Boulé, another native of Elbeuf.

We joked a great deal about the military life. But if it were necessary, all these young citizens were capable of making strenuous efforts. I remember that toward the middle of June our adjutant, a strict, fierce Corsican named Sacams, announced gruffly that we were to march in the review on the Fourteenth of July with the garrison of Eu which was composed of a battalion of the 39th.

"It will be a disgrace," he added, rumblingly, "because you 'exempts' maneuver like tramps . . ."

It was true that we were negligent in drill. Our hundred right hands did not strike the slings of our rifles with a single thud; the butts of our rifles did not hit the ground at a single instant. The old sergeants who drilled us suffered, swore at us, but got no results. Suddenly Sacams' contempt piqued our vanity and we decided that our parade on the Fourteenth of July should be a masterpiece of military art. I reminded my friends of a scene in Kipling's *Stalky* and the stupefied adjutant saw us practicing the manual of arms outside drill hours under the direction of one of our own number. Presently the platoon became a crack troop. This resulted in unexpected joys. Perfection, when it is collective perfection, brings its own reward. I retain from that review, held in the broiling sun, a memory of the same sort that certain fine concerts have left in my mind. This little experience helped me later on to understand the technique of military dictatorships and their fascination for young men. It also shows the value of close order drill and the manual of arms for molding a troop. From the Fourteenth of July on, in actual battle we would have been good soldiers.

At the end of July the platoon was given its examination. This was conducted in the most formal manner. Colonel Boelle of the 39th presided over the board of examiners; he had with him a Commandant from the War College, an austere and brilliant Alsatian named Ringeisen, and our Captain Moulin. We were supposed to know all about troop movements in open country, formations in close order drill, how to write orders, draw plans and expound the theory of war. I had the good fortune in the general drawing to get the fine preamble to *Home Service*, which I admired as much as certain passages from Bossuet: "Since discipline constitutes the principal strength of armies, it is imperative that every officer shall exact from his subordinates complete obedience and submission at every instant . . ." Commander Ringeisen who asked me to comment on this passage could see that I was deeply serious about it. My company maneuvers also went smoothly, and I stood first in the platoon. All was well.

The return to Rouen was less pleasant. The eight who stood highest were made corporals, so that in rejoining the regiment I found myself in charge of a barrack room. It was a difficult task. The corporal was responsible for the condition of the room and the men; but since he slept among them and felt disinclined to punish his comrades who but a short time before had been his equals, he had much trouble in obtaining from those subordinates "complete obedience and submission at every instant." If he gave the order: "Sweep out the room," there would often be some drunken oaf who would reply: "Sweep it out yourself, you loafer." What could one do? Give the insolent fellow two days confinement to quarters? For insubordination of this sort the Captain was likely to hand out fifteen days in the guardhouse, and the Colonel two months—of which a week would be solitary confinement. Pretend not to hear? One would soon lose every vestige of authority. Nevertheless, if the barracks room was not swept out the Captain would come in and say:

"This barracks is a stable! Who's the corporal? . . . Confined to quarters."

For a whole month I was not allowed to go out. I paid dear for my two red stripes.

But living constantly with my *bonhommes*, as they were called in those days, I learned a thousand character traits of the French workman and peasant. Up to that time in the Lycée and with the platoon I had mixed only with young men of the middle class, and I had had no opportunity of knowing the people. In the barracks of Seven-Four I slept, I ate, I lived with them. What did I find? Much intelligence and shrewdness. My *bonhommes* formed opinions of their superiors that were seldom wrong. Our Captain was held in contempt by them;

ten years later the war of 1914 showed that he was unworthy to hold command. They adored our Lieutenant, who in the same war died a hero. They entertained an invincible distrust of the powerful and the rich. Patriots by instinct, they did not question their duty to defend the soil of France, and they were ready to give up their lives for their country, always provided it was not for the profit of the "big fellows."

At first, because they knew I was the son of a great manufacturer, they made life miserable for me. There was nothing easier for them than to get me punished. All they had to do was not execute an order or execute it to the letter. Then, seeing me defenseless in the face of their malice and, moreover, full of good will, they adopted me with a strange rough sort of tenderness and from that moment did their best to protect me from Captain Pétry, a nasty beggar, who continued in pure meanness to make a point of honor in finding reasons to confine me to quarters: *"Being mess sergeant, he served thirteen portions to squad thirteen which is composed of fourteen men, and fourteen portions to the fourteenth squad which is composed of thirteen men: Four days confinement to quarters . . ." "For not requiring his men to clean adequately under their beds: eight days confinement to quarters."* This became intolerable. Then came the catastrophe of the general inspection. Pétry called together the sergeants and corporals:

"The General," he said, "has a horror of brooms. He believes that the dust raised by them spreads tuberculosis . . . He desires that the floors should be cleaned with mops made of wet rope . . . And so mops will be distributed to you and you will see to it that the brooms disappear until after inspection. Explain this to your men . . . Do you understand?"

I returned to my barracks and passed the word around. Two days later the General arrived. The mop was much in evidence beneath the rifle rack. The General stopped in front of one of my men, unfortunately an illiterate peasant, the stupidest of the lot.

"What do you use to sweep the barracks?" he asked.

"A broom, General."

"And where is the broom?"

"It's been hidden, on your account, General . . ."

After this incident Pétry began to hate me in earnest and he spoiled my last months with the regiment.

Nevertheless I enjoyed rejoining Seven-Four two years later. It was the rule that "the exempt" who had had only one year of service should go back to "meet again with their class" which had served three. In the interval I had been made a sergeant and I set off for the grand maneuvers as a section leader. I had sworn to myself that I would serve at this trade just as well as I possibly could. Participating completely in the life of my men, I slept with them in barns, refusing the room "with a feather bed" which the farmers invariably offered a sergeant. Each morning I explained as well as I could to my section the maneuver for that day. Other nations fight tolerably well on mechanical discipline. Frenchmen have to understand. My men, once they had "caught on," played the game with enthusiasm and intelligence. Feeling that I had established complete control, I was able to demand great exertions from them. Before long the Colonel took notice.

"There's a fine section," he said to the captain of my company. "The sergeant ought to be promoted to second lieutenant . . ."

But I neglected to make application, and the war eight years later found me still a non-commissioned officer, a fact which, as will be seen, saved my life.

.   .   .   .

I who might so easily not have been a soldier at all if I had not wished to be, was destined to spend more than six years of my life in the army. I do not regret it. In the furious Europe of the Twentieth Century, a country was as strong as its army, and no one could say that he understood France unless he was well acquainted with the French army. I believe I was well acquainted with it, and I loved it profoundly although I was sensible of its faults. It had fine traditions inherited from the Old Régime, the Empire and the colonial wars. It was one of those rare institutions in France which had traversed the bridge of the Revolution. Educated in excellent schools, most of its officers attained in their youth a very creditable degree of intelligence and culture. Many of them entered the army, as Lyautey later informed me, full of a mystical loyalty that was almost religious.

The trouble was that in most of the corps there was too little nourishment for their enthusiasm. An army that has no well defined task goes to sleep. In the colonies the officers worked. At the War College various enthusiastic professors inspired the best of them. But in the garrisons, routine gave rise to indifference. It was noticeable that little effort was being made in the modernization of methods or in taking advantage of scientific progress. Not enough was said to the soldiers about the glory of France and the immense patrimony she had to defend. Politics, especially after the *Affaire Dreyfus*, had crept into the army and divided it. Parliament was interested first of all in making sure that the principal leaders of the army were Republicans; they should have demanded that they be leaders as well. That was easy enough to see in 1914 when the men whom the Ministry had kept in the shadow shot up to the highest posts because of their talents.

As to the rank and file, they were the immemorial Frenchmen, "Frenchmen, sons of Frenchmen under the same oriflamme." They were grumblers, always discontented and always ready to sacrifice their lives provided someone took the trouble to tell them why. A Frenchman has to understand. During maneuvers I had been able to do with my men what I liked because I had treated them as intelligent, free, human beings. The Frenchman asks nothing better than to work if the task seems to him worth while; if he gets the feeling that he's wasting his time he becomes embittered. In short, a Frenchman has a need of justice; promises must be kept and offenses must be judged fairly. Such were the lessons I learned in the army; they were to stand me in good stead in industry.

CHAPTER VI

Between Alain and Kipling

I T HAD been decided by my father, in consultation with the Uncles, that I should enter the factory at the conclusion of my year in the army. When the time came the Uncles had been reduced to "Monsieur Henry" alone, for "Monsieur Louis" had had his second stroke and, with his body half paralyzed, was engaged in dying in that apartment above the factory whence he had reigned over the family. All the Fraenckel brothers had been stricken in the same way. They would work without vacations and without recreations until they were sixty or sixty-five, then one day they would collapse and lose consciousness; they would revive with a twisted mouth, thickened tongue, and an arm and a leg immobilized. Then would begin a life at reduced rate. One of the old Alsatians from the mill would become nurse for his disabled boss. The voice would come back, brokenly; the invalid would take a few steps supported by a strong arm, or read stretched out on a couch like Uncle Adolphe. All "the gentlemen" would come in each evening, after they left the mill, to spend five minutes sitting at the bedside.

"What's new?" the living dead man would ask.

A brother, a son or a nephew would then give him the number of pieces woven and sold, the price of wool, the results of the inventory, and for an instant a brief ray of intelligence would light up the glassy eyes. Thus it would be up to the moment of the second stroke which would precede the end by only a little while.

In 1904 the general staff of the mill was made up of "Monsieur Henry," my great uncle Henry Fraenckel, a strangely inhuman old man (whom I have described under the name of Monsieur Achille in *Bernard Quesnay*); "Monsieur Paul" and "Monsieur Victor," sons of Louis Fraenckel; "Monsieur Ernest" and "Monsieur Edmond," my father and my uncle. Who was the head of the business? By right of seniority old Henry Fraenckel, but he was a modest and taciturn technician who, although he had a thorough knowledge of manufacturing, was wholly ignorant of the general business of the firm. In all social contacts Paul Fraenckel took the lead. Cultivated, ambitious, deliberately pompous in manner but devoid of malice, he loved all representative functions. It was he who was a member of the Chamber of Commerce at Elbeuf and was destined to become its President; he who would call at the office of the Prefect in Rouen when there was some labor question to be settled, and he who insisted upon receiving the Legion of Honor immediately after Uncle Henry—an unvoiced and humiliating sorrow for my father, his senior in years and service with the mill.

These decorations succeeded one another in the family with the same regularity as the attacks of apoplexy. They were the occasion for great banquets which the mill gave to its fifteen hundred workmen. On the day when the news appeared in the Official Bulletin, a delegation from each of the workshops would arrive in the Show Room carrying flowers, and the personnel would present to the new chevalier a bronze by Barbedienne: *Work* or perhaps *Thought*. A month later the banquet would take place in the immense wool sheds which would be decorated with greens, with red hangings and with flags. Paul Fraenckel would assume the task of inviting the Prefect, the Senator of the Department, a Minister or, if worst came to worst, an Under Secretary of State. There would be champagne and speeches. Then the Norman workers would sing *"Long live the cider of Normandy,"* the Alsatian workers would sing *"Hans am Schnockenloch,"* and there would be dancing. Paul and my father would open the ball with two of the pretty girl employees. In Alsace my father had been a good waltzer and he still remembered how. These celebrations were gay and good-humored.

But if you call the *head* of a business the one who controls production, then the real head of the Elbeuf mill was my Uncle Edmond. Each week on Wednesday evening he left for Paris. He spent a day visiting all the big stores, all the wholesalers of cloth and all the clothiers, and returned Friday morning laden with orders or, in periods of crisis, with complaints. The report that he made every Friday to the assembled "gentlemen" was the high point of the week. The ceremony took place in the Main Office. This was an immense room hung with army blue draperies on which were secured portraits of the dead Uncles. There a meeting was held every morning at seven-thirty to read the mail; an enormous rectangular piece of furniture with an easy chair on each of its four sides, bore on its top the high pile of letters as yet unopened. The rule was that the first of the partners to arrive had the right to open the mail. But if while he was at work an older partner came in, the younger would get up without a word and the new arrival would continue the opening of the envelopes. I have seen on certain mornings four successive changes. Then the time came when Death had carried off my betters and I myself opened the mail, an honor as prodigious as a stool at the Court of Louis XIV.

On the morning of "Edmond's return" the mail was relegated to second place. Of what importance were letters from the provinces when Edmond might be bringing back from Paris orders for a thousand, yes and sometimes for three thousand, pieces? Besides he had the knack of giving dramatic form to the story of his day, without ever spoiling his effects by announcing his successes at the start. If during the afternoon he had succeeded in snatching the orders of the *Bon Marché* away from Blin, which was the supreme triumph, rendered even sweeter by the defeat of the hereditary enemy, he would not say so until the time came, and would begin coldly:

"At eight o'clock I went to the *Samaritaine* where I saw Mellino. . . . He complained about the weave in the overcoats . . ."

For Edmond's report was often an indictment of this or that branch of the mill. When he had finished, my father who was in charge of the weaving and Paul Fraenckel who was in charge of the finishing, would explain the measures to be taken to fill the orders or to make good the complaints. If the discussion took too long, old Uncle Henry would become impatient and his bony and hairy right hand would begin very rapidly winding up an invisible machine. This was the signal that enough time had been spent in talking and that the moment had come to disperse to the workrooms.

My father, who knew all the technics used in the mill, hoped to have me learn how to spin, weave and cut. But first of all I must learn about wool. That was the most difficult of all the apprenticeships, for it required an aptitude of eye and hand which time and practice alone could give. It was decided that I should spend every morning with the chief sorter Ursin, an old Norman, who worked with his daughter. Mademoiselle Ursin, a handsome and vigorous young woman, made me think immediately of Balzac's *Rabouilleuse*. She would stand facing her father in front of a large frame on which the wool to be sorted was laid. The fleeces came in the form of bundles of greasy wool, that had been tightly compressed in ironbound bales and these it was necessary to open up. Then one separated the wool from various parts of the animal: backs, flanks, stomachs, necks. If the wool came from Australia, the tufts were small and fine with black tips; if it came from Buenos Aires, the tuft was larger; from France or Morocco, the staple was very coarse. Père Ursin taught me to take out the "ganders," that is, the shiny hairs that will not take dye and spoil the finished piece of cloth. Then he made me distinguish between first and second choice and separate them. At the end of a few days my father came to observe my progress.

"Is he getting on all right?" he asked Père Ursin.

"Faith," said the old man, "he has a good will, Monsieur Ernest . . . But he's not very intelligent."

Mademoiselle Ursin laughed heartily. She had a robust, peasant charm which made it easier for me to accept the boredom of this monotonous work. But however delightful she appeared, I was on my guard against flirting with her. I had read *The Man Who Would Be King* by Kipling, and I understood that a future chief loses his authority if he gives way to his instincts.

In the afternoon I would go to the spinning and weaving depart-

ments. The spinning mill, with its silently turning carding machines
and its winders drawing out the trembling tufts of thread twisted by
the spindles, was a place of order and beauty. But I disliked the in-
ferno of the weaving mill. The noise of the looms made the building
tremble. In all the streets of Elbeuf you heard this harsh rhythm
which was the heartbeat of the town. In the fulling mill I was the
pupil of Père Fritz, an aged magician from Alsace who taught me the
art of "teaseling," that is, of smoothing the wool in a rough cloth and
making it shine. Wool workers were provided with natural thistles
to perform this task. These thistles, sorted and classified into thirty
varieties according to the age and size of the spikes, played an amazing
role in the perfection of this finishing operation. Old Fritz examined
the pieces to be treated with the authority of a great physician. He
fingered them, tested their strength and gave the prescription:

"No new thistles for this one," he would say.

The mills in the north had adopted mechanical carding machines
with steel spikes, but Père Fritz remained loyal, with cause, to the
inimitable suppleness of nature.

Unfortunately, as I quickly learned, these fine heavy clothing materials, of which my father was so proud, were selling less and less.
Men's clothes were changing. One seldom saw "frock coats of Elbeuf
cloth" except in old-fashioned novels. Even Brittany abandoned waist-
coats of embroidered cloth for the republican jacket. The success of
our mill had been based on the wearing of "blacks," but the decent
middle class sadness of the Nineteenth Century was being supplanted
by an appetite for colors and designs. The women helped us to survive
by wearing plain black cloth. But at the moment when I entered the
mill, the gross business was slowly declining. It had attained ten million francs; now it was nearer to nine. Since the running expenses
remained the same, this slight but steady decline presented grave problems. In all the departments in which I worked I inquired what the
workmen earned. I was shocked and seriously disturbed by the low
scale of the salaries. At that time a weaver received twenty to thirty
francs a week; a carding girl, twelve francs. This seemed to me altogether insufficient to live on.

"But what can we do?" said my father with whom I discussed the matter. "We earn a bare three to five per cent on our investment. Even if you took no profit whatever, which isn't possible because the capital has to be renewed, and if you divided the entire proceeds between fifteen hundred workers, that would give very little to each one of them. . . ."

"Nevertheless, it would give them something."

"Not enough to change their standard of living . . . And how would *you* live?"

I asked:

"Couldn't one increase the selling price a little?"

"You know perfectly well our competitors wouldn't allow it . . . The instant we increase the price of cloth by ten centimes we'll be beaten by Blin or by the Northern mills."

"And if all the French manufacturers should get together and agree to increase prices and wages simultaneously?"

"Then the foreign firms would monopolize the French market."

"It could be protected by import duties . . ."

"Yes, but there is a limit that would be quickly reached in a country like ours that depends on export. There would be immediate reprisals against our wines or our luxury products, and these industries would complain to Parliament."

"But then what can we do?"

"I'm trying," my father said, "to reduce the cost price by improving the quality of the machines and increasing production . . . A mill that works under more favorable conditions can pay its personnel better . . . You have seen the new automatic loom? One woman can operate two of them. That means she can be paid more . . ."

"But it eliminates one employee?"

"Obviously . . ."

And my father, long-suffering but weary of my complaints, raised his hands in a gesture of helplessness.

This question of labor threw me into a distressing quandary. As I have said, Alain, who was not a socialist, had talked to us about socialism with intelligence and understanding. Influenced by him,

I was anxious not to make myself an accomplice of injustice or exploitation. I pictured miserably the sufferings of a working woman encumbered with children and unable to provide decent lodgings. On the other hand, when I examined the life of a man like my father I found him so different from the cruel employers described by Zola in *Germinal* that all the dramatic side of the class struggle seemed to me false and ridiculous. "If an ideal society," I thought, "were seeking a director for a great mill, a competent, just, hardworking, modest, frugal man of simple tastes, it could not find a more perfect one . . ." Moreover I saw clearly, since all the account books were open to me, that, as my father had said, the profits of the mill represented a tiny percentage on the investment. And so what was one to think? And where did one's duty lie?

．　　．　　　．　　　．　　　．　　　．　　　．

Mouchel, my former teacher of mathematics, had become the socialist mayor of Elbeuf. I used to encounter him often on the streets with his moist mustache and his chalk-covered vest. He would stop me and explain his projects:

"This unhappy city," he would say to me, "has been exploited by certain vested interests: the Gas Company and the Water Company . . . I have decided to get along without them, not to renew their contracts, and to build a gas company of my own . . . Do you understand? Besides I am going to build an incinerator for the disposal of garbage which will give me free power . . . *Hein?* Do you understand? . . . In ten years from the profits of these municipal industries I shall make this city the most advanced in France in social institutions . . ."

I submitted my scruples and distress of mind to him; he, naturally enough, was hostile to all forms of capitalism:

"The thing that's unjust," he would say to me, "is that the united effort of the workers produces a surplus value and this surplus value is confiscated under the name of profits by the capitalists . . . Do you understand? . . ."

No, I did not understand. I could not see that it was true to say, as Mouchel did, that the surplus value was produced by the workmen alone. Around me in the industrial world of Normandy I saw that two mills that were almost identical and employed the same number of workmen might make, one a profit, the other a loss, if the first was well managed and the second ill. Production itself could be increased or diminished by the methods of management. Therefore, from a scientific point of view, the Marxist theory seemed to me, at least in part, false; viewed sentimentally the idea of class warfare filled me with horror. But a certain form of Christian socialism continued to attract me. I was ready to admit that my father was a Just Man. It seemed to me it was possible to go further and be a Saint, to give all to the poor, to turn over the mill to the workmen and nevertheless to continue to manage it for honor's sake. On certain nights of enthusiasm I proposed this sort of life for myself. In the light of dawn I realized it would not be easy to go into the Main Office for the morning conference and explain my plan beneath the eye of the defunct Uncles.

.   .   .   .

My evenings were my own. I almost always spent them in my parents' house. To this provincial and retired life I owe the best of my reading. It was then that I read all of Saint-Simon, Taine, Sainte-Beuve (and in particular *Port-Royal*), Auguste Comte and many books on science. I made notes as I read and I still owned, up to the time of the last war, large notebooks in cardboard covers, in which I had written down my impressions each evening. A theory of light and sound by Helmholtz would rub shoulders there with an analysis of *Capital*; an emotional comment on *Déracinés* with a dry and precise note on Pearson's *Grammar of Science*; Henri Poincaré with Vilfredo Pareto. My intellectual appetite was voracious. However, for my own pleasure, I kept coming back to the same authors: Balzac, Stendhal, Tolstoy, Kipling. I loved the moral preoccupations of Tolstoy. In the beginning I felt very close to Levine in his discontent with life and his constant readiness to renounce the world and devote himself to austerities. Then I came to believe that Prince André in *War and Peace*, the disciplined soldier, silent and ready to submit to fate at his post without a murmur, was the finest human type. To this I added the thought from Marcus Aurelius that it is not difficult to be a sage in solitude but it is a rarer and nobler thing to be a sage on the throne and in the press of great affairs. There it seemed to me lay the solution of my problem of conscience. It was not a wholly safe solution, for the devil might choose this round-about way of reassuring the Emperor or the Rich Man.

Meanwhile Kipling played a role of the first importance in my little spiritual drama. To the radical views of Alain—those of the embattled citizen defying the authorities and fearing tyranny above all—Kipling opposed the idea of a necessary hierarchy. A society divided against itself will perish, the Stories of Kipling said to me; a society that will not accept a leader will perish. Even the beasts submitted to the laws of the jungle in order to survive. But, on the other hand, Kipling's leaders had to show themselves worthy to command through their courage and abnegation. I loved the type of Anglo-Indian he held up for our admiration: A good technician devoted body and soul to his task, mysterious and silent, loyal to his friends and severe with the rebels. There again I found a picture of what I believed a captain of industry should be. In my copy books of that time I find impassioned dialogues, by myself with myself, in which I defended by turns the thesis of Kipling and that of Alain.

Every writer has his personal themes, the projections of strong sentiments that have forced him to write, and despite himself most of his books are built around these themes. Thus Stendhal, engrossed with the young man he would have liked to be, pictures him under the names of Fabrice, of Julien Sorel and Lucien Leuwen. Thus Dickens is obsessed with the idea of the child wife. Although I was not conscious of it, these interior dialogues were slowly forming in me a writer whose essential theme would be the opposition of two equally sincere sentiments and the necessity of reconciling these two halves of himself in order to go on living.

Little by little, through the daily contact with things and people that comes from working, I learned that abstract concepts do not exist in the real world, that capitalism and socialism are words like idealism and romanticism; that the realities are quite different—human beings with their bald or well-covered heads, their myopic or long-sighted eyes, their thin- or thick-lipped mouths, their violent or lethargic appetites, their passions, their desires, their loves, their follies. "What one must draw," I said to myself sometimes, "is not an abstract world in which words contend vainly with one another, but a universe of flesh and blood where bodies work together . . . In the mouthings of an orator, Catholics, Protestants and Jews may seem three hostile groups, but on the streets of Elbeuf the Abbé Alleaume, Pastor Roerich and my father, walking together, make a single human group . . . In a propagandist's harangue employers and employees become enemy factions; at work in the mill these factions mesh together and complete one another . . . What one must draw . . ."

During my sleepless nights I outlined magnificent novels that would be fair to both sides, and on awakening I found that I was, alas, totally incapable of writing them.

CHAPTER VII

The Technician Writes Me . . .

D URING my childhood and adolescence I had always dreamed of being a writer. My arduous life in the factory scarcely seemed to favor this plan. But my hope persisted. During my last years at the Lycée I had written a few stories; the army had inspired a long novelette, *Corporal Gaucher*; from the life of Rouen and Elbeuf I had derived another, *Suze*. Taken all together this was enough to make a volume. I wished to publish it. But how? I knew no one in the literary world. An editor in Paris seemed to me a powerful and unapproachable divinity. I did not know that every manuscript sent to a publishing house is given to a reader and gets an honest chance. I hit on the scheme of taking my collection to the printer in Rouen who published the little magazine of the Lycée, and asking him to print it at my expense.

Some weeks passed and then I received a packet of proofs. To see my compositions in print was a brief pleasure. I reread them. Alas! I had been too well nourished on good literature to preserve, after that reading, any illusion of having written a masterpiece. One of the novelettes, *The Last Story of the World*, was original, at least in idea. I imagined that through the great advances in technology mankind toward the year Ten Thousand had succeeded in getting along entirely without physical effort both in work and in war. Then the women, little by little, had gained control and, being conservatives by nature, had converted human societies into hives. Most of them, unsexed, had become workers, always dressed in gray uniforms, whose duty was to look after the young of the hive or to accumulate reserves of food. A few queens assured the continuation of the race. As for the males, drones clad in brilliantly colored doublets, they sat on the steps of the hive awaiting the brief hour of the nuptial flight and playing on guitars or composing sad poems. The women prohibited reading and writing on pain of death, for they feared revolution. The man in my story, who wrote down these facts, was the last who knew how to write and he went into hiding to do it; but probably he had been denounced, for suddenly he saw advancing toward him one of the amazonian workers, brandishing a little poisoned dart—the sting. The story broke off abruptly in the middle of a sentence, and it could never be continued, for after the death of the narrator there was no longer anyone in the world who knew how to write.

It was ingenious and, if not perfectly written, at least fairly well done. The story about the regiment was very Kiplingesque and it, too, had qualities; it illustrated a high but at the same time realistic idea of the art of leadership. But the rest were feeble, and the collection on the whole gave the impression of a work lacking in cohesion. No doubt it was the individual stories that mattered, but the volume didn't have that unity of tone possessed by a collection of Kipling's stories or of Maupassant's. I had the wisdom to realize this, and I went to see my printer and told him sadly that I had given up the idea of publishing the book and that he could distribute the type. He tried to dissuade me, but my critical instinct won out.

"Run off at least a dozen copies," he said to me. "That won't cost you much more. . . ."

To this I consented, and of that first endeavor of mine all that remains is a dozen slender volumes bound in covers of pale blue on which there is neither title nor author's name.

There remained, too, a feeling of despair which no one around me noticed, for I could be very secretive and I did not like complaints. "Now," I thought, "it's over and done with. I shall sink little by little into this life of routine. For three years, five years, ten years, the impulse given me by Alain and Stendhal will still have some effect. Then inertia will win out. Like the Uncles, I shall no longer talk of anything except machines and cloth and salaries. An old and respected million-

aire, I shall succeed Paul Fraenckel as president of the Chamber of
Commerce. Each morning I shall make a tour of the workshops as my
father does until the day when I, in my turn, shall be stricken, having
lived out in this sepulcher my brief and only life . . ." When I gave
myself up to this reverie I would spend frightful evenings over an open
book which I could not read, and for a while this despair turned me
toward the frivolous social life of the community which I had hitherto
neglected in favor of my evening studies.

.   .   .   .

Elbeuf, like most small French cities, contained a number of cultured
and amiable families. The wife of my comrade in the regiment, Jean
Boulé, was a charming woman with sweet and tender eyes; my cousin,
Robert Fraenckel, a very intelligent man only a trifle older than I and
enthusiastically interested in history, had married Olga Allatini, a
beautiful Italian woman who shared my taste for music; a Blin household and a Bessand household rounded out an entertaining little group
in which the women were pretty, the men gay and the conversation
lively and unconstrained. Soon I was giving up my evening work two
or three times a week in order to join them. Since I could not get along
without writing, I composed a revue for this group of amateurs and
then a comedy. The rehearsals entertained me a great deal. For a young
man in love with all women, they provided a proper opportunity for
intimacy with indulgent friends. Then we performed the revue for the
benefit of charity, and I tasted, on a tiny scale, the joys of successful
authorship.

Nevertheless I retained enough perspective to realize the futility of
the kind of life I was now leading and the miserable poverty, not to
say blameworthy vulgarity, of the scripts that brought me this small
local glory. But in my disenchantment and desperation I took the
same somber pleasure in degrading the noble profession of authorship
that women, disappointed in true love, take in throwing themselves
into lives of dissoluteness. Only one man during this period understood
what was happening to me: that was Alain. Although he had left Rouen
he still remained for me, as for so many others, the Master. When I

had the opportunity to spend a few days in Paris, which happened rarely enough, I went to see him. He had become professor at the Lycée Condorcet and lived not far from there in the Rue de Provence in a little room furnished with a bed, a divan, a piano and that library of thirty volumes which he considered necessary and sufficient. Seated beside him on the tattered couch, I felt transported out of this world and free to express myself without reserve. He listened to my angry descriptions of the life in Elbeuf and what I called, with adolescent hyperbole, "my spiritual decadence."

"Frivolity," he said, "is a violent state."

When he was talking about women, Alain would alternate between cynicism and adoration. In this, of course, he resembled his favorite, Stendhal. I have never heard anyone talk better about romantic novels such as *Le Lys dans la Vallée* or the *Chartreuse de Parme*. But he used to say too: "Woman's greatest fascination lies in being late or being absent." Or again: "Suppressed desire is a poison. If you want to see naked women, go to a brothel." I believe he thought me dangerously inclined to romantic excesses, for he commended cynicism to me. When I read Sainte-Beuve's *Volupté*, I recognized myself in the hero who is passionately in love with an unattainable woman and, on leaving her company, goes to explore the disreputable quarters of Paris. In the evenings in Elbeuf I would silently admire the respectable young matrons and write them verses which I would not show them; Saturday evening I would go to Rouen and, with the help of an usher, make a rendezvous with one of the little dancers at the Folies Bergère. These girls of easy virtue would give me a good supper, lodging and the rest. Then, since I was always a pedant, I would talk to these poor creatures about what I had been reading and about my scruples, and I would bore them to tears.

Later on, when I observed in America the freedom enjoyed by the young men and girls at the universities, and when I realized the charm imparted to the first blossoming of love by a certain equality in culture, I regretted bitterly the mediocrity and venality of the first women with whom I had been able to consort freely. In our small provincial cities at that time girls were so rigidly guarded and early marriages so cruelly discouraged that a young man found himself forced willy-nilly to turn to the professionals. It was a sorry introduction to love and life. Body and soul acquired dangerous habits. When the soul could not find passions that would answer to its own, it became bitter and cynical. The body grew accustomed to dissociating desire and admiration. Some even reached a point where they would feel desire only for women they despised. All this was unhealthy, and dreadfully disillusioning.

In 1906 the People's University at Rouen, where Alain had formerly reigned, asked me to deliver a lecture. I accepted, and discovered to my great surprise that I entered into immediate contact with the audience. Silent enough in everyday life, I felt no fear whatever once I was on a platform. The multiplicity of those present constituted a solitude. I talked aloud to myself and people listened. These lectures in Rouen brought me back to serious work, for they required preparation. Their success was some comfort to my wounded spirit. On the other hand, when I tried to make a speech at the People's University at Elbeuf, I was astonished to find myself attacked for the first time in my life in the local socialist paper: "Let the workers beware," said the article, "of this young capitalist who, beneath the pretext of popular education, is attempting to lull the working class to sleep. Behind a capitalist's every action one must seek out the economic motive. Here it is all too clear . . ." I had talked to them on the first occasion about Victor Hugo, and on the second about *The Child in French Poetry* and I was sure of the purity of my intentions. I was stupefied and hurt. I was destined, alas, to encounter more serious injustices and to accustom myself to hatred, but at that time I was thin-skinned and I stopped speaking in public.

Another thing that wounded me was my adventure with young Duruflé. He was a boy about my own age, a weaver and the son of a weaver, whom I saw every day when I made the rounds of the workshops with my father: his fine, intelligent features had made an impression on me. With his narrow face and eyeglasses he had the look of a student or, more precisely, a pupil at the Polytechnique. I often stopped to talk with him and I discovered that appearances had not deceived me. He had a taste for intellectual activity and for reading:

he complained about the town library which was little to his taste. I
put mine at his disposal and invited him to come once a week to borrow
books at my house. For several weeks he came, and I took pains to treat
him as a friend.

"What I want to do," I said to my father, "is to make him forget
completely while he's here that I am the son of his boss."

"I doubt you will succeed," my father said.

Three months later there was a short strike at the mill. The trade
unions in this locality were moderate. They disputed questions of salaries and hours, as was their right, but up until that time the tone
of the debate had been without violence. On this occasion, for the first
time, a truly hostile and malevolent speech was delivered against us,
and the orator was young Duruflé.

"What did I tell you?" my father remarked.

I admitted that I must have been very inept.

"But what got into him?" I asked. "Can it be that I offended him
without knowing it?"

"You couldn't do anything but offend him," my father said, "and
it was for that reason that I disapproved of your methods. Even your
kindness would offend him, and your library and the room in which
you received him . . . And I don't blame him. What you meant to be
the treatment of an equal was condescension in his eyes, and I imagine
that despite yourself your words supported this misunderstanding.
Believe me, an employer must stay in his place . . . He is more respected for doing it, even better loved."

"It's too bad," I said.

.   .   .   .

In those days the political life in Elbeuf was lively. Up to the time of
the *Affaire Dreyfus* Normandy had been conservative. Then the radicals had gained the upper hand and we had had a deputy, Monsieur
Maille, a worthy Norman with the visage of a Roman senator, whose
radicalism was so pale that even the most timorous of the middle classes
could support him. But at the following elections Mouchel, my ex-
professor in mathematics, who was already mayor of Elbeuf, had

decided to be deputy as well. Jaurès had come to make a speech in his behalf, and his poetic eloquence had inundated our crowded stadium with beautiful metaphors. At the outset of the campaign the local political wheelhorses had laughed at a candidate without money or experience who delivered technical discourses to the electors and said to them: "*Hein?* . . . Do you understand?" They forgot that Frenchmen love professors.

"That fellow," Père Ursin, the old chief sorter, said to me, "is didactic. I like that."

Mouchel promised that he would have the salary of deputies reduced, that he would remain poor, and that he would resist the temptations of Paris. When the day came he was elected by a large majority.

From the very start he provoked some excitement in the Palais-Bourbon, for he dared to propose, as he had promised he would, a reduction in parliamentary salaries.

"Why," he demanded, "should we live better than the majority of our constituents?"

Unanimous murmurs silenced this upstart. A little later he protested that the Chamber didn't do enough work:

"Why not come at seven o'clock in the morning," he said, "and pass the budget on time?"

Right and Left treated him as a demagogue, but he was acting in good faith. I still used to meet him on the streets of Elbeuf.

"Our municipal works are in operation," he told me proudly, smoothing his moist mustache.

This I knew, for the works functioned badly and a dreadful smell of gas had penetrated a whole quarter of the city. The Lane of Sighs where lovers used to stroll on summer evenings had become unbearable. But Mouchel was living in a Seventh Heaven.

"To be deputy and mayor!" he said to me. "What a fine career! Each day brings some extraordinary incident. I believe you once thought of being a novelist? Oh, if you could observe the stories that I see! Listen, this very morning I was called to the Municipal Prison. A man had just hanged himself . . . He was still warm . . . And why

had he committed suicide? I started an inquest immediately . . . It's
fascinating. *Hein?* . . ."

Some disturbing rumors began to circulate through the city. Not
only did the gas works function badly but, it was reported, it did not
meet expenses. The unhappy Mouchel had unsuspectingly given jobs
to all his campaign workers. A certain sly and artful Norman named
D., who was a weaver in the Blin mill and one of the leading socialist
politicians, had been made director of the gas works in recompense for
ill-defined services. He was incompetent, like most of those employed
in the enterprise. There was no money in the tills. The town had borrowed two million francs to pay the costs of construction; it would have
to borrow anew in order to continue operations. Then the Prefecture
protested: It could not authorize the new loans. Was the town of
Elbeuf going bankrupt? One morning when we arrived at the mill the
watchman said in great excitement to my father:

"Does Monsieur Ernest know that Mouchel has killed himself? . . ."

I hurried to the town hall. The body was still on the sidewalk awaiting the coroner. The deputy-mayor had spent the night in his office,
bringing his accounts up to date; then at dawn he had come downstairs,
had got out his big, reserve-officer's revolver and had put a bullet
through his head.

His secretary, a nice young man who was devoted to him, told me
amid tears that on the day before the mayor had said repeatedly:

"I was mistaken . . . I must pay the price . . ."

But the sacrifice of an honest man makes up for nothing. This was
a triumph for the conservatives who had been predicting disaster from
the beginning of the enterprise:

"Just see what socialism leads to!" they said.

Alain, who sent an article from Paris each day to the *Rouen Dispatch*, wrote a beautiful funeral eulogy on Mouchel: "In this occurrence at Elbeuf," he said in substance, "we have nothing to regret,
nothing to take back. To draw from the death of a Just Man arguments
against his creed and faith, that is the sort of talk one might expect to
hear at the tables of the rich . . ." The article was admirably written
and it moved me, but for the first time I allowed myself to be in funda-

mental disagreement with my master. I wrote to him. My theme was: "I mourn as you do the death of a Just Man, but I do not think there is nothing to regret. Is one to understand that to hope a business will be well run, to regret the bankruptcy of a town—that these are topics for the tables of the rich? . . . Would not true victory over the rich consist in managing the gas works and the town better than they? . . . You, Alain, are like a man off sailing in a yacht; it makes no difference to you when you return. But I am a pilot aboard a merchantman; the harbor lights alone spell repose for me."

Two days later, to my great surprise, when I opened the *Rouen Dispatch* and turned to Alain's *Comments*, which were its honor and ornament, I saw that he had published my letter. "The Technician writes me," he said, and then quoted my text in full. Next day in his *Comments* he replied to me. I rejoined in my turn. "I have received," Alain wrote, "a new and striking letter from the Technician about the sad occurrence at Elbeuf . . ." From this time on it often happened that my letters and also my conversations with him became part of his *Comments*. He loved to have me talk shop or describe "the Uncles" whom he regarded, with reason, as equal to the characters of Balzac. Based on them he created for his *Comments* a man whom he called Castor and who was a sort of industrial Grandet, narrow, prudent and sensible. Some of "Monsieur Henry's" maxims delighted him: "All reports are false."—"It's not enough to give an order; you must also carry it out yourself." A remarkable characteristic in this radical was that it did not displease him to see me evolving a political attitude in consonance with the role I was destined to play in life. I even have a feeling that he would have been displeased to find me too faithful a disciple.

"I've been afraid for a long time," he said to me one day, "that you would become too intelligent. I am reassured."

This pronouncement, harsh though it sounded, gave me a strange pleasure. It came from a reader of Balzac and Comte and from the man who used to say: "In my eyes every proof is clearly discredited."

.   .   .   .

My father had decided to give me a month's vacation each year.
I spent the first one in England. For years I had fed on English poets
and novelists; I felt a profound affinity with them and wished to
become better acquainted with their language. I put an advertisement
in one of the London papers asking for lodging in a private home for
a young Frenchman. A hundred replies came. I selected a widow who
lived in Richmond on the bank of the Thames and who had three
daughters aged sixteen, eighteen, and twenty. My memory of this first
month in England is a mixture of the Micawber family and Italian
comedy. My hostess was the widow of a dancing teacher of good Norman stock, who had left an honored name but no estate. At the time
of my sojourn the only money there was in the house was the thirty
shillings I paid each week for my board. On that all of us had to
live; and the meals consisted of such stuff as dreams are made on.
But the three girls, Florence, Mary and Daphne, were ravishing. If
I wished to take one of them to the theater or out on the river, I had
to buy her an evening dress or a hat, for they lacked everything. It
made no difference to them. They were young and gay. In their company I saw the first plays of Shaw and Bennett, and musical comedies
whose songs we sang on the way home, and the *Follies* of Pelissier,
which were then the rage in London.

At first I went out impartially with each of the three sisters in turn.
Then Florence, the eldest, took the lead. Gentle, brown-haired, with
the face of a Botticelli virgin, she was unexpectedly bold. I used to go
with her every day to Richmond or Kew; I would rent a boat and take
her out on the Thames. To be honest, we never went very far. The
islands in midstream were surrounded by willow trees. We would moor
our boat to one of the trunks, stretch out beside each other on the
bottom of the craft, and that day we would row no farther.

"Do you know," Florence would ask, "what in this country we call
a butterfly kiss?"

I did not know but I was quite willing to learn.

"As for me," Florence would say provocatively, "I have never liked
French kisses."

I would try to make her change her mind. Thus the hours fled.

When evening fell, the continuous sound of laughter, of sighs and songs would rise from the innumerable boats that encircled the islands. What charming irresponsible days "written on water" I have passed thus between Richmond and Kew beneath the willow trees of the happy isles.

These pleasures of the enchanted isle, however, were not without danger. First of all, one had to be careful of the tide which is quite strong in the Thames. Sometimes in the sweetness of the hours Florence and I would forget to let out the painter of our boat and we would suddenly discover that the river had receded so far that the bow was hanging in midair. To avoid a catastrophe, I would have to clamber the length of the boat up to the bow and release the rope which had jammed under tension and refused to run. Nearby couples would be entertained at our plight and blond heads would shake with laughter in the moonlight.

The second and more serious danger was love. Florence was engaged to a rich banker in Riga who had been the boarder of the year before; she was to leave at the end of August to marry him. It was sad to acquiesce in losing her so soon. But what had I to offer? When the day came, I went to see her off on the boat in company with her mother and sisters. In traveling costume she looked, as Stendhal would have said, divine. She took me to her cabin:

"Why don't you make the crossing with me?" she implored . . . "You can go directly from Riga to France and we'll have a week more of happiness."

It was a great temptation. But I had agreed to be back at the mill on the first of September, and I had a fanatical respect for promises. I gave her a last kiss, disengaged myself from her, and ran all the way to the gangplank. Her mother and sisters, who knew very well what was going on, surrounded her and stood guard over her in her cabin until the final whistle.

CHAPTER VIII

The Sylphide

A T THE time I entered the mill, it was agreed by all "the gentle-men," my father included, that I should spend a long appren-ticeship in the different workrooms before being allowed to participate in the management of one of the departments. Events decided other-wise.

Every year at the end of July the ceremony of the "Inventory" took place. Theoretically it was the drawing up of a very simple balance sheet. In the *debit* column capital and debts were set down; in the *credit* column the plant, machinery, accounts receivable and the stock; the difference between the two columns was the loss or profit. But the evaluation of the stock in a large mill, an operation that today is simplified by new methods and new machines, remained at that time a painful task and the result was in doubt up to the very end, which made of the Inventory an exciting drama with frequent crises. For two weeks all the employees were engaged in calculating the value of cloth that was in the process of being woven, cases of thread and thread on the looms. My father, surrounded by a whole staff, would call out:

"883.772 . . . Hannibal skin . . . fifteen kilos of warp at 3 francs 50; sixteen kilos of thread at 3 francs 15 . . . 883.775 . . . Debussy Amazon . . . Six kilos of warp at 8 francs; eleven kilos of thread at 3 francs 50 . . ."

The calculators would send him the results of their multiplication. In the main office the department heads would bring in each evening the estimated results:

"Goods on hand will come to one million three hundred fifty thousand francs . . . There are eleven thousand pieces on the looms and the average will be about 215 francs . . ."

But since each one strove to guard against excessive optimism, and named a figure well below the one he actually hoped to arrive at, the advance estimates always seemed ominous. On the eve of the great day immense losses appeared certain. On the great day itself there would be a series of dramatic surprises, almost all agreeable, and in the evening the result would turn out to be what it had been every year since 1871: a normal profit.

The second year that I spent at the factory saw the rupture of this reassuring tradition. That year the nearer the hour of the decisive addition came, the clearer it became that the final result would be bad. When it was known, there was no escaping the fact that the year had been disastrous. This was serious. To have worked hard only to find oneself impoverished would have seemed painful enough in itself, but my father's real anguish was for the future of the firm. A mill that does not make a profit moves rapidly toward its death. What sickness had attacked ours? What cancer was gnawing at it? "The gentlemen" had a clear conscience. They had done their best. There had been no shirking, no extravagant expenditures. The thing that had betrayed them was Style. The fine black cloth, these woolens of uniform color, at which they were past masters, were being more and more neglected. If they were losing money, it was because their gross business was diminishing while the operating costs remained the same. For several years Edmond had been saying to them in his Friday reports:

"If we persist in refusing to make fancy cloth, I will not be responsible for maintaining our volume of sales . . ."

At first "the Uncles" shrugged their shoulders. Patterns were not their stock in trade:

"A little flower, more or less red or more or less green . . ." Monsieur Henry would say disgustedly. "Is that what you want us to make? No! We are manufacturers of Blacks . . . Each to his trade."

But the disastrous inventory called for heroic measures. It was decided that a department of design should be created, that a certain specialist, Monsieur Denis, should be engaged to manage it and that I should be put with him to learn this new trade.

Monsieur Denis was a big fellow, elegant, nonchalant, indifferent; he smoked cigarettes all day long and wore a flower in his buttonhole. "A flower! . . . In the office! . . ." said Monsieur Henry with· indignant contempt.

Monsieur Denis came from the Breton Mill in Louviers, a little town near Elbeuf, and would have been able to teach us their secrets if he had known them. As a matter of fact he knew nothing. The real creator of designs in the Breton Mill was Monsieur Breton himself, and we were forced to recognize very quickly that Denis was incapable of designing "the lines" that we lacked. Baffled and discouraged by the complete incapacity of my new master, and spurred on by the anguish of my father in the face of diminishing orders, empty looms and the threat of closing, I finally said to myself: "After all, what do we really need? . . . To devise certain new designs each season, to follow a certain tendency in style and to discover the appropriate raw materials?" This seemed to me far less difficult than to write a Latin composition or solve a problem in geometry.

What I lacked for this task was technical knowledge. I knew only the rudiments of setting cloth. What I possessed was method, a love of work and determination. One morning when everyone in the Main Office was aware of the complete checkmate of Monsieur Denis, I dared to speak out:

"Dismiss Denis," I said . . . "Hire a simple setter and let me try with his help to produce 'a line' . . ."

I was criticized for my audacity but I got what I wanted. The languid Denis and his flowery boutonnière were replaced by Martel, a vigorous technician in a blue blouse, with whom I went to work. First, I had to know what the public wanted. What were these English and French lines that were so highly praised? Some old clients, friends of the firm, informed me. They gave me samples. Martel unraveled them and pointed the elements out to me. My desk was covered with little bundles of threads of a thousand different shades. I saw with apprehension that to produce these all-important patterns hundreds of gradations and blendings were necessary. Would my elders, who were so timid, consent to give me the necessary funds?

When Martel and I had drawn up a plan I showed it to my father. He found it too ambitious . . . I reduced it. The peddlers of samples who came to see me taught me that one could know in advance what designs and colors the English were going to feature the following season. It was like an incredibly well informed Secret Service in the textile trade . . . On the themes indicated by them it was necessary to invent new variations. Here the general principles of the Fine Arts stood me in good stead: "Beauty," Alain had told us, following Kant, "is that which is intelligible without reflection." It was as true of a piece of cloth as of a monument, a painting or a poem. I set to work to have Martel produce designs that would be intelligible, simple and elegant. We made our experiments on little Jacquard looms, relics of an age that had disappeared, which old weavers used to manipulate by hand. Martel and I worked that winter as hard as men can work. Finally our first line was ready for the following spring. It comprised too small a number of series, but it had variety and grace.

"Now the thing to do," Edmond said, "is for you to come with me to Paris next Thursday . . ."

The Main Office sighed but resigned itself. A young man in Paris! What an innovation! Wednesday evening, in morning coat and high hat, for such was then the custom, I departed with Edmond. My reception was kind. All the old clothiers, the Dormeuils, the Pezés, the Chérets, who had known our firm for a long time, had been sorry not to be able to give us any more orders. They inspected my poor efforts with generous tolerance. I returned that evening having placed all my patterns and sold three or four hundred pieces. The only trouble was that my selection was now exhausted. I had not foreseen that each of the important firms would demand exclusive designs, which rendered an immense variety necessary. Our preparations had been on much too small a scale. But this comparative success inspired my elders with confidence and I obtained more generous appropriations for the following season.

Three years later, my department of designs was manufacturing eight to ten thousand pieces a year, and the gross sales of the mill had passed by several million francs the high mark of the most prosperous years of the past. This was no special credit to me. The old factory was a robust and powerful organism ready for action. My role had been confined to evoking from it an effort adapted to the new times; it had immediately carried it out with its traditional perfection. I was a little like the governor of a colony who has as support behind him the power and riches of a substantial empire. But success sometimes gives an unearned prestige, and as it happened I found myself at twenty-three the independent and uncontested head of a vast industrial domain. I had acquired some knowledge through experience. The Uncles' generation knew nothing of this new trade. They let me do my work in peace and, since they had great need of me, they treated me well. I had retained the memory of the injustice from which my father had previously suffered, and I promised myself as soon as I felt I had more power to see that the legal name of the firm should become: FRAENCKEL AND HERZOG. In this I succeeded a little later.

This power and responsibility transformed my life and, to some extent, my character. I now had so much work to do and so many daily decisions to make that I had hardly any time to meditate sadly about myself, or to analyze my scruples about the rights of a captain of industry. "Hamlet is a poor prince because he speculates about a skull," Alain wrote me. I was subject to the laws of action and the duties of one in authority. Now I dreamed of writing: *Industrial Servitude and Grandeur*. For the desire to be a writer still preyed upon me. At the mill I had my own office full of thread, felt-cloth and woolens. In a secret cupboard I had hidden some novels by Balzac, a Pascal, a Tacitus, *The Memorial* and the large notebooks in which I continued to set down my plans and thoughts whenever I had a few free moments. Mixed with my great happiness in successful and triumphant action there was a regret—for the books that would never be written and also for a way of life for which I felt myself made and which I would never know. At the Lycée I had dreamed of meeting Anatole France, Barrès, Kipling. Now I was living in a world which had no point of contact with such men. How would this narrow, exacting life of a manufacturer ever bring me the opportunity of meeting them? When would it allow me the time to write? I no longer saw any possibility of it, and this made me suffer.

The marriage of my sister Margaret gave me an instant's hope. During a visit in the mountains she had met a brilliant young professor of history, Jean Bloch, son of Richard Bloch, one of the principal officers of the Orléans Railroad Company. She fell in love with him and married him. Now her husband, like me, wanted to write, but being a Parisian by birth and education he knew the literary world infinitely better than I did. He founded a little review called *Effort*, and I contributed some articles on Bernard Shaw and Maurice Barrès. *La Nouvelle Revue Française* commented on one of them; perhaps this was an opening wedge. But my brother-in-law and I were of such opposite temperaments that any collaboration or even friendship was out of the question. It was one of those cases in which differences of feeling run so deep that even the most honest explanations can change nothing. My mother, who attached so much importance to family unity, persuaded me, for a long time, to an armed neutrality. Then the abyss became so deep that I ceased to see my sister and brother-in-law. I regretted it on my mother's account, since she suffered from the break, and also because of my sister whom I had loved very deeply in my childhood.

Now that I had become master of my own actions, I went to Paris every week and I made Monday my business day, which permitted me to spend Sunday away from Elbeuf. I had discovered the Dominical concerts and they provided me with constantly renewed delight. The elder Dupré had already taught me to love Bach, Chopin, Schumann. Colonne and Lamoureux revealed Beethoven to me. It was an immediate communion. Everything that I had thought and not been able to say, everything that I hoped for and had not been able to express, was sung in the wordless phrases of these symphonies. When that mighty river of sound began to flow, I let myself be carried on its waters. My soul was bathed and purified. The necessity of giving orders had tended to harden me. Beethoven called me back to kindliness, charity, and love.

This lesson was especially necessary for me at that time. Preoccupied, overworked, harassed, naïvely certain of the importance of my activity and once more spoiled by success, I was becoming temperamentally difficult to get along with. Women in my eyes had ceased to be what they had been at the time of the forked lilac tree, the Queen of the *Young Russian Soldiers*, Helen, Andromeda or the fair ladies of a reverent knight, and had become mere instruments of pleasure and servants. However, one of those whom I saw at that time was especially worthy of being loved. She was a student of medicine whom I had met on the train between Rouen and Paris. Chance had led to a conversation. I had found my fellow traveler cultured and remarkable for the scientific turn of her conversation: since she was also very pretty, with the freshness of a Flemish blonde, I was eager to see her again. This was not difficult to arrange, for she was studying to be an intern and the courses, the hospital and, in case of need, a substitute for the night, gave her a great deal of liberty.

We dined together two or three times on Sundays and then, wishing to receive her in my own establishment, I rented a ground-floor apartment at the end of a courtyard in the Rue de Madrid. This was the time of bachelor apartments, of the novels of Bourget and of *The Red Lily,* and Madame N. took pleasure in hiding her face behind a thick veil and stealing into forbidden lodgings. Surely there was never a less exacting mistress. I was incapable of any effort of kindness or sacrifice for her, no matter how slight. Twenty times Suzanne (this was her first name) said to me:

"Stay over Monday night . . . I can take a night off . . ."

"What are you thinking of?" I would reply. "I have to be at the mill Tuesday morning at seven-thirty."

"Then give me part of Monday afternoon."

"But you're dreaming, Suzanne! What about my work?"

Perhaps this conscientiousness was laudable, but it was carried out gracelessly, and I am amazed that this charming woman was able to put up with me for as long as she did.

When my vacation came, I went mountain climbing with a team of good Alpinists in the massif of the Vanoise, and on my way back stopped at Geneva. I had promised while there to call on an actress named Maggy Bertin, a friend of one of my friends. She was playing at the theater of the Parc des Eaux-Vives. During the intermission I went to see her in her dressing room. A girl was seated nearby. She introduced her:

"Mademoiselle Janine de Szymkiewicz . . ."

I stood motionless, transfixed by the astonishing beauty of this stranger. How often I had dreamed of the perfect face in which the pensive seriousness of the adolescent should be combined with the delicate grace of the woman. The countenance of my dreams was before me.

"Mademoiselle de Szymkiewicz," Maggy said and I hardly heard her, "has come to ask my advice . . . She is not happy at home and is thinking of going on the stage . . ."

I could not take my eyes away from the apparition which had suddenly fulfilled all the longings of my heart. The young woman was wearing a dress of natural tussur silk; it had a blue silk sailor collar trimmed with white beads and a belt of the same material. Her large straw hat was tied with a white ribbon trimmed with blue beads. She, too, was staring at me and, embarrassed by my silence, she smiled.

What was Maggy talking about that day? I don't believe I ever knew. I remember my impatience for the intermission to end and my tremendous desire to be alone with the stranger. Finally the prolonged, insistent ringing of the bell drove us out. As the door closed I said:

"Are you going back to the play?"

"No," she said, "I have no ticket . . . I just came to see Mademoiselle Bertin."

"May I accompany you through the park?"

"If you like."

When I recall that evening, the sentiment that I recapture is a mixture of admiration, enthusiasm and assurance. From our very first words the conversation moved on a plane of intimacy, tenderness and, one could probably say, love. I fell in love immediately with her precise, slightly husky voice and the poetic sadness of what she said. And what did she say? She told me the story of her life. Her mother, a very beautiful woman from Lyons, had captivated a Russian gentleman, Count Constantin de Szymkiewicz. The latter had died very young, leaving two children. His widow had come to live in Switzerland and had put her daughter in a convent at Lausanne and her son in a boarding school at Neuchâtel. Janine had left her school a year before. She was unhappy.

"But why?"

"Oh! It would be too hard to say . . ."

"Why? Is it so complicated?"

"No . . . but it is distressing."

"Talking about distressing things is one way of getting rid of them."

An instant later we were seated side by side on a bench in the Parc des Eaux-Vives in the moonlight and she was telling me why life in her home seemed insufferable to her. From the instant when I first saw her the soul of the Knight of my childhood had re-awakened in me. She was the Queen of the *Young Russian Soldiers*, the Natasha of *War and Peace*, the Irene of *Smoke*.

"It's strange," I told her, "but I have been waiting for you for twenty-five years . . ."

Our hands met in the shadows.

"You're like the Reynolds angels," I told her.

"Don't place me too high," she said, "you will be disillusioned . . ."

"I don't believe it."

The moon disappeared behind the trees. My new friend got up.

"I'll have to go home," she said, "the Lions will be furious."

"Who are the Lions?"

"My mother and my grandmother."

I went with her to her door.

"And may I see you tomorrow?"

"Yes. Come to the park at four o'clock near our bench. I will be there . . . We can have tea together."

I walked back toward my hotel along the shore of the sleeping lake. I felt joyful, lighthearted and confident. Suddenly all my cynicism had vanished.

CHAPTER IX

For Better and for Worse

NEXT day I had lunch with Maggy at the Café du Nord and questioned her at length about the angelic apparition that had brightened her dressing-room the night before.

"But, my dear," Maggy said, "you're not talking about anything except her. You're being rude . . . You didn't even come to see the end of my play . . . However, I forgive you; the child is unbelievably beautiful . . . What do you want me to tell you about her? I met her at the home of friends here in Geneva . . . They said she was charming and of a very noble Slavic family . . . Her mother had left her Russian husband, who was the girl's father, for a Swiss diplomat whom she loved. Hence the residence in Geneva . . . Now the husband is dead; an uncle, Jean de Szymkiewicz contributes a small allowance for the education of the children . . . I have seen the mother; she is still beautiful; she is gay and generous, but there is also great disorder in her affairs. The children suffer from the situation . . . You can well imagine in this puritan city they are not allowed to forget that, despite their excellent birth, they will not be received by the small local aristocracy . . . Hence the girl's desire to work, to earn her own living, in short to get away from here . . ."

At the appointed hour I was waiting in the Parc des Eaux-Vives. An instant later Mademoiselle de Szymkiewicz arrived, and I was enchanted to find her even more perfect than I had remembered.

"Good afternoon," she said.

On her lips the syllables were smooth and long drawn out. Her very musical voice had modulations in the minor key. She suggested that we hire a carriage and have tea at one of the farms near Geneva. Thus began a week of enchantment, understanding and tenderness. From morning till night we were together. Sometimes we took one of the steamers that make a tour of the lake, and she showed me her convent at Lausanne and the beautiful cathedral from whose tower a watch-man sings out the fleeting hours. Sometimes we wandered afoot through the old quarters of Geneva; she made me look at the ancient wall of the Escalade and hummed its song for me.

Finding, as always, an added pleasure in combining memories of books with my strongest sentiments, I determined to take her to visit the Château de Coppet, as a pilgrimage in memory of Madame de Staël, and the Château de Chillon as a pilgrimage in memory of Byron. "How sweet are the first steps of love," Goethe wrote, "when the young woman likes to learn and the young man likes to teach." I do not know whether Janine liked to learn but she wanted to please me and she listened with patience. At that time I could not see a woman whose beauty I admired without immediately hoping to make her mind re-semble mine. I used to like to quote Baudelaire's phrase: "A man's mind in a woman's body," and another from La Bruyère: "A beautiful woman who has the qualities of an honest man affords the most de-lightful companionship in the world." I did not understand that a woman of seventeen, however intelligent she might be, remains a woman. To poor Janine, who had read a great deal for her age and who sincerely loved poetry and music but also loved the windows of jewelers and florists, I talked about philosophy and mathematics. With the end of my cane I drew geometrical figures for her in the sand of the paths, and in the evening I told her the names of the constellations reflected in the waters of the lake. Then she would turn her head and look at me laughingly. And suddenly my pedantry would dissolve and I would be just a young man desperately in love. Time fled. It was already two days past the time when I should have returned to the mill. I had sent a telegram saying that I had been detained in Switzer-land but giving no further explanation. Ah! How deeply in love I must have been suddenly to show such boldness in wrong-doing!

What was to come of this romantic adventure? I had no idea. No doubt it would have been possible to ask Mademoiselle de Szymkiewicz to marry me. But that seemed bold to the point of insanity. Could I return to the Main Office and announce my engagement before the portraits of the terrible Uncles?

"To whom?" I would be asked.

"To a young Russian girl who lives in Geneva."

"To a young Russian girl! How old is she?"

"Seventeen."

"What do her parents do? . . . What dowry will there be? . . ."

"No dowry . . . Her mother has nothing but debts."

"Are you mad?"

No doubt in the end my father, a romantic beneath his surface timidity, would have taken my part. But what sort of reception would the little industrial town give to a stranger from fairyland? Wouldn't she be very unhappy? The answer seemed to me all too clear. Moreover, after a week of happiness, there had been no mention of the future between Janine and me. She was afraid to think of it. Her own destiny seemed to her dark and full of obscure dangers. She often quoted a sentence from some novel: "Beneath the sway of Mars, sentenced without reprieve, O maid of the golden tresses, beware . . ."

"Sentenced without reprieve," she would repeat often, melancholy foreboding in her melodious voice, and for the first time in his life the self-assured and logical boy that I was then understood that there were more things beneath the heavens than were dreamt of in his philosophy.

Janine's sorrows contributed as much to her prestige in my eyes as did her beauty. From childhood the idea of love had been linked in my mind with that of devotion. To be the Perseus of some Andromeda, the Chevalier de Maison Rouge for some Marie-Antoinette had been my favorite dream. Life now imitated the dream.

"And the Lions?" I asked her. "What do the Lions say about our daily excursions?"

"The Lions?" she said. "They are speechless."

She decided to introduce me to her mother; I found a woman of jovial plumpness, still beautiful and a little hostile toward me, which was only to be expected. The day after this visit a telegram arrived from Elbeuf: *"Fail to understand—designs held up by your absence—return immediately."* However intense my desire to stay, I could not and must not disobey this order. I had to tell Janine about my departure. It was at Nyons beneath the trees that border the lake; before us the vague, recumbent profile of Mont Blanc dominated the flowery slopes. The sun was setting. I had waited until the final moment so as not to spoil our last day.

"I must leave, Janine, this very evening . . . I am going by the night train."

I saw tears in her eyes.

"What will become of me without you?" she said. "For a week I have been so used to having you always with me."

"I promise I will come back."

She said eagerly:

"When?"

"Very soon. I shall not even wait for the Christmas holidays. At need I can take a train from Paris on Saturday evening spend Sunday with you, and be back in Paris at seven Monday morning to go on with my work."

"Oh, do that!" she said. "Swear to me that you will do that."

I gladly took the oath, for I myself was very unhappy at leaving her.

"I'm going to try," I said, "to spend five minutes without looking at you so that I can get used to it."

I turned my head away; at the end of ten seconds our eyes met.

"I *cannot* do it," I said. "And in my turn I have to ask: What will become of me without you?"

She sighed:

"Oh you! . . . You will see other girls . . . You will forget me."

"They will not possess your sweet moonlight radiance."

She accompanied me to the Geneva station, and at the instant when I had to get into my compartment she raised her lips to mine. We were both weeping but we smiled through our tears.

"I have been too fond," she said, quoting Shakespeare's Juliet, "and you may be afraid that if you marry me my conduct will be too light . . ."

A sympathetic Swiss guard pushed me gently:

"Come on! Come on!" he said. "All aboard!"

I returned to Elbeuf transformed and distracted, but no one at the mill noticed it. I got through my work as usual. The colored threads and the samples of cloth had piled up on my desk in my absence. The clients were clamoring for me to call. On the following Sunday I did not go to Geneva, but I did find in the Rue de Madrid my learned and voluptuous friend. She had a premonition of danger:

"What's the matter with you?" she said. "You have changed . . ."

I denied it, but in the second week I could not keep it up and informed Suzanne by telegram that on the following Sunday I should be absent. The night train took me to Switzerland; another brought me back Monday morning to Paris in time for my work. I then adopted the surprising, but for me delightful, habit of going to spend *all* my Sundays in Geneva. Janine would come at eight o'clock in the morning to meet me at the Cornavin station. As she was very pious and did not want to miss mass, she took me with her. She had been stupefied and disconcerted to learn that I was not a Catholic.

"I shall convert you," she said.

I experienced an infinite sweetness in finding myself close to her in a church. The music and the singing were so beautiful, the Latin of the liturgy so sublime and the lesson of the day, each Sunday, so perfectly and mysteriously in accord with our thoughts.

"How happy are those," I thought, "whose lives are framed by such a combination of religion and poetry . . ."

Janine had said to me one day at the beginning of our friendship:

"Promise me that you will never try to make me lose my faith . . ."

"Dearest," I replied, "I would rather try to give you one if you were without it."

This life went on until the beginning of December. Then one day in Elbeuf the doorman at the mill handed me a telegram:

"*Arriving Rue de Madrid Saturday—Lions have become dangerous— Love—Janine.*" This piece of news upset me. Not that I was less delighted to see her in Paris than in Geneva, but what was I to do with her? To ruin the life of such a charming, proud, young girl seemed to me hideous. Moreover, I was only living two days a week in Paris.

What would she do alone the rest of the time? Should I marry her? I eagerly wished to, but I judged it impossible to talk to the family about it until Janine was at least twenty years old and until my position was more firmly established. I passed two sleepless nights thinking of possible solutions, and arrived at a project which many will consider ridiculous and which only an academic mind like mine could have imagined. "Since she is not happy at home," I thought, "and since I expect to marry her, why not take advantage of these two years to complete her education? . . . And why shouldn't I send her to England at my expense to spend a year at some young ladies' finishing school, and then another year at the university?"

When she arrived, artless and unconcerned, with her suitcase ("My light luggage," she said in appealing tones, referring no doubt to Manon) I informed her of my plan. She was surprised and a little upset:

"To England? But why? I shall never see you."

"I shall do what I did when you were in Geneva. I shall come to see you on Sundays."

"Is that possible?"

"Yes, by taking the night boat."

"You'll die of exhaustion."

"I am never exhausted."

"But I don't know a word of English . . ."

"That's why you must learn it. There's nothing that will be more useful to you."

After much weeping she agreed:

"On one condition . . . You'll take me there."

"That's what I intend to do. I want to pick out your school myself."

It took a little time to prepare for the trip, provide her with clothes and inform the Lions. Meanwhile I rented a room for her in the home of a friend of mine. Then at the time of the Christmas holidays I obtained from my father, under some pretext which I have now forgotten, three days leave during which I took her to Brighton, where I had discovered by correspondence a school that seemed excellent. I took great pleasure in shopping with her in the Paris stores where her ex·

cellent taste delighted me. There was already a sort of conjugal note
in our friendship and this seemed to me a propitious sign.

It was an odd feeling to receive each day from an English school the
letters of a student who was at once my daughter, my pupil and my
fiancée. I was amused to compare myself with the tutors in Molière
and Beaumarchais who educated their pupils in order to make them
their wives. At Brighton and also at Clacton-on-Sea, where she went
later, I presented myself to the headmistresses as Janine's brother. This
explained my paying her school bills and enabled me to go out freely
with her. At Clacton she formed a very close friendship with Louise
Baumeister, an Alsatian girl, to whom she told the story of our intrigue.
So romantic a situation fascinated the blithe and charming friend who
became, as will be seen, an invaluable aid to us.

After a year of school Janine knew enough to take courses at Oxford.
There I boldly arranged to have her board in the home of Monsieur
Berthon, the professor of French at the university. He had an English
wife who was an excellent hostess and who contributed a great deal
to the formation of Janine's tastes and taught her the art of running a
household. Twenty years later when my books were used as texts in the
classes at Oxford, the Berthons knew that we had played an innocent
Italian comedy in their home and that their pupil's brother had been
in reality her future husband. They had the good grace not to harbor
a grudge against me. Monsieur Berthon undertook to enroll Janine in
the different courses at Oxford which a girl could attend. She happily
followed those in literature but was bored with the class in political
economy which, for reasons which escape me, we forced upon her. I still
own a notebook which she covered with humorous sketches alternating
with scraps of a theory of prices.

In all the courses she attended her beauty turned the heads of the
young men. Soon she was besieged with admirers wanting to take her
out on the river or to the theater. When I came to see her and she
described her success, with amusement but without vanity, for she was
modest, I was somewhat jealous. What would happen if one of these
handsome blond or red-headed young athletes offered to marry her?

"Don't worry," she said to me, "several have already proposed. I have replied each time that I was engaged . . ."

"So you are," I said.

In her company I learned to know Oxford. She took me to see Magdalen, Christchurch, All Souls and at University College the Cenotaph of Shelley.

Beneath the willow trees along the river we talked about our future. I was now determined to marry her. In the course of her year at Oxford she had acquired I know not what quality of assurance which inspired me with confidence in our designs. My own independence in Elbeuf was now great enough for me not to fear that my family would stand in my way once they felt that I had definitely made up my mind. I knew that my father had thought of a different alliance for me which would have brought together in my hands great industrial and financial power, but I knew too that he had a tender heart and that our romance would touch him. What were the best means and the best moment to break the news of this romance?

It was a characteristic of my family that it was impossible for them to transmit a message that was painful or simply important directly to the person for whom it was intended. A telegram announcing a sickness, a death or even an engagement had to be addressed to an uncle or a cousin who would then have the duty of "preparing" the person concerned. Faithful to this local tradition, I asked my sister Germaine, an energetic girl who was acquainted with the situation, to "prepare" my mother. As almost always happens, the latter replied that this was far from being a revelation to her:

"Of course I haven't said anything to your brother," my mother said, "but for a long time I have believed that he was secretly married in England . . . He has made so many visits there in the last two years . . . He gets a letter from there every morning and always in the same handwriting . . . Yes, I was convinced that he was married . . . But I have not yet dared to talk to your father about it . . ."

And so the problem still existed. Louise Baumeister, Janine's Alsatian friend, who had finished her studies in England and returned to Haguenau, suggested an excellent plan.

"Why don't you come," she wrote to Janine, "and spend your vacation at Haguenau? Your fiancé's family can become acquainted with you there. Since they are Alsatians they will probably be happy to revisit their province and this will dispose them favorably. As for my parents, to whom I have talked so much about you, they will be delighted to meet you and to render you this small service. My mother's meals will sweeten all dispositions. Tell me when you will arrive . . ."

I believed with her that nothing could be more helpful to me in making my parents accept this "exotic" and, in their eyes, extraordinary marriage than the cordial and savory atmosphere of an Alsatian household. How many times my father had talked to me of Haguenau! It was quite close to Bischwiller where he had had his first mill and to Bouxwiller where he had been brought up. He had never returned to Alsace since the war. I knew that he would feel freer there than in Elbeuf where the shades of the Uncles, harsh and sarcastic, wandered through the offices keeping censorious track of thoughts and of hours.

I have already said that my father and I had great difficulty in broaching to each other any intimate or delicate subject. Twenty times I volunteered to go with him to the Caudebec mill or to the one at Saint-Aubin, determined to talk to him on the way. The curious thing was that he knew perfectly well what I had to say to him, for my sister had discussed it with my cousins who had told him my secret. But he was as timid as I, and we would return to the mill without having said a word. Finally an urgent letter from Loulou Baumeister, which showed me how painful Janine's false position had become, gave me the necessary courage. The news was received sympathetically but with some concern:

"Are you quite sure," my father said, "that you are not making an immense mistake in linking your whole life to that of a stranger who is so different from us?"

"But, Papa, I have known her for three years and I get along with her infinitely better than with the girls of Elbeuf or of Rouen. Moreover, I am not asking you, at this moment, to consent to our marriage but simply to see her."

"And who are these Baumeisters with whom she is living? Her rela-
ives? . . ."

"No, they are friends, but they treat her like a daughter."

"Formerly," my father said, "I used to know a Dr. Baumeister . . ."

And I felt that everything was going well.

The trip to Alsace was a great success. My parents were delighted to
see Strasbourg and Bischwiller again. The Baumeister family pleased
them greatly; their crusty forthrightness, their friendly familiarity, their
Alsatian solidity, brought back all their youth. The *Kugelhopf*, the
mussel-plum tarts, the roast goose recalled the festivities of their childhood. Janine, pale, delicate and deeply moved, stood out from this
robust background like a saint in a stained glass window above the
stolid, kneeling Donors. Her fragile beauty touched my father.

"I don't know whether you're right," he said to me, "but I understand."

The presence of this patriarchal Alsatian family around her reassured him. Unwittingly he forgot that she was in this house by chance
and through the courtesy of a friend. My mother, who was more critical, remained polite and reserved. I divined that she would have
preferred to have for a daughter-in-law Loulou Baumeister, who was
as pretty, as poised and as brilliant as a *soubrette* in a play by Molière,
and who had staged this whole pageant and was animating it with her
spirit. But on the day of our departure when Monsieur Baumeister,
admirably coached by his daughter, served us champagne for dinner
and proposed the toast: "To a happy event that is not far off," my
parents embraced us. The game had been won.

"And the Lions? What will the Lions say?" I asked Janine when we
had left the table and were alone in Loulou's room.

"The Lions?" she said. "They will be flabbergasted!"

She undertook the negotiations with her mother and her guardian
uncle who lived in Varsovie. That could not have been very difficult.
All that Madame de Szymkiewicz asked was the promise that the children should be Catholic. That had been my intention anyway. In
Elbeuf, the Main Office received the news of my approaching marriage,
for which they had been prepared, with coolness. They dared not

criticize; they would not praise. Monsieur Henry put an end to an embarrassing silence by winding up with his hairy, bony hand an invisible machine.

We needed a house. I found one near the Caudebec mill that was modest but comfortable and was surrounded by a fine flower garden Janine went to look at it and loved it. On the other hand, she was terri fied by Elbeuf, by the noise of the looms, and by the silently censorious reception of "the gentlemen." After a few words, Monsieur Henry gave a flick of the wrist, dismissing us to unspecified labors.

"Are you sure he's alive, that uncle of yours?" she asked me as we left the factory.

I felt that she was on the point of giving up our beautiful plan.

"I don't know," she went on in a serious tone, "whether I can live here. It seems so sad, so sad . . ."

"Not at all," I said. "You'll see. The town is full of young couples. You'll find them in due time."

The entertainment of buying furniture and a trousseau soon made her forget her dismay. Up to this time she had never had any personal belongings except a little ebony elephant with a broken trunk, which she solemnly brought me as her dowry. The marriage took place in Paris on the 30th of October 1912 at the town hall of the Ninth Arrondissement. Some months before, I had left the Rue de Madrid and had rented a small apartment in the Rue Blanche opposite the Church of the Trinity. It was in that church that an amiable, aged curé united us. To hold Janine's hand in mine and to slip the ring on her finger was very sweet.

"For better and for worse," she said to me gravely as we walked down the steps of the church. In Trinity Square flights of doves were wheeling in the sun.

CHAPTER X

O Time, Stay Thy Flight

OUR house in Caudebec was simple but charming. Janine's taste had done wonders. Fresh from Oxford, she had selected English furniture at a Paris upholsterer's. Everywhere the rich billiance of mahogany reflected vases of flowers. "Doing her flowers" was one of my wife's greatest pleasures. She loved long slender vases, Chinese vases with lustrous surfaces, Venetian glass, Wedgwood vases, engraved Lalique crystal. She would spend a long time studying the curve of a stem or a green cloud of asparagus fern. She knew how to thin out and lighten bunches of flowers that were too heavy. I owned a great number of books and all our rooms were adorned with shelves bright with the mosaic of bindings. Our garden, like all those in Elbeuf, was an old-fashioned garden: beds of begonias and geraniums with borders of forget-me-nots or heliotrope; but Janine quickly added a well-designed kitchen garden and a cutting garden crowded with a profusion of brilliant variegated flowers like the high borders of the Oxford gardens. She proved to be a good housekeeper and kept up a correspondence with her grandmother (whom she loved very much), with her mother and with Loulou, in which recipes played a large part.

Was she happy? I don't believe that question can be answered by a simple yes or no. Certainly she found pleasure, after having suffered so much uncertainty and disorder, in being sure of her ground, mistress of her own little world and free from all material worries. We had many tastes in common and the evenings we spent together while I read novels or plays aloud to her or she played the piano for me or told me about her childhood were almost always gay and full of tenderness.

With my incorrigible professorial instincts I tried to make her love what I loved; Stendhal, Balzac, Mérimée, Tolstoy. Desiring nothing more for myself, I believed with naïve egoism that she too was completely satisfied. I learned long after her death from letters she had written that she had had great difficulty in acclimating herself to a family that was austere and, on the whole, sad. "Our hermit's life," she used to say. No doubt she had suffered in her mother's home in Geneva from an excess of caprice and lack of foresight. But she, together with her brother, had acquired there habits of frivolous gaiety that had no scope in Elbeuf.

For me, who spent the whole day in an office between the blue blouse of Père Martel and the grumbling of my partners, to come home at mealtime and find beneath a bower of lime trees a fresh and ravishing young woman in a bright dress, always ready to listen to me or to love me, was delightful. For her these hours of intimacy were separated by the vast desert of the days. What could she do? She did not get along with my mother as well as I had hoped. She admired her virtues and respected her, but she suffered from a feeling of being constantly supervised and she sensed a constant unexpressed criticism which disturbed and chilled her. Completely engrossed in her charities, my mother would have liked a daughter-in-law capable of helping her in managing them. Janine was too young, too lacking in patience. She liked my father very much and sometimes accompanied him on the piano in the evenings when he sang the *"Bells of Corneville"* or *"The Little Duke,"* but he was at the mill all day long, and moreover he was too old and too reserved to be her confidant. It took her a long time to form friendships with the young women of Elbeuf. Two of them, my cousin Olga and the wife of my friend, Jean Legrix, could have and should have been congenial. But beneath her detached and almost haughty manner, Janine was shy. She stayed at home and was bored.

If I attempt after thirty years to imagine what impression our family life made on Janine, I think she must have felt great amazement and, on some occasions, fear. All was honor, work and austerity, but we lived there, she and I, beneath the constant menace of Things Not Said. Mute monsters floated invisibly amid our vases of flowers and our shelves of books. My family surrounded us with melancholy reticences and unexpressed reservations. There were days on which Janine felt herself blamed without knowing why, and on these occasions I would say to her that to question my parents about it was inconceivable. Repression, which in the Freudian doctrine serves principally to conceal impulses of sensuality, in our household also hid shades of feeling, wounded pride and conflicting ideas. Nothing was openly expressed and for that reason everything took on a disproportionate importance. Experience was to show the dangers of this attitude. Nature too long compressed ends by bursting the bonds imposed upon it. For a long time I believed in the virtues of silence; I have now come to understand the liberating virtues of confession.

Luckily for Janine there was the trip to Paris that came each week to break the hold of Elbeuf and the monotony of our recluse life. I now stayed there two days in addition to Sunday, and we decided to rent a more comfortable apartment than my bachelor quarters in Trinity Place; we found one in the Rue Ampère that was new and furnished with taste; and of this Janine made "a thing of beauty." At this time we knew no one at all in Paris. I had a strong affection for my mother's family and I found a subject worthy of Dickens or the Brontës in the four sisters who, at the age of fifty, came every day dressed in black to sit for hours around their seventy-year-old mother in the drawing room in the Rue de Tocqueville like almost silent statues of filial devotion, happy to waste silently away amid the family heirlooms. But if I admired the vigor of my grandmother's mind, her unimpaired memory, her sane and lively judgments on Gide, Romain Rolland, Anatole France, and the prodigious prestige which she retained in the eyes of three generations, I perceived that Janine was horribly bored by these collective meditations in the Rue de Tocqueville, and I rarely took her there. As for my clients, I was seeing them all day and had no wish to meet them again socially. And so actually we were very much alone, but we had no need of others. The theaters, concerts, museums and, for Janine when I was away, the dressmakers and milliners, sufficed for a time to fill our lives.

The mill was growing steadily; it now employed almost two thousand workers. Monsieur Henry, the last survivor of the Uncles' generation, had had his first stroke. One morning he had felt a tingling in his right hand, that hand which by winding up an invisible machine had so often cut short my proposals and my thoughts, and two days later paralysis had immobilized half his body. Now that man of iron was no more than a living corpse watched over with insolence and devotion by an ancient Alsatian whom he would summon when he had need of his services during the night by pounding with his cane. Every evening on leaving the factory the three Fraenckel brothers and the two Herzog brothers would come to sit by his bedside.

"What's new?" he would ask, moving his thickened tongue with difficulty.

They would answer him in figures: production, orders, prices of raw materials. To be sure there were certain events abroad: the campaign in Morocco and the hostility of Germany, but no one ever mentioned them to him.

My father had finally received the Legion of Honor, after having been nominated by the Prefect with this handsome citation: "For having in 1871-1872 saved for France through his efforts and devotion four hundred Frenchmen. For having founded and supported numerous charitable institutions. Forty years of industrial activity." The workmen had greeted this award with a hearty, triumphant and tumultuous joy which gave him the keenest pleasure. Not only had one delegation followed another into his office bearing flowers and the classic bronzes of Barbedienne, but he received numerous simple letters from spinners and weavers all saying: "Bravo, Monsieur Ernest, this time the government has done the right thing . . ." It was agreeable and touching to see that this unaffected man had been judged by those under him at his true worth and that work, impartiality and justice retained their value in the eyes of French workmen. My father of course held a banquet in the wool shed for the personnel, and opened the ball with Philomène, eldest of the Alsatian women, who had been brought to Elbeuf in 1871 in a wheelbarrow pushed by her father. Some weeks later he retired. His health was not good and, moreover, with his habitual generosity he wished to give me his place now that I had a household of my own to support.

I myself was already becoming an oldtimer. Two of my young cousins, Pierre Herzog and André Fraenckel, entered the mill in 1912, having taken their bachelor's degrees and done their military service. Both of them had taken the course for Cadet Officers of the Reserve, a new institution which had not existed at the time of my service. Pierre was in the infantry, André a *chasseur à pied*; both possessed the finest qualities of leadership. With them there, I was confident of the future of the mill. Together with Robert Fraenckel we composed a unified and enthusiastic young team imbued with the same theories. Like me, Pierre and André had the highest ideals of the duties of an industrialist, a desire to get along with the workmen, innate respect for the interests of the nation and a sense of sacrifice. I was so happy to find in them collaborators after my own heart that I forgot for some months the still bleeding wound of the literary vocation I had missed. Moreover I was not writing any more now; I was too busy. All signs pointed to the life of a great industrialist for me, sovereign of his little kingdom and perhaps happy.

On the 27th of May, 1914, there was born in the little apartment in the Rue Ampère our daughter, who was called Michelle, from the name of the heroine in one of Henry Ardel's naïve romances which her mother loved. My wife, who liked to bestow nicknames, called me Minou and (baptized Jeanne) had named herself Janine, then Ginette, transformed her little daughter into "Poucette."

It was a difficult delivery; Janine was very sick, had a violent hemorrhage and remained weak for a long time. But she was pleased to have a baby. An English nurse, an ageless person, red-headed and authoritarian, came into our house. With her we returned to Elbeuf at the end of June. In the train at the Saint-Lazare station, as I opened the paper I had just bought, I read in the *Latest News* the murder of the Archduke, heir to the throne of Austria-Hungary, and his wife at Sarajevo. I mentioned it to Janine, who had taken her daughter on her knees and was trying to make her smile. She raised her head:

"Who's been assassinated?"

"The Archduke Francis-Ferdinand, and the Duchess of Hohenberg."
She pouted with indifference.

"Look at Poucette," she said to me, "the little darling likes being
in a train."

This news, this instant, marked the end of our peace and happiness,
but how were we to have guessed it? Without further comment on the
news item, we bent over the little red face and our eyes met above
our daughter.

The whole first part of the month of July was devoted to Michelle.
Her bottles of milk, the chart of her weight, her pram, had become
the sole subjects of conversation. Janine was suddenly showing herself to be very maternal, and this revelation modified the feelings of
certain members of my family toward her.

"Up to now," my Uncle Edmond said with candor, "I had considered her a stranger, an imported ornament, a duck's egg, or even
a parakeet's egg . . . But now that she has a daughter and looks after
her I have adopted her."

Meanwhile the mill ran normally, the "lines" were nearing completion and we were all making plans for vacations. About the 20th
of July the news became disquieting. There was talk of an ultimatum
to Serbia, but the idea of a European war did not even cross our
minds. Two days later it was necessary to face that danger. I went to
get my instructions for mobilization out of the bottom of a drawer.
On the first day I was to go to the depot of the Seven-Four at Rouen.
I was still a sergeant.

"How careless I have been!" I said sadly to my wife. "All I had to
do was to say a word and I should have been made second lieutenant,
and now here comes the war and I shall have to go as an N.C."

"But you don't really think that we are going to have war?" Janine
said.

"I don't know . . . Things are moving that way."

"And what will become of us, your daughter and me?" she asked
in distress.

I myself was sadly disturbed. Janine's life in Elbeuf was possible as long as I was there. Alone in the midst of a family that was not hers at heart, what would in fact become of her? I could not picture it. In vain I tried to make arrangements, to look ahead. Already I found myself caught in the teeth of huge gears and deprived of all liberty. The headlines in the papers became enormous: "STATE OF ALARM IN GERMANY . . . GENERAL MOBILIZATION IN RUSSIA . . . WHAT WILL ENGLAND DO?"

On the 30th of July it was no longer possible, even for those who, like me, wanted to be optimistic, to preserve the slightest illusion. I went to the shop of Bonvoisin, the Elbeuf shoemaker, to buy military boots, distrusting the army issue. Then I went to look for a belt with a pocket for gold pieces, for I had been brought up on the stories of Captain Parquin, soldier of the Empire, who was always saved at moments of crisis by a napoleon drawn from his belt. My wife, despite her fatigue and weakness, went with me everywhere.

"I'll not leave you for an instant!" she said. "As long as I still see you I don't believe that I am going to lose you."

I had never seen her more beautiful nor more touching since the day when she arrived in Paris with her "light luggage." In the same tone that was at once sad, childish, plaintive and imperceptibly mocking, she repeated:

"Poor Ginette! . . . Poor Poucette! . . ."

The streets of Elbeuf, ordinarily so empty when the factories were running, were filled from morning till night with distracted families. At our mill we cleared for action. All the young executives, Pierre, André, and I were due to leave the first day. Robert Fraenckel, exempt from service because of his nearsightedness, refused to stay behind and went to Rouen where he hoped to enlist. My father, who had recently resigned and had great need of rest, announced that he would take my place for the duration of the war and that he refused remuneration. Patriotism was present everywhere. In August 1914 France showed itself marvelously united. Young workmen came to shake hands with their employers.

"Well, Monsieur André, you're in the *chasseurs?* . . . I'm in the
biffe, Hundred Twenty-Nine, the Le Havre regiment . . ."

Saturnin, the man who carried the pieces of cloth on his head in
the storeroom like the drawers of water in Oriental pictures, a veteran
of the African campaigns with a scar that bisected his face, told us
about war:

"You'll hear the bullets, Monsieur Pierre; it's nothing much. You'll
see . . . They go *pish* . . . *pish* . . ."

The Alsatians made an appointment with my father in Strasbourg:
"We'll get Bischwiller back for you, Monsieur Ernest . . . And
you'll open a factory down there."

Janine and I spent a sweet and melancholy evening. The weather
was clear and warm; we went to sit in the garden beneath the trees.
We held hands and hardly spoke.

"I hope you have not been too unhappy?" I said.

"I have been so happy," she said, "that I wish now all my life had
been like this last year . . . But I'm so afraid of what is coming . . ."

"My family will take care of you; I have solemnly asked them to."

"Yes," she said, "they will do their best, but they won't know how
. . . Once you have gone, there will be no further bond between them
and me."

Above us the stars revolved gently, but we talked on in the warm
night until dawn. Very shortly after we had finally retired we were
wakened by the drums of the mobilization. Only once when I was
with the regiment had I heard the lugubrious beat to arms. It overwhelmed me. From street corner to street corner the drum beats answered one another and re-echoed in our hearts. Then the bells of the
churches in Elbeuf, in Caudebec, in Saint-Pierre fell to ringing out
the tocsin. The die was cast.

I had to be in Rouen before evening. We spent our last morning
in the garden. The nurse, silent and icy, as Englishwomen are in time
of catastrophe, had come and placed Michelle's carriage in front of
us. After the rolling of the drums and the breathless summons of the
bells, the calm was so complete that we seemed to be living through
enchanted hours that could never end. Was it possible that such sweet-

ness should serve as the prelude to so much horror? From the town, which was no doubt full of silent farewells, there arose neither songs nor cries. We could hear the bees busy gathering honey in the lime trees of the arbor, and the quiet breathing of our daughter. This morning, which was one of the most tragic in my life, has left me with an impression of unbelievable beauty, of sweetness unbearable in its intensity, and of sad and solemn communion. I felt that these hours so cruelly and tenderly fleeting were the last of my youth.

My parents arrived to say good-by and broke the enchantment. I went to put on my uniform which my father wanted to see. The Infantry still wore blue tunics and red trousers. Mine had been got out of a wardrobe the day before and smelled of camphor. The puttees felt uncomfortable on my legs which were used to the freedom of civilian clothes. My father looked me over with the severity of an old soldier:

"You must polish up your buttons," he said.

He was sad at my leaving but full of hope for France and happy to see a son of his taking part in the war of revenge of which he had dreamed ever since 1871. Jean Boulé, who was to take me to Rouen in his car, was announced. He too was in uniform. I had asked Janine not to go with me to the barracks so as not to weaken my courage. On the threshold she embraced me. Tears hung on her eyelashes but she did not cry. At the moment when I was getting into the car she rushed to the garden, returned with our daughter, and held her up to me; the baby, terrified by the red caps, started to cry. But the car was already moving toward Rouen.

"Poor Ginette!" I thought. "Poor Poucette!"

British Expeditionary Force

THE barracks of the Seven-Four in Rouen had acquired a warlike air. In the courtyard, behind a long table made of three boards supported by trestles, the quartermaster-sergeants were seated leafing through mobilization papers. Huge figures at the end of each table identified the companies. Men in civilian clothes—bourgeois, workmen and peasants—stood in queues in front of the quartermasters waiting to check in. I took my place among them. When my turn came, an officer standing beside the table looked at my papers:

"Oh no," he said to me, "you are not to go with the regiment . . . Special Mission H . . . Report to Room 52, building B; you will find the others there."

In Room 52, building B, I found Boulé who had brought me, Legrix, André Blin, some men from Rouen, others from Paris . . . But what was this special mission? The better informed members of the group said that we were to be in charge of liaison with the English and that we would go with them.

"With the English?" I said. "But I don't want to fight this war with the English! I'd rather stay with my regiment."

"Don't get excited," they said to me. "It is not even certain that the English will come. They haven't declared war yet."

I went to see a commandant whom I had known well since the last maneuvers.

"*Mon Commandant,*" I said to him, "I do not know what this Mission H may be, but if it really is a matter of being an interpreter with the English, it seems to me absurd. I do not speak English at all well, whereas I think I would make a good section leader."

"You are right," he said, "but there is nothing I can do about it. This mission was assembled independently of the regiment. It is in charge of General Huguet; he alone has authority over the men."

I learned later that Mission H had been got together very secretly. One day a *gendarme* had come to my parents' house and had asked my mother if I spoke English. When she said yes, he put my name down. There had been no examination; no one of those concerned had been officially notified. This *gendarme* had played the part in my life of one of those messengers incarnated in humble form, which the Gods in Homer made use of to control the destiny of mortals.

When I returned to Room 52 I learned that we were allowed to go out. A huge crowd full of confidence and enthusiasm filled the ancient streets of Rouen. In front of the Café Victor a band was playing the national anthems of the Allies: the *Marseillaise,* the *Brabançonne,* the anthem of Imperial Russia and the Serbian anthem. Then someone shouted for *God Save the King.* The people of Rouen listened bareheaded. Near me an old Englishman with a red face and a white mustache was weeping:

"By God!" he said, "I hope the boys will come."

As the last notes died away the crowd shouted: *"Vive l'Angleterre!"* I went into the café and asked if I might telephone to Elbeuf. It was permitted. I called Janine. To hear her voice was a delightful experience.

"How wonderful!" she said. "I was picturing you already on the battlefield . . ."

"Oh, no," I said, "I'm still here in Rouen. Come and see me tomorrow . . . What have you done all day?"

"Nothing," she said in the tone she had used in referring to her *light luggage.* "I cried a little; I rocked Poucette; I thought of you."

Next day she came to Rouen with Germaine Legrix whose husband was also a member of Mission H. We now had a leader, Captain Ridel, an artillery officer in the Reserve and a Parisian industrialist; he was a little man, lively, precise, epicurean, lovable and mercurial. He had brought with him to Rouen his wife, who was a beautiful red-haired woman, warm-hearted and cultivated. Our two families immediately became friends and I grew to be the Captain's right hand man in the group, a circumstance which turned out to be both good and bad luck for me. Good luck because the Ridels were to remain our friends for a long time; bad luck because Suzanne Ridel, touched by Janine's isolation, insisted, with tender sympathy, that her husband keep me in Rouen as long as possible.

"When the English Army leaves," he said, "I shall have to stay here myself for some weeks, perhaps for some months, to organize its service of supply and its bases. I shall need you."

"But, *mon Capitaine*," I said, "I should rather go with the others; I want to fight in this war."

"You'll have plenty of time to do that," said Ridel. "It will be a long war. And you must think of your unfortunate wife. She has explained the situation to my wife: she has no family in this country; she has not yet become a part of yours; she has not recovered from the nervous shock of her confinement. She is concealing her condition from you, but she is desperate."

Later I often blamed myself for my blindness at that time. Men never understand the dreadful weariness of women. The woman I adored was suffering from nervous exhaustion, and I saw nothing; I made her take a trip each day for the pleasure of seeing her during one hour; I thought, not about arranging my life to make her happy, but about seeing that her existence was compatible with my duties as a soldier. Captain Ridel wished to do me a service in selecting me to stay in Rouen; I believe he unwittingly did much harm to our marriage.

Janine had married a young leader of industry, a power in his own domain and master of his actions. She suddenly found herself sharing the life of a non-commissioned officer, a tiny cog in a terrible machine, a small employee subordinated to innumerable superiors. At the moment when I left Elbeuf I had, in her eyes, the prestige that comes from danger courageously and sincerely accepted. At parting she had passionately embraced a warrior. What she recovered on the station platform was an unimportant functionary. I felt this contrast and I suffered from it.

My regiment had set off with flowers on their rifles accompanied by a throng of singing women, old men and children. How handsome it looked, how well they marched and how I regretted not parading with them! There followed two days of silence; the town, emptied of its youth, was waiting. Then one morning the captain sent me an order:

"Report at ten o'clock at Cavalier de la Salle Quay to receive Colonel Moore, and place yourself at his disposal."

I have a noble memory of the arrival of the first English regiments in Rouen, in August 1914. The great transports loaded with soldiers in khaki, so closely pressed together that they seemed to form a single living mass, came up the Seine. On the bank French girls waved flowers and handkerchiefs.

"Hip, hip, hurrah!" the soldiers replied with a single voice.

When they disembarked we admired their discipline, their numbers and the evidence they bore, in a thousand details, of the ancient tradition of a great people. For us foot soldiers of the Third Republic, the army meant an odor of coal tar, scanty coats, stiff boots. These English regiments had preserved the elegance and finery of the armies of the old regime. Their beautiful drums painted with the royal arms, their horses with white harnesses and the brilliantly colored tartans of the Highlanders filled me with admiration, surprise and misgiving. How would these bright paladins setting out for the Crusade receive us poor beggars of the French rank and file, jabbering horrible English?

On this point we were quickly reassured. Not only did they receive us with courtesy but they quickly became attached to us as though to mysterious, strange and useful animals which France had given them. Whether the man in question was Boulé, Legrix or André Blin or myself, in a week's time no English Colonel could get along without "his Frenchman" who, in this strange country of incomprehensible customs, had become a sort of Providence for him and the battalion. Colonel Moore, my colonel, was an Irishman, energetic, ambitious and anxious to astonish his superior the Quartermaster General by the speed with which he carried out orders. In this I helped him to the best of my ability. Organizing a military base is a business very much like any other in civil life. My days and nights were spent in renting stores, negotiating with the port authorities and military authorities. Because I spoke in the name of the British Army my modest rank was forgotten. Once more I dealt in large affairs. I got on well with my superiors and my comrades. But I was not happy.

In the first place the news was bad. The Germans were advancing. At Charleroi my unfortunate Seven-Four had lost half its effectives. It was said that Rouen might be menaced from one day to the next. One night at the beginning of September Colonel Moore woke me up and said in a whisper:

"You're leaving with me immediately. The car is at the door . . . Not a word to anyone . . . We're going to Nantes to establish a new base there in case Le Havre and Rouen should become untenable."

The Germans at Rouen . . . But what of my wife and daughter? I mentioned them to the Colonel. He was sympathetic:

"Send word to your wife and advise her to leave for Nantes tomorrow, but do not tell her why nor that she will find you there."

Poor Janine traveled for two days and two nights in a third-class carriage because the refugees from the north had crowded the trains and troop transports had overburdened the railways. When she arrived, exhausted and ill, the news of the victory of the Marne had just been announced.

"We have nothing more to do in Nantes," Colonel Moore told me. "We must return to Rouen with all haste."

Once more I had to break my wife's heart by abandoning her in this strange city. She was at the end of her strength.

Weeks passed. Everything was different from what we had expected. I had left Elbeuf to take command of a section, to maneuver and shoot, to risk my life. My desire for sacrifice had been denied and I had lost my equilibrium. After the Marne I hoped for a quick victory. But the armies had entrenched themselves and did not move. Now they were requesting wood charcoal for their braziers, the only fuel that was not dangerous. There was hardly any left in France. Colonel Moore said to me:

"I need tons of charcoal . . . Produce it."

With the aid of Captain Ridel I created a whole industry in the

forests of Normandy. The braziers in the trenches did not lack for
fuel. But I suffered from carrying on this overseer's task while my
friends were under fire. I received somber but courageous letters from
my cousins Pierre and André. Both had been handsomely cited in the
orders of the day. André, a lieutenant in the *chasseurs à pied* had no
doubts about his fate: "The certainty of a fine death," he wrote to me,
"leaves no place at all for fear." At the beginning of 1915 he was
killed by a bullet through the forehead while leading his company in
an attack. I had loved him dearly, his death overwhelmed me. I said
to Ridel:

"Don't make me stay in Rouen, sir, I implore you. I cannot bear
to remain in safety when this boy has sacrificed his life for the ideas
which I helped him to form . . ."

"But your wife?" Ridel asked.

"Do you think this life is making her very happy?" I replied.

I knew that she was not. In Elbeuf she was often at cross purposes
with my family; in Rouen she complained that she never saw me except surrounded by tiresome majors and colonels. My departure for
the front would leave her free to go and live in Paris in our attractive
small apartment in the Rue Ampère. We did not lack money, for
contrary to expectations the mill which I had believed condemned to
run at a reduced rate was working at full capacity. Although it had
lost a large part of its workers through mobilization, it had acquired
hundreds of refugees from the North who had repleted its working
force.

In March 1915 Ridel was appointed liaison officer with the Ninth
Scottish Division and promised to have me come to the front with him
as soon as Colonel Moore consented. Colonel Moore, whom we called
in the Hindu fashion "our father and our mother," fought like a fiend
when the Mission talked of suddenly taking away *his* two Frenchmen
and replacing them by strangers. Finally he himself was promoted
and I was able to rejoin Ridel. Trips at that time were difficult and
mysterious. A Railway Transport officer would give you a "secret"
route order which simply contained the number of your unit, then

he would put you on a certain train with orders to get off at a specified station where another R.T.O. would shunt you on again.

Finally after long hours of jolts, waiting and slow progression I arrived at Béthune and learned that the Headquarters of the Ninth Division was located there. Gunfire was audible on all sides; part of the city bore visible evidence of bombardment; the trains stopped outside the station because the latter was an enemy target. I found my Captain in a little office near the station. He was the same as in Rouen, gay, mercurial, energetic and friendly:

"We're in luck," he told me, "this Scotch Division is a picked troop . . . With it we'll go places."

And he confided in me as a great secret that the British Army was preparing a gas attack in imitation of the one the Germans had launched at Ypres. This battle, the first I saw, was the battle of Loos. For the great day Ridel had put me at the disposal of the Division Commander, General Thesiger.

Several days before the attack Divisional Headquarters was moved from Béthune and installed in a small château on the road to Loos. The spectacle of the troops on their way to take up combat posts with heads bent before the passage of shells like wheat bowed down by the wind, the fresh shell holes smelling of earth and powder, awakened in me a keen longing that I had not felt for a long time—the desire to write. The contrast between the calm of the khaki-clad soldiers, who stood at the crossroads directing the movement of traffic with the calm gestures of policemen in Piccadilly Circus, and the danger of their position seemed to me beautiful and worthy of being recorded; sadder, but not less beautiful, was the contrast later on between the appearance of the General on the morning of battle, very courteous and dignified, in a uniform resplendent with red and gold, and the return that same evening of his corpse stained with blood and mire.

My role during the battle was exactly that which I later assigned to the interpreter Aurelle in my first book. It was my duty to maintain liaison with the French batteries which supported the Division. My route through the damp woods where lost soldiers wandered seemed to me fantastic and romantic. I fancied I was Fabrice on the battlefield of Waterloo. I thought of nothing in the world except the proper execution of my tiny role. Unfortunately this offensive of Loos was a complete failure. The wind changed and blew the gas that had been destined for the enemy back on our own troops. The losses in the Ninth Division were so great that after the failure of the offensive it was decided to send us back for a rest. Then it became necessary to reinforce the region of Ypres and G.H.Q. sent us there. It was a hard sector for tired troops.

All this Flemish country appeared strangely inhuman at that time. A house that was not disfigured by any scars was something to look at. The little village of Poperinghe had been cut in two, one half being in ruins while in the other prosperous shops survived where Tommys and Jocks purchased lace from young Flemish girls who were undismayed by the danger. Ypres was nothing more than a location and a name; Vlamertinghe, Dickebusch, Reninghels, where our Division was encamped, contained only the phantoms of houses in which we found shelter for our sleeping bags. When I arrived in this sector I stayed with Captain Ridel in the Hoogegraef Convent which was inhabited by six aged nuns and their Mother Superior. These kind sisters had generously allowed us two beds in a room situated at the end of their own dormitory, on condition that we should come in after nightfall and wait before going out until they were at matins—stipulations which were of course scrupulously respected. Later I shared the tent of an English doctor in a field.

It rained. Oh, how it rained! The rich earth became a morass which was rendered treacherous by the beetroots over which we constantly stumbled. Since I had no rubber boots my feet were wet all the time. Sometimes rain squalls would upset our badly secured tent during the night, and we would have to crawl about in the mud under the wet canvas in order to get out. The British Army had given me a very nice horse and, remembering the lessons of Charpentier, I attempted to school him. One day in jumping a ditch he slipped in the clay soil and fell on me. I can still see that great horse crashing down on my chest and beyond it a livid sky across which black clouds raced. This accident sent me to the Field Ambulance Station where I met doctors

whose conversation delighted me. It was while listening to
conceived for the first time the idea of writing dialogues
describe the English and Scotch from within, with no comments by the author; and it was then that I composed a first chapter,
The Horse and the Faun from an anecdote told by Dr. James, a brilliant and sarcastic alienist with whom I had made friends.

Little by little there emerged from this arduous life a mad and
melancholy poetry. It took, at first, a musical form. At the officers'
mess, night after night, the Colonel's gramophone ground out the
same songs: *Destiny Waltz, We've Come up from Somerset, Pack Up
Your Troubles in Your Old Kit Bag;* then came Kreisler's violin,
Caruso's voice and that of Mrs. Finzi-Magrini, who was the Colonel's
favorite. Outside the detonation of the cannon and the rattle of the
machine guns provided an excellent counterpoint. From time to time
one of the rough and gallant fellows would tell some story of the
Indies, of Egypt, or of New Zealand. I would listen with a sort of rapture as though some fine foreign book had come to life before my eyes.
Then when the music alone traced designs in the silence, I would
dream of Janine, of my daughter and of my parents. What were they
all doing? I would summon up my wife's ravishing face bending over
the cradle of the sleeping Poucette. Would she not forget me? Every
day long letters came from her and packages of food, of woolens and
of books. I sent her verses written beneath the tent to the accompani-
ment of gunfire and wind.

What was she thinking about? Whom did she see? I asked her these
questions constantly and complained at the lack of preciseness in her
replies. That she should be living the life of Paris disturbed me. "I
am taking lessons," she wrote, "I am learning Italian. I am riding
horseback. I am learning to drive in the Bois. I saw all the Aunts at
Rue de Tocqueville." Her mother and brother had come from Geneva
to live in Paris, and I was afraid their influence would be opposed to
mine. Anyway, without having any specific reason, I was worried to
the point of distraction. My acute anxiety ran like a melodious plaint
through the harmonious life of my foreign comrades. A secret voice,
hardly audible, kept murmuring within me: "And if you could de-

scribe this anguish wouldn't it, too, contribute to the beauty of your book?"

Occasionally some officer would take me with him to Ypres. With an elderly Colonel in the Medical Corps I went to see my friend, Dr. James, in Maple Copse, a little wood in the front line. At the entrance to the town a violent bombardment stopped us in the midst of a military transport which was blocking the road. The shells came closer. Around us red explosions blew bits of machines, men and horses into the air. For the first time I knew the feeling of fear that twists your entrails and contorts your face. The Colonel, seeing me grow pale, offered his flask:

"Drink," he said. "Dr. Johnson said that brandy is the stuff from which heroes are made."

He was right. A few swallows of good cognac brought back my natural optimism and the bombardment became a spectacle. I have remembered this receipt and made use of it successfully through two wars.

Despite the way the days dragged, the weeks and months passed fast enough. General Furse had replaced General Thesiger who had been killed at Loos. Furse was what the men called a *strafer*. As soon as he arrived in a quiet sector he would order bombardments and attacks and provoke the enemy to reply. Ridel had left us, summoned back to the artillery. With Georges Richet, who had replaced him, I translated a very good English book on the war, *The First Hundred Thousand* by Ian Hay who, under the name of Major Beith, was one of our officers. Nelson accepted our translation and published it. Another of our officers was Winston Churchill, a lieutenant-colonel in command of one of our battalions, but I barely saw him at that time. When we left the Ypres sector we were sent to recuperate at Outersteene in the rear of Bailleul. There happily I found a true French village living and working as in time of peace. And I formed a real friendship with the beautiful and sensible daughters of the local tavern keeper.

During this period of recuperation I became better acquainted with my Scotsmen. I had a chance to visit all the regiments, with their diverse tartans: the Gordon Highlanders, the Seaforth Highlanders,

Argyll, Black Watch, Camerons. Everywhere I picked up types and anecdotes which were to prove useful for the book I was dreaming about. I saw boxing matches in barns and football matches on muddy fields which were inaugurated by the solemn ritual of the bagpipes and drums. When Christmas came, I was requested to supply the division with turkeys and with sage for the stuffing; on St. Andrew's day I saw the bagpipes precede the *haggis* into the officers' mess. Thus little by little was filled in the background against which I was to draw my characters. I began to see those characters, as well, in obscure confusion, and I let their transparent shades draw nourishment from flesh and blood and from the conversation of my friends.

I was in no hurry; I knew that one day, when the time had come, the ripe fruit would fall from the branch.

After the Bailleul sector, General Headquarters sent us to the Armentières sector. It was less rough than Ypres but, overworked and stunned by fatigue and nervous shocks, I fell ill. The Army doctors decided to evacuate me in the direction of Le Havre. On the card I was not supposed to see I read: *"Aneurism of the aorta."* Did I really have so serious a disorder? I could not believe it. I felt exhausted but not dying. In the hospital train that took me away, beautiful, rosy, blonde English nurses treated me like a fragile object. I let them do as they liked. Life had been so hard for ten months that a little feminine tenderness was sweet. And then I was going to see Janine again . . . To the devil with doctors and their diagnoses! My heart leaped, but with joy.

CHAPTER XII

Colonel Bramble

FROM the British hospital train I was taken to the French military hospital at Le Havre where by good luck I found Doctor Leduc of Pont-de-l'Arche who was a friend of my family. He examined me and auscultated me with care.

"I solemnly assure you," he said, "that you have no aneurism of the aorta. What you have is an extra-cardiac murmur and incredibly violent palpitations. I am going to put you on the inactive list."

I begged him not to do it; I had finally been recommended for the rank of second lieutenant and I had set my heart on becoming an officer; this would not be possible if I stayed behind the lines.

"All right," he said. "I shall put you under observation for three months, during which time you will live here at the Base. Then I shall examine you again myself and if it isn't too unreasonable I shall send you back into active service."

The French Mission with the British Army, when it was informed of this decision, attached me to the staff of General Asser, Commandant of the British Base at Le Havre.

General Asser, a superb giant of a man, who had been Commander-in-Chief in Sudan and whose eyes, beneath bristling eyebrows, remained half closed from the Egyptian sun, was as Kipling said, "a Presence." A born commander, energetic and even harsh when necessary, he nevertheless listened to complaints, knew how to soothe wounded pride and had formed a staff that was devoted to him to the point of abnegation. His second in command, Brigadier General Welch, a little, dark, austere man with a hard face, served him like a faithful dog. British soldiers called them the White General and the Black

General; in reality General Welch was as "white" as his master and a perfect soldier, but he had assumed an implacable mask because his rapid promotion had given him as subordinates men older than himself. Fear secured respect; justice maintained it.

Before my arrival the liaison work had been carried on by Lieutenant Raymond Woog, a talented painter and charming companion, and by Sergeant de Chabaud-Latour, a courteous and meticulous elderly gentleman who served as the General's authority on etiquette. Having some free time ahead, I rented a pretty, old house at the foot of the hill of Sainte-Adresse and had my wife and daughter join me. It was against the regulations since Le Havre was in the Army Zone, but all my superiors had become my friends and closed their eyes to it. Seeing my daughter again was a great and delightful surprise. At that age children change rapidly. Michelle was now talking and running about. Her mother was proud of her and called her *Miss Non-Non-Non* or *Ta-peti-peta*. In that beautiful garden at Le Havre we spent hours that recalled the sweetness of the past.

"Your husband will soon be our best liaison officer," Black General Welch said to my wife. "He understands us and we understand him."

Janine seemed contented. She had found friends in Le Havre. She loved the sea and the harbor and the fine pattern of masts and rigging against a dramatic sky that reminded one of Jongkind and Boudin. I believe she would willingly have stayed permanently in that lively city.

But in time of war nothing lasts. Since the British armies were complaining of the poor organization of transport and supplies, General Asser, who had succeeded so splendidly at Le Havre, was suddenly made G.O.C.L. of C. (General Officer Commanding the Lines of Communication) with the rank of Army Commander and the grade of Lieutenant General and with residence at Abbeville. Lieutenant General Sir John Asser (he had received a K.C.M.G. from the King) took Welch, who had become a Major General, with him and requested the Mission to make me an officer and attach me to his staff, which was granted at once.

.   .   .   .

Abbeville . . . A charming cathedral, surmounted by a graceful watch tower, dominated the town. The ancient wooden houses with sculptured beams were situated around a statue of Admiral Courbet holding out his hand "to see if it's raining," as the inhabitants used to say. The latter, shrewd and suspicious Picards, resembled the 15th Century burghers carved on the beam ends of their houses. Although the city was attacked nearly every night by German airplanes the trades people who were doing magnificent business with the English General Staff refused to be evacuated. Energetic girls braved death to sell postcards and beer to the Tommies. I had sumptuous lodgings in the home of Mademoiselle d'Aumale and took my meals at mess with the General Staff, a group of officers to whom I became more attached than to any I had met up to that time.

The Colonel in charge of operations (G. Branch) was Warre, son of the famous headmaster of Eton. Colonel Warre was an elegant little man celebrated in the British Army for having won the Kadir Cup, for pig sticking. This exploit of his youth conferred great authority upon his strategic views. His adjutant, Major Wake, also an Etonian, was a descendant of Hereward the Wake, the last Saxon who fought against the Normans at the time of William the Conqueror. Sarcastic, paradoxical, brilliant and highly educated, he became later on the Major Parker of my book but with a mixture of Colonel Jenner, Assistant Adjutant General and descendant of Jenner, inventor of vaccine. Douglas, the General's Aide-de-Camp, was a young artillery officer who had been seriously wounded and who shared my office; he played ragtime on my typewriter, tossed my papers about and gave voice to hunting cries whenever I was struggling with the telephone. Much simplified, he was the Dundas of the book.

I had a great deal of work. General Asser was responsible for the defense and organization of an immense territory administered by French authorities. The relations with the latter were close and sometimes difficult. Often I would have to jump in a car and rush to make peace in some small village which believed it was insufficiently defended against airplanes, or in the heart of some French general wounded by a too-peremptory British order. My friendship with General Welch was invaluable. Every day I had tea alone with him and at that time could tell him frankly and unofficially a thousand important things. Even the English generals, knowing that he listened to me, would seek me out to explain ticklish cases:

"If you could say a word about it to Welch, it would help . . ."

I was the Grey Eminence of a Grey Eminence, a Father Joseph of the second degree. Moreover, now that I had become an officer, I was in command of a detachment of about thirty liaison agents and had to watch over them, pay them and keep an eye on their conduct. One of "my men" was Jacques de Breteuil, a friend of the Prince of Wales and another was the orientalist Eustache de Lorey. They all did their work well and gave me little trouble; for my part I let them alone and paid them no more attention than I was forced to.

General Asser was much less intimate with me than General Welch, rarely descending from his Olympus to mix with mortals (except occasionally like Jupiter and for the same reasons) but he often made use of me in his work and on official visits. When Clemenceau came to the Somme front we went with him. Later President Poincaré and King George V were to meet at Abbeville, and I was instructed to go to the station and accompany the President.

"You will detain him for a quarter of an hour," General Asser said to me, "because the King wants to talk to some Kaffir chieftains and this will delay our schedule a bit . . ."

This curious mission earned me the imprecations of the French general who was accompanying the President and my first highly embarrassed conversation with Monsieur Poincaré.

"What's the meaning of this?" the General demanded. "The King keeps the President waiting because he wants to talk to Negroes? It's unbelievable!"

"But, General," I said, "there is a reason . . . These are the head men of the Kaffir workers who made an agreement for just one year and who now want to go home . . . These workmen, however, are urgently needed to dig trenches, and it is hoped the King's prestige will make them stay."

"All right," Monsieur Poincaré said resignedly. "But it's ridiculous for me to wait in this station. Can't the itinerary be extended a little?"

"Alas, no, *Monsieur le Président,* because police measures have already been taken along the appointed route."

"Very well! Then we'll go slowly, but let's get off!"

The General seized me by the shoulders:

"Let's get off! Good Lord, let's get off!" he cried.

I had almost gained the prescribed quarter of an hour and we set off. Above us wheeled the Stork Squadron, on watch above the leaders of the two nations.

.   .   .   .

During the latter part of the war Abbeville was bombarded by German airplanes every night that was clear enough. We had anti-aircraft guns, but they never hit anything. Never were attacks more uniform. About ten o'clock in the evening a cannon would sound the *alerte.* Twenty minutes later one heard the broken-winded whine of the German bombers. Flares illuminated the town and the nearby munitions depots. There would be a quarter of an hour of pyrotechnics. Then it was over for that night. People went to see the craters which were sometimes very large; the dead, few in numbers, were counted; and everyone went to sleep with his mind at rest. After the break-through in the Fifth Army front the attacks at times became heavier and we tried sleeping in the suburbs and returning to work in the morning. But this was exhausting and uncomfortable and the General Staff soon got tired of it. Surprise plays a large part in any fear of danger; as soon as it's well known, familiarity puts an end to fear and laziness to precautions.

I was entitled to a leave at regular intervals. I spent the first one in Paris in the little apartment in the Rue Ampère. It was spoiled by an indefinable and distressing feeling of uneasiness. As might easily have been foreseen, Janine alone in Paris and so beautiful had been discovered gradually by very diverse groups whose life was not the studious, retired and modest one that I had planned for her. I was far away and, knowing that some of her new friends would displease me, she had never mentioned them in her letters. Now she found herself embarrassed and disconcerted by my return. Through the whole of that leave she made a kind and tender effort to make me happy, but I was not happy and I left with a memory poisoned by mysterious telephone calls and incomprehensible allusions. This she felt, and on the platform of the Gare du Nord she embraced me with solicitous and desperate tenderness.

Another of my leaves coincided with the first shots of "Big Bertha." When I left the station I could find neither a porter nor a taxi. Paris was in a state of *alerte*. I walked through empty streets with my heavy suitcase in my hand. At regular intervals there was the sound of an explosion. This was a strange kind of raid. That evening the papers were still talking about airplanes, but in the course of my stay the truth became known and I advised Janine to take our daughter out of Paris. She had spent the preceding summer at Bagnoles and at Deauville; from this time on she traveled, spending a few months in Brittany and then renting villas in the Midi. The war had broken up our household like many others; and this was not the least frightful of its woes, this severing of so many domestic ties.

At this time I wrote my wife many letters in verse, but they were addressed to the Natasha and Irene of my imagination rather than to the real woman, homeless and unhappy, who needed a living presence rather than poetry. I remember two stanzas:

> Ton coeur est transparent pour moi comme un ruisseau.
> Comme des poissons d'or, j'y vois fuir tes pensées
> Et j'y sais deviner, aux frissons d'un roseau,
> L'invisible réseau d'actions effacées.

> Si quelque jour, venant s'y refléter, une ombre
>   Met notre bonheur en danger,
> J'y verrai le premier, penché sur le flot sombre,
>   Le visage de l'étranger.[1]

[1] To me your heart is like a crystal stream.
   I see your thoughts like goldfish dart and flash
   And from the trembling of a single reed
   I guess the vanished pattern of your acts.

The end of 1917, for me as for everyone else, was unhappy. The war seemed endless, victory improbable. A vague shadow darkened my personal life. I sought refuge in fiction. For a long time, as I have said, the characters had been growing inside me nourished by my reveries. They were inspired in part by imagination, in part by the officers I had met in the Ninth Division and in part, too, by my friends and comrades on Asser's staff. A taciturn Colonel Bramble, made up from ten colonels and generals compounded and kneaded together; a Major Parker, who was a combination of Wake and Jenner; a Doctor O'Grady, who was in part Dr. James; and a padre whom I had met and learned to love among the Scotsmen, had little by little taken shape. During the nights in Abbeville, while I waited for the whine of the German planes, in order to escape my somber thoughts, I set to work recording the conversations of these men.

Very soon these dialogues became a book. In my leisure moments I tapped it out on the staff typewriter while Douglas gave voice to hunting cries. Then I found a title: *The Silences of Colonel Bramble*. What was I to do with this little work which I kept polishing and repolishing? I really had no idea at all. Publish it? No, that seemed too difficult, if not completely impossible. But I could give it to a few friends and, most important of all, I could record in it the fantastic duets of gramophone and artillery fire, the tremolo of the machine guns and the melody of anguish—and thus be delivered from them. When the book was finished Raymond Woog, who had come to Abbeville to paint General Asser's portrait, read my manuscript:

"It *must* be published," he said.

Such was also the opinion of Captain de Mun.

"But I don't know any publisher," I objected.

One of my friends replied that nothing was simpler, and undertook to deliver my manuscript to a young publisher of whom he spoke very highly—Bernard Grasset.

If ever shadow mirrored there should cloud
　　Our happiness,
I first, bent over darkened waters, will descry
　　The stranger's face.

Soon a reply came: Grasset liked the book and was ready to publish it. Since I was an officer on active service I had to have authorization from the Mission. The latter was very reluctant. Commandant de Castéja, who was our chief of personnel, summoned me to Montreuil: "I find your little book very entertaining," he said. "But you can't publish it under your own name! . . . The English officers with whom you are living or have lived might recognize themselves and be offended. If there is the slightest complaint it will be this unhappy Mission that will be blamed . . . No, we give you our moral authorization, but you must use a pseudonym."

This disappointed me, because as a young and unknown author almost the only readers I could count on were my friends in Normandy and my old comrades in the Lycée and the Regiment, who would not be able to recognize me under a pseudonym. Finally I resigned myself and selected the first name André, in memory of my cousin who had been killed in action, and Maurois, the name of a village near Cambrai, because I liked its sad sonority . . . André Maurois . . . How strange and new those syllables sounded to me then!

Meanwhile Grasset was printing *The Silences*. He sent me the first proofs. They arrived at the time when the Germans were advancing on Amiens in March 1918. For several days I believed the war was lost. Long streams of refugees pushing wheelbarrows full of furniture, children's toys and potatoes, came through Abbeville. To establish and provision a new front we worked day and night. The bombings were redoubled. Thousands of trucks, rushing up French troops to seal the breach, maintained an uninterrupted rumble beneath our windows. I found reassurance in the calm of General Asser:

"It will be all right," he said to me.

When my book appeared the battle was still raging and the fate of Amiens, where I often went, remained undecided. One day in Abbeville I received thirty small gray volumes printed on filled paper and with covers bearing the portrait of a Scotch Colonel drawn for me by Raymond Woog. The hour was so dark that I got no pleasure from seeing my first book.

"Send these copies," Grasset wrote me, "to the critics you know . . ."

I didn't know any critics or, for that matter, any writers. I decided to send the copies to my friends and also to the men I admired. For Anatole France I composed an oddly archaic dedication in verse:

> Sans un regard de vous, ma Muse ira peut-être
> Dormir loin du séjour de vos belles amantes,
> Esclave dédaignée, mais encor frémissante
> D'avoir passé si près du Maître.[2]

And for Rudyard Kipling, I am not quite sure why, this adaptation of a little English poem of the 16th Century (by Robert Herrick, I think):

> O mon livre, en t'écrivant,
> Je t'aimais comme un enfant.
> Comme un enfant, ô mon livre,
> Tu me fuis pour aller vivre.

> Aux demeures étrangères
> Lors je t'abandonne, ami,
> Aux fortunes passagères,
> Mais tu demeures mon fils.

> Et mon paternel amour,
> Indulgent donne toujours
> Un soupir à tes défaites,
> Un sourire à tes conquêtes.[3]

I sowed this poor grain hopelessly at the time when Ludendorff

[2] Without a glance from you, my Muse perhaps will seek a place to slumber far from the abode of your fair loves, a disregarded slave, but still atremble from having passed so near the Master.

[3] O book, while I was writing you I loved you like a child. Like a child, O book, you leave me now to go out into the world.

Henceforth I relinquish you, my friend, to strange abodes and uncertain fortunes, but you will remain my son.

And my paternal love, ever indulgent, will vouchsafe a sigh at your defeats, a smile at your triumphs.

was attacking in Champagne. The harvest and the victory came with equal speed. Because this slender volume appeared at a time of anguish, because it directed a melancholy humor on our woes, because it opened the door to hope, because it portrayed our allies sympathetically, its success was immediate. From this circumstance I draw no argument in favor of its literary merit. But it is a fact that the little pile of copies at the bookstore in Abbeville, which remained open despite the bombs, melted away like snow in the sun. The bookseller had at first ordered ten, then twenty-five, then a hundred. All of them went. At the end of ten days Grasset wrote me that it was the same in Paris, that he had been surprised and was caught unprepared by the sale, and that he was ordering a new printing of five thousand. Then it was ten thousand, then twenty thousand, then fifty thousand. The game was won.

More important to me than the numbers of my readers was the quality of the criticisms. My first reviews were delightful. Since I was completely unknown I had no enemies, I irritated no one and I could be praised without reservation. I was an officer in the army and this further entitled me to everyone's kindness. But above all there was in France, and there still is, a real generosity in the Republic of Letters which prompts men of established reputation to help new writers. Abel Hermant, Daniel Halévy, Pierre Mille and Lucien Descaves, who did not know me at all, spoke of *The Silences* with a warmth that touched me. Anatole France wrote me (or rather caused to be written to me) an amiable letter in which he asked me to come and see him at La Béchellerie. Kipling replied to me himself. Marshal Lyautey, to whom I had not sent my book but who had read it, wrote me in care of my publisher a dazzling letter: "My dear comrade,—Good Lord! what an astonishing book . . ." The leaders of the French Military Mission, who had hitherto treated me, naturally enough, as an almost indistinguishable part of the military machine, suddenly discovered my existence. The Commander-in-Chief Sir Douglas Haig when he came to Abbeville asked to see me and talked to me laughingly about Colonel Bramble, as also did Monsieur Clemenceau when, with his felt hat cocked for battle and cane in hand, he inspected our armies.

.   .   .   .   .   .

The tiger still roared, but the victory placated him. From the time that the German attack against Gouraud's Army was stopped, we went on from victory to victory. Beneath the blows of the French, English and American troops, the enemy line which had been so long invulnerable staggered and gave ground. One felt the end was near. I ought to have experienced an unmixed happiness—and naturally I was happy at the salvation of France—but by that time my personal life had suddenly been wrecked. Without warning a telegram, signed by a doctor, had summoned me to the Cap d'Ail to my wife who was very ill. I had great difficulty in getting permission to go there for two days. Her condition seemed so serious that I implored my superiors to allow me to remain with her. General Welch replied with friendly sympathy but with firmness that at that moment my post could not be filled without preparation by any other. I had to take my wife back to Paris and leave her in the hands of doctors, abandoning the being I loved most in the world at the instant when she had greatest need of me.

I was so worried that the victory itself seemed to me a distressing routine. On the day of the Armistice my British comrades, from General Asser to General Welch, from Colonel Warre to Childe Douglas, decided to give me a surprise. At the end of dinner they rose, forced me to remain seated and sang with great seriousness: *"For he is a jolly good fellow, and so say all of us . . ."* Then they presented me with a beautiful silver platter on which they had had their signatures engraved. I was highly gratified. Their affection, as I well knew, was sincere; for my part I had learned to esteem and love them. Our paths were soon to part. What would be left for me in the new world of the Peace? The mill? I felt myself very far removed from that calling. My cousin Pierre Herzog, after being wounded ten times, had been killed at Château Thierry a few days before the Armistice. Thus the two brilliant and dependable young men who were to have formed a team with me were both gone . . . My family? I felt that even if Janine should recover, my home had been cruelly shaken by absence, by hostile influences, by Destiny.

No doubt I had found a new form of happiness in writing, but what does success amount to, even in a profession which one pursues with enthusiasm, if one has no one with whom to share it? My wife had seemed indifferent to this new aspect of my life. My dearest friends were dead. My daughter, the sole hope of the future, was four years old. Almost nothing remained of the edifice patiently constructed in the first part of my life. On this evening of victory, when I found myself alone in my room I felt exhausted and beaten. A few days later I developed a high fever. It was the famous Spanish grippe which was then ravaging the armies. An English doctor came to see me:

"I'm very depressed," I told him, "but on the whole I am not suffering."

"I've seen more than one case like yours," he replied, "in which the patient did not suffer but died next day."

This ominous prediction seemed to me at the time a very desirable solution of my problems. But the prognosis was in error. I did not die and, after a long convalescence, was demobilized at the beginning of 1919. I was thirty-three years old. In a few months my hair had turned white.

·   ·   ·   ·   ·   ·   ·

This was not the only change that had occurred in me. When I had left Elbeuf in 1914 I had been a provincial business man convinced that nothing in the world was more important than the happiness of my home and the successful operation of my factory. My little town, my little house, my little family seemed to me the center of the Universe. I and mine were a part of an enduring and immutable system with established laws the knowledge of which allowed one to foresee events and to act wisely. The war had shown me that Empires under the impact of violence may fall in ruins in a few days, just as the noblest edifices of a great city may fall in a few seconds beneath the shock of an earthquake, and that the collapse of a state may bury beneath its debris the greatest fortunes and the happiest homes. To be sure, I had resolved to return to Elbeuf and take up the yoke there once more, but I prepared to do it without enthusiasm or confidence. I had lost my faith in all that. I had too clearly realized the existence of a larger world. I no longer believed in the eternal necessity, or even in the solid durability, of the machine in which I was a wheel, and already in the bottom of my heart I was forming, without ever putting it into exact words, a project that four years earlier would have been inconceivable—to leave my mill, my town, my province and go out and rebuild elsewhere, according to new plans, a life which the war had left in ruins.

CHAPTER XIII

Home Coming

IN THE tumultuous brooks of Elbeuf still flowed the blue, green and yellow waters of the dye works. The loud, monotonous pounding of the looms made the air of the town tremble. In the long courtyard of the mill trucks loaded with bolts of cloth, barrels of oil and cases of thread, recalled the past. I breathed again the moist, vapid odor of steam and the heavy odor of greasy wool. But close to the main gate a second black marble tablet had been erected, bearing in gold letters the names of the owners and workmen who had died for France. It was a long list, beginning with these two names:

CAPITAINE PIERRE HERZOG

Chevalier of the Legion of Honor, Croix de Guerre . . .

LIEUTENANT ANDRÉ FRAENCKEL

Chevalier of the Legion of Honor, Croix de Guerre . . .

And so the young chiefs led once more and for the last time the invisible company of the dead. My two cousins had been loyal to their ideas of the duties that privilege entails; both had commanded, had led their troops in battle and had perished. In that year of 1918 it was legitimate to hope that common sacrifices might lead to a better understanding between classes and parties for the greater good of France.

Every morning when I arrived at the mill I would meditate for a few moments in front of that tablet covered with Alsatian and Norman names. All of us, both employers and workmen, now came to work later. Clemenceau had had the eight hour day voted. The Uncles were no more than uncouth memories. We had trouble—after four years of surprises and dangers—in accustoming ourselves to an easy, routine life. With the veterans, I preferred to talk about the war rather than the mill. Saturnin, our friend with the scarred face who worked in the warehouse, had come back a sergeant with the Military Medal, having campaigned in the Orient and later been a prisoner in Germany. He would discuss Cairo and Alexandria like an American tourist. In Bavaria a rich woman who owned a farm had offered to marry him. He had preferred to return to Elbeuf and, as formerly, carry on his head pieces of black cloth and of Amazon blue. The workrooms were full of unknown heroes who feared nothing and were getting bored. I myself was amazed at my comfortable civilian clothes and at the fact that thenceforth I was answerable to no superior.

For the period of my wife's convalescence the doctors had advised me to live out of town and I had bought a house surrounded by a little park at La Saussaye, a pretty village near Elbeuf on the Neubourg plateau. No estate was ever more precisely laid out. The four hectares formed a perfect rectangle. The house, of brick and stone with a slate roof, was in the exact center of the grounds. One quarter of the park was an apple orchard; one quarter a flower garden; one quarter a kitchen garden; one quarter a grove of fine lime trees. A garden of climbing roses adorned, with Dorothy Perkinses and Crimson Ramblers, the central path that led down to the gate, through which a belfry was visible. The tiny village had been built in very ancient times by a chapter of Canons whose little houses, decorated with sculpture, surrounded the church. Originally a fortified wall had protected the town. All that now remained of it was two gates with Roman arches which formed graceful and decorative boundaries. I at once fell very much in love with our house at La Saussaye. It was surrounded, as far as the eye could see, by fields of wheat sprinkled with poppies, corn-flowers and daisies and one could

it from afar, when returning from a walk, by the three
which rose like masts above lime trees where the bees hummed.
Janine become fond of her new home? I do not think so. She
had returned from that other war, illness, bruised in soul and body.
This was not visible to strangers because her beautiful face remained
young and her smile sweetly childlike. But to her natural melancholy
was now added a strange bitterness. Abandoned without a protector
and without advice in a world rendered pitiless and perilous by the
disorders of war, she had learned the meaning of treachery, perfidy
and cruelty. From her brief encounter with life she had acquired a
distressing cynicism which she hid by playfulness, by poetic gaiety
and by a forced lightness, but which rose to the surface occasionally
despite her. As at the period of our Geneva walks she would sometimes murmur:

"Beneath the sway of Mars condemned without reprieve," and she
would add: "Mars . . . the God of War . . . You see, darling, I had
cause to be afraid of him . . ."

She who had formerly loved solitude and put up with simplicity,
now revealed an appetite for luxury, for gowns and for jewels, a taste
for dancing, for night clubs and for jazz, which perhaps was natural
but which wounded the austere moralist that lurked deep within me.
Observing her way of life I thought of a comment by Alain: "Frivolity
is a violent state."

Perhaps I could still have made her happy if I had accepted her
as she had become and if I had given myself without reserve to the
task of reconciling her to life. I believed that I was full of good intentions; I wanted with all my heart to sacrifice my desires to hers;
I granted her everything she asked: a fine apartment at Neuilly, a
visit to Deauville, trips, countless presents, but it was all done in a
way that made each gift a concession and a reproach. I would say to
her:

"All right, but why don't you help my mother instead? There are
so many unfortunate people since the war! . . . Why don't you interest yourself as she has done in the Wards of the Nation? . . . Why
drag me to Deauville when I could stay here and work on a book?"

When I reread, with greater maturity of mind, Claudel's plays and in particular *The Hostage*, which gives such a clear statement of the doctrine of total sacrifice, I understood too late what had warped our reunion after the conflict. In order to win back Janine I was ready to make any concrete sacrifices but not the intellectual sacrifice that would have consisted, I repeat, in accepting her as she was. The pleasures of the artist which I had commenced to taste now attracted me more strongly than those of love. The writer's egoism, more concerned with his work than with the people who surround him, that strange combination of maternal solicitude and paternal ambition, grew visibly in me. Our household, so peaceful in appearance beneath the beautiful lime trees of La Saussaye, suffered from it.

.   .   .   .

This egoism became all the more exacting inasmuch as I was at that time discontented with my efforts to write. *The Silences,* with its wide success, had proved to me that I could write a book and find readers. And so while I was still living at Abbeville I had begun a second novel. From the time of my first visits to Oxford I had been thinking with eager interest about a Life of the poet Shelley. It seemed to me if I wrote that Life I could give expression to certain feelings that I had experienced and that still troubled me. Like Shelley, I had become a doctrinaire under the influence of my youthful reading, and I had tried to apply rational methods to the life of the emotions. Like him I had encountered material that was alive and sentient and did not yield to my logic. Like him I had suffered and caused suffering.

I was irritated at the adolescent I had been and also indulgent because I knew he could not have been otherwise. I hoped at once to expose him, to condemn him and to explain him. Shelley, now, had met the same reverses, with a hundred times more grandeur and grace, but for reasons that were very much the same. Shelley's attitude toward Harriet, his inability to understand and to respect the frivolity of that child wife, his lessons in mathematics and lectures in morals, his Address to the Irish People, all these mistakes, I realized, were ones that in the same circumstances and at the same age I might have made and that perchance I might still make. To the pride and the certainties of adolescence there had succeeded in me a pressing need of pity and of humility, and here also I recognized traits of Shelley; those of his last days . . . Yes, in every respect, the subject seemed excellent.

But at that time I was living in Abbeville with no English library and no source materials, and as long as the war lasted it was clearly impossible for me to do the research work necessary for writing a biography. One day the idea came to me that perhaps it would be possible to make a novel out of this real life. Could one with any appearance of reality transpose the story of Shelley and Harriet Westbrook and Mary Godwin into modern life? Would that degree of romanticism be bearable outside the romantic period? The problem occupied me for a long time. I could have solved it more quickly if I had not retained at that time a fierce disinclination to make use of my own experience. The freer I felt to express myself beneath the mask of persons who were obviously distinct from me, the more incapable I felt then of writing a book that might be considered a confession. Unable to confront my hero with the real problems that had been mine, I was forced to recognize that it would be absurd, if I made him my contemporary, to confront him with anachronistic problems of Shelley.

I was much attracted by the city in which the hazards of war had decreed that I should live. I loved its churches, the lovely paved courtyards of its mansions, and its houses with carved wood decorations. I began to read the histories of Abbeville and, among others, the correspondence of Boucher de Perthes, a learned citizen of the town. He had an agreeable way of writing and his period interested me. It was the end of the reign of Louis Philippe, the Revolution of Forty-Eight and the beginning of the Second Empire. It seemed to me that 1848 was the epoch in France in which it would be appropriate to place a Shelley. His sentiments, his grandiloquence, his idealism would then seem plausible. And since I loved Abbeville so much, why not have him live in Abbeville? All this seemed fine. It remained to be seen what had happened at Abbeville during that Revolution.

I got permission from the Subprefect to examine the archives, and I became very much interested immediately in the file on Civil Engineering. There I followed the disappointments of an unfortunate engineer at grips with the sea, whose most carefully calculated works were being constantly destroyed by the waves. The symbol pleased me; thanks to my Uncle Henry I was familiar with the technique; I decided that my Shelley should be an engineer. From this moment my novel developed with a rapidity that surprised me. My hero, Philippe Viniès, was a former *Me* to whom I had become hostile but whom I continued, without realizing it, to resemble.

The book was published in 1919 and had no success. One hundred thousand copies of *Colonel Bramble* had been sold; *Neither Angel nor Beast* sold seven or eight thousand. Bernard Grasset blamed the title which he had always considered "unpopular." I condemned the novel. Nevertheless Alain liked it, a fact that surprised me and kept me from complete discouragement:

"You have throughly understood the lesson of Stendhal," he said.

I had indeed understood it, but I had not been able to liberate myself from the Stendhal pattern.

After *Neither Angel nor Beast* I had given Grasset a second batch of English military stories of the same type as *Bramble—The Conversations of Doctor O'Grady*. This time the public had welcomed the book but the critics expressed disappointment: "Is André Maurois going to continue forever rewriting his first book?"

It seemed to me nevertheless that I had something serious and perhaps important to say which should have been in *Neither Angel nor Beast* but was not there and was linked obscurely but intimately with the character of Shelley; no doubt it would be better expressed if, instead of transforming Shelley into an engineer of 1848, I should write his life directly and openly. Hence sprang a keen desire to have time to read everything that had been published about Shelley, to reread his correspondence and his poems and to write a biography that would be, not the literary study of a poet, but the picture of a human conflict.

This desire, which became a need, made me impatient. Both the life in the mill and that at home seemed to me full of futile acts and words. Ah! To shut myself up to read, to write, no longer to have to listen to meaningless complaints, to live the life of a writer surrounded by creatures born of my imagination, such was now my dream. Later I gave it to Shelley himself: "It seemed to him that in the crystalline mansions of his thought, Harriet and her daughter had fallen like blocks of recalcitrant living matter. In vain, with all the strength of his logic, he tried to rid himself of them; the ponderous reality was too much for his fragile arms . . ."

.   .   .   .

My work at the mill weighed heavily upon me. No doubt it was because other occupations to which I was better suited attracted me, but also because post-war industry no longer resembled that of the pre-war days. Before 1914 if competition had been sharp and profits limited, at least a prudent man could pilot his ship with some intelligence. The costs of raw materials served him as landmarks, the value of currencies fluctuated only within narrow limits, salaries increased only by slow stages.

After the war all the compasses began to spin. Francs, pounds, dollars, marks, pesetas shot up and down without order or understandable rhythm. Immediately after the Armistice the needs of Europe were such that an unheard of prosperity seemed to lie ahead of industry. Before 1914 clients had been heartless monsters, to be spoken of only with respectful dread, and they had easily imposed their capricious demands on manufacturers who were disunited and always starved for work. At the slightest sign of rebellion F-B would find himself menaced by B-B. In 1920 manufacturers, stuffed with orders, entered into agreements to deal with the buyers. The Brothers Blin approached us to form an alliance—a diplomatic revolution as astonishing as the one which at that time was bringing England and Germany together. When I went to Paris the triumph no longer consisted in bringing back orders but in canceling them. On paper we were amassing fortunes; in reality, if one took purchasing power as the standard, the mill was growing poorer every day, but we were too ignorant of monetary matters to realize this.

The workers, seeing the factory gorged with orders and prices rising, quite naturally demanded their part in this prosperity; they hoped by some miracle to see their wages rise and the price of manufactured goods fall. Almost every week one trade union or another demanded ten per cent or twenty per cent increase. The employers agreed to everything. What difference did it make to them? Selling prices seemed to have no limits. They did not become hostile until professional agitators took over the question of wages in order to make it an instrument of domination. Then their pride as employers rebelled. Elbeuf entered upon a period of political strikes. In *Bernard Quesnay* I have described the most serious of them and the sadness of silent workrooms with their glittering and motionless machinery. Workers who had been my father's friends and my own put their names to insulting notices. Those who wanted to keep on working and who were few in number, were attacked, humiliated, beaten. This state of war between Frenchmen made me suffer more than I can say. Ever since I had been at the mill I had tried my best to be fair, but the adversaries in these two camps loved their prejudices more than justice. Who was grateful to me for my efforts? The executives said to me: "You're weak"; the workers: "You are our enemy." I was tired of this struggle in which I had no allies. I even missed the war. There if you suffered, at least you had the satisfaction of feeling yourself united with your comrades.

Soon the excessive rise in prices brought a crisis. It was sudden and terrible. Our clients, who had been purchasing madly, brutally applied the brakes. In a few days half our orders were canceled. In a few weeks the strikes had been succeeded by unemployment. The workmen, haughty and hostile yesterday, were all of a sudden friendly and docile. Looms came to rest in the sleeping mill. The value of stocks in hand fell precipitately, and since the value had been assessed in a depreciated currency, we discovered that during these three years of folly we had lost our substance.

"We're children," my cousin Robert Fraenckel said to me sadly.

"We should have done our bookkeeping in terms of gold. By measuring our stocks and our prices with an elastic standard we have endangered the existence of our business."

He was right, but when he and I insisted that a double bookkeeping system be installed, in francs and in dollars, our elders shrugged their shoulders:

"How complicated!" they said. "And why do it? No one has done anything like that before!"

As for me, I was rapidly becoming more of a novelist than a manufacturer, and I consoled myself by deriving from our woes a short novel which I called: *Prosperity and Depression*.

.   .   .   .

In the spring of 1922 I received an invitation from Monsieur Paul Desjardins, Professor of Literature at the Ecole Normale in Sèvres, founder of the Union for Truth and estimable critic, to spend ten days during the summer at the Abbey of Pontigny. His gracious letter, written in a fine archaic hand, explained to me the nature of the Pontigny Conferences at which each year writers, professors and men of good will from all countries came together to discuss some literary or moral problem. That year the subject was to be: *"The Meaning of Honor."* André Gide, Roger Martin du Gard, Edmond Jaloux, Robert de Traz, Jean Schlumberger, the Englishmen Lytton Strachey and Roger Fry were to be present. The program tempted me. Many of the names were those of people I admired and I felt a strong, almost morbid, need to hear conversations about ideas and books and not about strikes and sales. I suggested to Janine, who did not want to accompany me and did not want to stay at La Saussaye, that she go for a visit to Trouville, and I accepted Monsieur Desjardins' invitation.

The Cistercian Abbey of Pontigny is in Burgundy near Auxerre, not far from Beaune. In my compartment on the train from Paris were a couple who immediately attracted my attention. The man, hardly older than myself and almost bald, had deep thoughtful eyes, long, drooping mustaches, and a vest that was too big for him, from the pockets of which protruded innumerable sharp-pointed pencils; his wife was a fresh looking curly-headed blonde with timid child-like grace; their conversation, which I heard despite myself, interested me. Presently, seeing the label PONTIGNY on my suitcase, they introduced themselves:

"Charles and Zézette Du Bos . . ."

This meant nothing to me, but that was my mistake, for Charles Du Bos had already published fine studies of Baudelaire, Mérimée and Proust which were very highly esteemed by a small but discriminating group of readers. He spoke with extreme slowness; his choice of epithets was admirable. What he said was not only fair and true, it was the object itself miraculously transformed into words. When he talked to me about the writers we were going to meet, I was impressed by his seriousness, the minuteness of his character analyses and his constant references to the English poets. I had a feeling that I was simultaneously meeting a character from Proust and a hero from Dickens. I did not and could not foresee that this eloquent stranger was to become one of my most intimate and dearest friends.

We were met on the station platform in Pontigny by Desjardins and Gide. The Master of the Abbey looked like Tolstoy. The same unkempt beard, the same prominent cheek-bones, the same faun-like look of genius. Though ceremonious and often meek, he was disconcerting because of his tone of raillery. Gide, on the contrary, was reassuring. Wrapped in a great mountaineer's cape, with his samurai's face framed by a wide-brimmed, gray felt sombrero, he made a startling first impression but quickly charmed one by the youthfulness of his spirit and by the immediate interest he took in new people. In this assembly, seething with talent, where I knew no one, I had feared I should be an outsider, but I quickly made friends. The rule of the house was monastic. We had our meals together beneath the Gothic vault of the old refectory of the monks and Madame Paul Desjardins, stepdaughter of Gaston Paris, presided at them with calm dignity and seated the guests herself. She put me beside her daughter Anne, a wild young creature with black hair, lively, ardent and bursting with eagerness and intelligence. A whole group of youngsters, pupils of Monsieur Desjardins, surrounded Anne who, as daughter of the house, had great prestige at Pontigny and judged us all with mischievous finality. She and I got on well together from the start.

The daily program was simple. The morning was free and it was spent by some of us in walks to Auxerre, Beaune, Vézelay or along the river; by others in the library of the Abbey which Monsieur Desjardins, with feigned modesty, called "the village library" and which was astounding in the quality of the editions and the selection of the books. After lunch we sat beneath the arbor and the discussion began. Each day brought its own drama, for there was an immediate clash between the morbid susceptibilities of Monsieur Desjardins, the meticulous and desperate seriousness of Charles Du Bos, the diabolical maliciousness of Gide and the naïveté of some of the strangers. Roger Martin du Gard, silent and with a sweetly impassive expression on his Norman lawyer's face, would listen and from time to time draw a notebook from his pocket in order to make a brief entry. The philosopher Edmond Jaloux waited in patient boredom for the moment when he could go to the Pontigny inn and drink a bottle of respectable burgundy. The Germans, Curtius and Grothuysen, enveloped the lucid ideas of the Frenchmen in profound and vague abstractions. Charles Du Bos (or rather, as all Pontigny called him, Charlie) who distrusted ideas that were too clear and would gladly have said of Voltaire or of Anatole France, like the Empress Eugénie: "I cannot forgive them for having made me understand things I shall never understand," glanced approvingly at Curtius and Grothuysen. Lytton Strachey crossed one of his long legs over the other, shut his eyes in amazement at our lack of humor and went to sleep.

"And what in your opinion, Monsieur Strachey, is the most important thing in the world?" Paul Desjardins asked suddenly.

There was a long silence. Then from the sleeping beard of Strachey issued a tiny falsetto voice:

"Passion," he said finally with suave nonchalance.

And the solemn circle, relieved for an instant, broke into laughter.

At four o'clock a bell announced tea. It, like lunch, was served in the refectory. After dinner we met in the drawing room to play subtle and learned games.

Portraits by Comparison:

"If it were a painting, what would it be?"

"A Venus by Raphael retouched by Renoir," Roger Fry replied gravely.

Portraits on a Scale of Twenty:

"Intelligence?"

(The subject this time was Benjamin Constant.)

"Nineteen," Gide replied.

"Dear friend," Charles Du Bos interrupted anxiously, "if you will permit me, I should rather say eighteen and three quarters . . ."

"Sensibility?"

"Zero," Gide said.

"What?" Charlie broke in again in distress. "But he is at least par, dear friend, or perhaps even twelve . . . or to be more exact twelve and a half."

One day the keyword was: *Mephistopheles.*

"Is he one of your friends?" Gide, who was being cross-examined, was asked.

"So I flatter myself!" Gide affirmed between clenched teeth in his most metallically infernal voice.

I was happy in this new world. Educated until I was eighteen among philosophers and poets in my old Lycée, then suddenly transplanted into a mill and cut off from my favorite occupations, I found again at Pontigny my true environment and thrived visibly there. At Elbeuf my extensive reading had served no purpose and I had to be on my guard against frightening people by my pedantry. At Pontigny all this reading became a factor in my success. I had been invited on the strength of *Colonel Bramble* as an amusing author but one not to be taken too seriously; what they found was a student of Balzac, which appealed to Gide, a man who knew Tolstoy by heart, which appealed to Martin du Gard. Charles Du Bos, put off by what seemed to him the levity of my first book and also by the fact that I had been one of Alain's students, for whose works and doctrines he had no great regard, remained aloof at first but our mutual friend, Anne Desjardins, seeing that I admired Charlie with all my heart, brought him to me in affectionate repentance before the end of "the decade." I made precious friendships that year at Pontigny. On the eve of departure, André Gide said to me:

"And what are you writing now?"

"A Life of Shelley."

"Why don't you come to my place in the country and show it to me? . . . I live not far from you."

"But the book isn't finished . . ."

"Exactly . . . I'm not interested except in unfinished things . . . One can still mold them . . ."

I accepted. I had promised to join Janine at Trouville and to spend some time with her at the Hotel Normandy in Deauville. I escaped for three days and went to Gide's home, which was on the other side of the estuary between Le Havre and Fécamp. Not knowing him well as yet, I expected to find the house "artistically" decorated in the manner of *Paludes*, very Nineteen Hundred. I found an old Norman country seat, a long white house, elegant and unostentatious, and an upper middle class French household. Madame Gide was simple and reserved.

"I hope," she said to her husband as we sat down at the table, "I hope, André, that you will like the menu . . . The chocolate cream is very thick, the way you like it . . ."

After dinner Gide asked me to read my manuscript aloud to him.

"It's a dangerous test for any script," he said, "but decisive . . ."

In my excitement I read very badly. But he listened to me with perfect attention well into the night. From time to time he made notes. When I had finished he told me that he found the book well put together and agreeably written, but that he had hoped for a more profound analysis of the poet Shelley and of his works. I replied that had not been my subject. Then he gave me certain detailed criticisms, all of them proper, about wrong words and superfluous ornaments. He advised me to sacrifice certain passages which were brilliant but in the wrong tone and which interrupted the action.

Gide had the most infallible taste, and the lesson he gave me was useful to me for a long time. From this brief visit I took away friendly and grateful memories.

The sojourn at Pontigny was repeated each year, and the friend-ships that I formed there exercised a profound influence on me. It was Pontigny that reconciled me to my real self. The place was not without its faults. It was capable of producing pedantry, abetting the formation of little groups of literary idolaters and encouraging hair splitting. But its virtues far outweighed its drawbacks, and the little groups of worshipers were dedicated to great saints. At a time when the violence of nationalism and of political creeds tended to create isolated and hostile human groups, men of goodwill from antagonistic countries, sects and parties could meet on friendly terms at Pontigny. For several years there was talk of giving Paul Desjardins the Nobel Prize for Peace. It would have been justified. So far as I was con-cerned, Pontigny saved me forever from frivolity of mind and hard-ness of heart. To my sojourns in the ancient Cistercian Abbey, to the walks beneath the cloisters and to the conversations beneath the arbor I owe some of my dearest friends and those worthiest to be loved.

CHAPTER XIV

Eurydice Twice Lost

THROUGH four years of war I had lived with the British. It would have been too bad if victory had broken the tie. In 1920 and again in 1921 my comrades of Asser's staff invited me to commemorative dinners. Some of them I entertained in Paris. General Byng (Lord Byng of Vimy), whom I had known in France and whom I met again in London, said to me:

"Now you know the English Army—good, but you don't know England. I am going to introduce the country to you. Come and dine with me at the Athenaeum . . ."

And he arranged an odd sort of dinner to which he invited a dozen Englishmen belonging to a dozen different professions and environments. I remember there was an Admiral there, a Minister (it was Sir Austen Chamberlain), a sporting bishop, a painter, a humorist (Owen Seaman of Punch), a manufacturer, a merchant, a trade-unionist and a gentleman farmer. After each course I was told to change my place so that by the end of the meal, having talked to everyone present, I should know England. When the champagne was served Lord Byng made a little speech in the course of which he said to me:

"We are all Brambles here . . ."

It was true.

The army was not my only point of contact with England. When my book had appeared the novelist Maurice Baring, at that time Major Baring serving with the R.A.F. in France, had written me an amusing letter which served as the starting-point of a friendship. When I went to London, Baring always arranged a little luncheon in his picturesque apartment in Lincoln's Inn. He himself had charming and unusual friends. At his home I met Duff Cooper and his future wife, the very beautiful Lady Diana Manners; Harold Nicolson, Desmond MacCarthy, Lady Lovat and Lady Wilson, Hilaire Belloc and all the Cecils. A convert to Catholicism, Baring was ardently and sincerely religious. He had the gaiety of the saints and their charity. The letters he wrote me (of which I had saved hundreds up to the present war) were typed in a bizarre mixture of black and red words in which whole lines were composed of w's or x's, alternating with scraps of poetic prose. The text was half French, half English, and the signature would be preceded by *"Amicalissiment"* or a *"Votre vraiment,"* a literal translation of *yours truly.* All this was a little mad, droll, full of delicacy and learning, with here and there a profound thought which would illuminate his deep feelings. That was Maurice.

All England called him that. He was much loved there and with reason. He was consistently and unobtrusively generous. When I introduced him to the Abbé Mugnier, he was pleased by the Abbé's admiration for Goethe. Maurice owned a first edition of *Werther*. As soon as he returned to England he sent it to the Rue Méchain where the Canon lived. He owned a collection of paintings of Carmontelle. One day a French friend said to him: "There's a collection that ought to be in the Carnavalet Museum . . ."

"Really?" Baring said. "I'll send them."

He did so the next day. When the library of Ronald Storrs, Governor of Cyprus, was burned by the natives during an uprising on the island, Baring sent him this cablegram: "Library on way. *Uno avulso.*" At the very moment he had learned of the catastrophe he had stripped himself of all his books.

Maurice also had a taste for the wildly imaginative and fantastic that was calculated to astonish a Frenchman. For many years he used to invite his friends to a dinner in a hotel in Brighton on his birthday, which fell in the middle of winter, and at the end of the meal would jump into the ocean fully clothed. I have seen him with my own eyes, during a luncheon at his home, get up, strike a match and set fire to the curtains because the conversation was languishing.

One day when he was an undergraduate at Cambridge and was crossing the courtyard of Trinity, a Hindu student whom he did not know tapped him on the shoulder. Maurice Baring turned around.

"Oh, I beg your pardon," gasped the student, "I thought you were Mr. Godavery . . ."

"I *am* Mr. Godavery," Maurice replied calmly.

These stories about Maurice amused me, but I much preferred his serious side and I kept urging him to write the serious, moving and profound novels for which he was fitted by nature. *Daphne Adeane* rewarded my expectations, and I introduced this book to the French public by a preface.

I was received in other homes in London. Lady Oxford and Mrs. Greville introduced me to men of politics; Lady Colefax to men of letters. It was at her home that I first met Rudyard Kipling whom I had admired so much. I was not disappointed. Kipling talked like Kipling. Kipling was a Kipling character. He was the first to put me on my guard against the optimistic pacifism which was then disarming England:

"Don't forget," he said, "that countries always end by resembling their shadows."

This sentence seemed to me sibylline at the time; history proved it to be prophetic. Later in 1928 he invited me to come and see him at Burwash where he had an old house, which had belonged to an Elizabethan iron master, and a wonderful garden. It was the country described in *Puck of Pook's Hill*. But this book had been written for his son who had disappeared in that same battle of Loos which had been my baptism of fire. His death had stabbed Kipling even to the quick of his creative power and he was doing almost no writing. I found him discontented with his own country, uneasy about mine, overly clairvoyant and prophesying misfortunes. But to see and to touch a man whom I had so long considered superhuman intoxicated me.

Another of my English retreats was Avebury Manor, an ancient

Elizabethan house, which belonged to Colonel Jenner, one of my Abbeville friends, and was surrounded by prehistoric tombs, fields of dolmens and thousand-year-old yew trees. Inside it was furnished with canopied beds, huge fireplaces with open wood fires, tables set with bluish Waterford glass, and with rare and ancient collections of books. It was through my numerous visits in this Wiltshire home that I came to know the country families of England, traditional, conservative and yet liberal. There I saw the life and way of thought of the country gentlemen who, together with the merchants of London, had so long constituted the backbone of the country and who still played such an important role in the Army, the Navy and at the Foreign Office. They had their faults, stubbornness and narrowness, and their virtues, courage and tenacity.

All things considered, I found them useful to their country and always ready to serve it. It was Colonel Jenner who first guided my readings in English History. He was well acquainted with it and would recount it from his viewpoint of Die-Hard Tory, with vigor and sarcasm; but he made me understand why parliamentary institutions, which were being so much questioned in France at that time, had gained acceptance in England. The two principal reasons seemed to me to be, first, that the English Parliament had begun by being the house of the aristocracy and had little by little been opened to all classes so that it did not appear as an instrument of tyranny to any group in England. And second, that the executive power in England was strong enough to govern, whereas in France, the Chambers claimed to be at once legislative and executive. Nothing seemed to me more important than to explain these differences to my countrymen, and from this moment I began to think of writing a history of England.

Finally, in 1923 my Life of Shelley was finished. I gave it the title *Ariel*. Charlie Du Bos, who read the manuscript, advised me to add an introductory note to indicate to the critics what I had tried to do. I listened to him and no doubt this was a mistake, for from this brief preface was born, much against my intention, the absurd and dangerous expression: *romanticized biography*. I had never used it; I had on the contrary said that a biographer has no right to invent either a fact or a speech, but that he might and should arrange his authentic materials in the manner of a novel and give his reader the feeling of a hero's progressive discovery of the world which is the essence of romance. But few people take the trouble to read carefully, especially prefaces, and the success of *Ariel*, a success which astonished my publisher and me, encouraged a whole series of *Romantic Lives* and *Private Lives* which were often very bad. For some time I suffered from the reaction against this avalanche of improvised biographies and I took great care, when I myself returned to this type of book, to respect the legitimate phobias of meticulous, distrustful and atrabiliar men of learning. Fortunately, to my great joy, Sir Edmund Gosse, the most eminent of the English critics, understood and praised my *Ariel*, a fact which intimidated the malcontents. On the other hand, my master Alain was by no means enthusiastic:

"Why don't you write novels?" he said to me. "Then you'll have a freer hand . . . I preferred *Neither Angel nor Beast* and above all *Bramble*."

He was now living in the Rue de Rennes. From time to time I would go to pick him up at the Lycée Henri IV, where he was teaching, and walk home with him. The war had changed him a great deal. Although exempt from military service, he had insisted in 1914 on enlisting as a private in the Artillery. From this experience of army life he had produced a cruel book: *Mars, or War Brought to Judgment*. For a man so jealous of his independence, the worst misfortune of war had not been death or danger but the suspension of civil liberties and public criticism. "Who is in the right?" To find the answer to this question in the army you count the stripes or the stars of the interlocutors. It is likely that Socrates as a private would have suffered from this method. Hence in the case of Alain, veteran of the Great War, there had grown up a bitterness that he had not possessed when he was at Rouen. In the mud of the trenches he had caught rheumatism which made him drag one leg, but he had acquired a better understanding than ever of Homer and Tacitus. He remained the man I admired most in the world.

He had said this to me about *Bramble*:

"You don't tell the whole truth in it, but you don't lie; and that's a great deal. Your Colonel is massive, terrifying; he will last."

After *Ariel* he wrote me:

"I know you well. You are a tender-hearted boy. Take care **not to** suffer too much."

.   .   .   .

Ariel found in Janine an attentive, disturbed and surprised reader. Prior to this book my wife had not attached much importance to my vocation as a writer. *Bramble* had appeared at a time when she was suffering from a serious illness. The failure of *Neither Angel nor Beast* had discouraged her. She had good taste, was a reader of Shakespeare and Swinburne and copied out her favorite verses in little classroom notebooks. But in me she had married a manufacturer; she loved the luxury and the pleasures that money provides; we now had three children (two sons, Gerald and Olivier having been born in 1920 and 1921); she had no desire to see me abandon a prosperous mill for labors the success of which was doubtful.

"Instead of scribbling in the evenings," grumbled the red-headed nurse, "Monsieur would do better to go out with Madame, and instead of scribbling during the day Monsieur would do better to look after his business."

Janine repeated this comment to me as a comic example of the churlish English, but she herself was not far from sharing her opinion. After *Ariel* she was more indulgent and more respectful of my work.

"I should never have thought," she said, "that you were capable of writing this book . . . In it you talk about women better than you've ever talked to me about them . . ."

"Perhaps," I said, "it's because you intimidate me, and who knows whether I didn't write this book just to tell you things I couldn't say face to face."

She had read the manuscript. She reread the printed book twice. She searched it for allusions and explanations. She copied out passages from it. I discovered that she was surprised to see me criticize

in Shelley precisely the same things that distressed her in me—
the inflexible seriousness which she called my "pedantry," the need
to surround myself with professors whom she considered insufferably boring, the unconscious and unattractive egoism of the artist.
"But since he understands so well," she seemed to think, "why doesn't
he change?"

I had brought my new friends of Pontigny to see her. The meeting
did not go off well. She considered them "dry-as-dust pedants." They
found her beautiful as a poet's dream but frivolous, mocking and too
well dressed. What they considered her "coldness" was perhaps timidity in the presence of creatures of a different species from her own
Nevertheless Charlie, endowed with a mysterious sense of the tragic,
had divined in her, beneath the ermine and the diamonds, "an authentic fatal being."

At my request Janine had agreed to loan our drawing-room at
Neuilly, which opened on a beautiful garden, for a series of lectures
that Charlie planned to give. Every Tuesday there met at the Rue
Borghèse some thirty or forty persons to whom Charles Du Bos
carried away sometimes to the point of tears, talked about Keats
Wordsworth or Katherine Mansfield. These lectures were often ex
cellent, for Charlie had prodigious learning. Since adolescence he had
been reading all day long, underlining with one of those innumerable
sharp-pointed pencils with which his pockets were always filled entire
pages which thereafter he knew by heart. His great knowledge o
music and of the plastic arts helped him to see analogies. He loved to
point out subtle resemblances between Mozart and Keats, between
a Chinese vase and a poem by Mallarmé. His listeners were society
women who had been brought there by Alfred Fabre-Luce who wa
dearly devoted to Du Bos, some writers from the *Nouvelle Revu
Française* and some professors.

Charlie and Zézette came to stay with us at La Saussaye during th
summer of 1923. Du Bos had now a great deal of influence on m
and I think it was good influence. He was a real spiritual directo
and his presence raised above themselves those who had the goo
fortune to be his friends. He lived in the highest regions of the spiri

The air that one breathed there was a little rarefied, but the light was brilliant and clear. He urged me toward greater profundity and toward the meticulous analysis of feelings. Others might have been in danger of going too far in this direction, as he himself did. But my natural tendencies were rather toward rapidity, excessive clarity and simplification. By his example Charlie made me take a cure that consisted in complexity, slowness and obscurity. It did me good.

But this intimacy, which furthered my apprenticeship as a writer, was not good for my married life. Tired of my solemn friends, Janine accused me of imitating their faults.

"My, but you're getting hard to live with!" she said to me half jokingly, half sadly.

At this time I had some literary friends in Paris to whose homes I used to go occasionally without her in the evening. For her part, Janine saw a good deal of her brother, who had become a well-known couturier. He introduced her to a world I did not know. We both saw with despair the chasm, created by the four years of the war, growing deeper between us. Like a man whose feet are caught in quicksand and whose vain struggles only thrust him deeper into it, so our attempts at kindness, our little sacrifices, often unnoticed, misunderstood, ill rewarded, made us realize all the more clearly the danger of our position. Nevertheless between Janine and me there were so many happy memories, our love had begun with so much strength and assurance, that we could not accept the idea of a spiritual divorce.

During that summer of 1923 Janine, who had once more become pious, held long conversations with the Abbé Lemoine, curé of La Saussaye. He was a young and enthusiastic country priest of severe morals, who courageously endured almost incredible poverty in this country of rich farmers. I admired his disinterestedness and his faith; he exhibited great friendliness toward me. I do not know whether it was by his advice, but Janine tried, during that summer, to recreate the atmosphere of the first months of our marriage twelve years before.

The three children in the garden were a delight to watch. Michelle rode around the lawns on her bicycle, the little ones, whom their mother called *Topi* and *Little Man*, played with the flowers, the rab-

bits and the chickens. Janine, who loved them tenderly, was with them
a great deal at this time, but she showed a surprising, foreboding sadness. Despite her youth, she talked constantly about death. One evening at La Saussaye she had a great open fire lighted in the library and
burned many of our letters. This distressed me.

"But why, Janine? . . ."

"I don't know . . . I don't want to leave anything behind me . . ."

"Why do you say behind you? . . . You'll be here for another thirty
or forty years."

"You mustn't believe that," she said, with a look that was filled with
terror.

In October Charlie Du Bos resumed his lectures. He spent a long
time discussing Browning who was one of his heroes. Janine, ill and
in bed most of the time, seldom attended the lectures. Toward Christ-
mastime she summoned up enough strength to prepare gifts and a tree.
She was so fond of festivities and presents. As a gift for me she had had
sent from London, in greatest secrecy, the sixty volumes of the *Dictionary of National Biography*, the absence of which from our library
she had heard me deplore. I can still see her joy the day she led me to
the shelves on which she had placed "the surprise." I also see her face,
thin but ravishing, as it looked through the glass door of the dining
room at the time when the children were having their meals.

At the end of December the doctors ordered her to spend some weeks
in the south. She begged me to accompany her:

"Make the most of me . . . You won't have me here long to make
you unhappy . . ."

She had adopted her *"light luggage"* tone which I was never able to
resist. Although it was not vacation time, and despite the complaints
of my partners, I abandoned the mill at its busiest season and went to
live with my wife and the children in La Napoule near Cannes. Janine
had a group of English and American friends there: the Henry Clewses
and Winifred Mackenzie whom we both loved. We hardly went any-
where beyond our villa and the beach. We had long frank conversations; these weeks might have been sweet if the weather had not been so
cold, the children sick and the servants irritable. But various catas-

trophes so marred our vacation that at the beginning of February we decided to return. Janine was five months pregnant; she was sinking into despair.

We had barely arrived at Neuilly when she was put to bed with a violent fever. Her teeth chattered.

"But what has she?" I asked the doctors in alarm.

"Auto-infection," they replied with ominous vagueness . . . "Septicemia . . . It seems to be extremely serious."

They decided upon surgical intervention. Janine agreed to the operation bravely but without illusions. She had asked to see her children again. The two little ones had been seated near her bed and had been playing at being doctors:

"Mammy, we are two piggy goctors . . ."

When the chloroform wore off and she regained consciousness she suffered a great deal. I remained near her with the nurse. She talked like a person who was going to die and knew it. She declared that she was a true believer and asked me to have masses said for the repose of her soul.

Suddenly she cried aloud in terror:

"I can't see any more! . . ."

Her head fell back on the pillow. It was the end. I could not believe it nor accept it. At my insistence the doctor, who had been summoned back by telephone, attempted to revive her by injections of adrenalin near the heart, but in vain. I remained until morning kneeling beside the small Directoire bed holding her hand as it grew cold.

At the time when the noises in the street began and the screeching of the iron shutters of the shops, I went out to look for flowers. I returned with my arms full of lilacs and roses which I arranged around her. "Poor Ginette!" I thought. "This is the first time that you've not arranged your flowers yourself . . ."

I talked aloud to the body lying there. I could not imagine that Janine would no longer answer me. She was so beautiful, so calm. A vague smile was etched around the corners of her pale lips. The strong perfume of the lilacs filled the room. In my mind it evoked the forked tree of my childhood, my first reading and the Queen of *The Young*

Russian Soldiers. I had found the Queen in the wide, wide world; I had chosen her, won her and lost her. The penetrating and tender fragrance of lilacs was to bring back, to my dying day, the memory of that funeral bed, that icy forehead and my tears.

In the forenoon the first friends arrived. I left two nuns to keep watch in the room and received Charles Du Bos, who was gentle and compassionate. He volunteered to arrange everything with the Church of Saint-Pierre in Neuilly. I desired to have Fauré's beautiful *Requiem* played and Händel's *Largo*, which was one of Janine's favorites. I feel an infinite gratitude to the Church for the poignant beauty of that Mass. I was consumed with sorrow and love. The divine music of Fauré, the sublime voices of the choir, the hieratic deliberateness of the evolutions, the solemnity of the absolution, comforted me. *"Requiem aeternam, dona eis, Domine . . . Requiem aeternam . . . aeternam . . . aeternam."* It seemed to me that I could be at rest, and that if another world existed in which she whom I had so greatly loved survived, she would be happy and like the angelic, childlike and ardent girl whom I had seen in the moonlight that first evening beneath the trees of the Parc des Eaux Vives.

CHAPTER XV

Life Must Go On

THE most terrible thing for the survivors in the death of a loved one is the feeling of irreparability. *"Nevermore . . ."* Nevermore should I hear that slightly muffled voice; nevermore should I see that beautiful thin face; nevermore would there be what she used to call a "palaver," one of those long discussions, concerned sometimes with painful subjects, but now seeming so precious that I should gladly have given what was left of my life to talk to Janine for a single hour, a single minute. The weather, in that month of March 1924, was beautiful and the sweetness of a premature spring, by its contrast, intensified my despair. Day after day the sun rose in a cloudless sky. I did no work. Each day I would go and buy flowers and arrange them as best I could, the way she would have done, moving a rose here, accentuating the curve of a stem, in front of the portraits I had placed in every room. Michelle, with a woman's instinct, would come and sit opposite me after dinner, and her grave sweetness re-established my connection with life.

Colonel Jenner, when he learned of my bereavement, wrote me: "Do come to us in Avebury. The old house is very large. We will give you half of it. You won't even see us. The change of scene will do you good . . ." I accepted this very kind invitation, but I did not find tranquillity of soul in England any more than I had at Neuilly. In vain I tired myself out with long walks among the upright stones and the turf-covered downs of Avebury. Each night in my dreams I found Janine again. Each awakening was a torture. When I returned to France the vault that I had had constructed at La Saussaye was finished and I had the coffin brought there. In front of the tomb I had placed a little semi-circular bench of marble, a willow tree and a large urn for flowers. I formed the habit of going every day to sit in the cemetery and dream of the past. We spent the summer at La Saussaye. The children in the garden were charming. Often they came with me to the cemetery.

"Let's take flowers to Mammy," they would say.

Michelle had become serious, thoughtful, reserved. Although she had the grace and beauty of her mother I found in her, in a different form, my own scruples, shyness and reticence. The two boys, blond and rosy, looked enchanting on the green grass in their bright-colored overalls. I loved to follow their simple and happy little lives. Each day they made a tour of the garden, as my father had formerly done of the mill, and with the same seriousness. They coveted the strawberries, looked at the sweet peas, admired the roses, counted the eggs that had been laid and went to visit the gardener. Then, as I had done at their age, they gathered wild flowers in the shadows of the trees and made fragile bouquets of them. Toward evening they would put on their tiny belted coats of pale blue and go for a walk on the uplands along paths that crossed fields of wheat, blond as their hair, in the midst of which their heads disappeared among the poppies and corn-flowers.

As soon as I was able I forced myself to work. For a long time I had been thinking of writing *Dialogues on Leadership*. On this subject there was a conflict of ideas that had troubled me since the time of Alain. The latter thought of himself as the Citizen on guard against the Authorities. He had taught me that the less a government governs the better governed a country is and that every leader is tempted to become a tyrant. But life had taught me instead (as had Plato's *Republic*) that for lack of leaders men fall into disorder and then into tyranny. Where did the truth lie? I hoped to put my thoughts in order and, as Renan says, make the two lobes of my brain argue it out.

In the preceding year at Pontigny, I had met a Lieutenant Blacque-Belair, son of the cavalry general who was commandant of the Academy of Saumur. Aimery Blacque-Belair was a district commander in Morocco in the rebel zone. He was an earnest young man, a great reader of Gide and full of ardor for the profession of soldier. He became one of the interlocutors in my dialogue; the other was Alain. During the whole month of July the Lieutenant and the Philosopher carried on their argument inside me. My mind tried to be impartial but my heart was with the Lieutenant. Horror of disorder has always been one of my strongest feelings. Not that I love tyranny; I *hate* it, because it too is a disorder and always ends by breeding anarchy. But I respect a just and legal authority. No successful action without discipline. Such was my theme.

The book was finished by the end of summer. The work had not been interrupted except by a visit at La Saussaye of André Gide, the Du Bos' and Anne Desjardins, with whom Michelle and I made a friendly and memorable trip to Chartres. I was delighted by the encounter between Gide and the cathedral. My friends of Pontigny now replaced the friends of my youth who had died in the war. My publisher, Bernard Grasset, was enthusiastic when he read the *Dialogues*; he said it was my best work. He would have liked a Greek title for it and proposed *Nicias*; the name sounded all right but the general had been mediocre; I refused. The *Dialogues on Leadership* made quite a stir when they appeared. They were judged, very mistakenly, not as a literary work but as a political manifesto. As a matter of fact, I was not the advocate of any party. "Not enough," Alain used to say. I clung tenaciously to those essential liberties which seemed to me, and still seem, the prerequisites of man's happiness and dignity. But I believed that these liberties could not be maintained except by a discipline freely consented to, and that an excess of liberty always kills liberty. Subsequent events have only too clearly borne me out. I loved my country passionately; I desired its security and greatness; I wanted to attract the attention of the young people—the future leaders of France, in politics, military affairs and industry—to the rules of action which experience and history had taught me. Nothing more. The fanatics of the Right and Left refused to believe that a dialogue could be nothing more than a dialogue and each tried to draw me onto their side. But certain distinguished soldiers like Marshal Fayolle, and certain distinguished servants of the state like Jules Cambon, wrote me wise letters. Bergson was kind enough to praise me for showing the role of intuition in the make-up of the leader as well as of the artist. Alain, who recognized himself, appeared not displeased.

"Wouldn't you like to meet Marshal Pétain," Grasset said to me one day in November, "and discuss with him your *Dialogues* which he has read? He is going to have lunch on the second of December at the home of one of my friends, Madame de Caillavet, together with Robert de Flers, Henri-Robert and Paul Valéry. She has asked me to invite you."

"You know very well, Grasset," I said, "that I am in mourning and don't go out socially."

"This isn't a question of going out socially," Grasset protested, "it is a professional luncheon. You are interested in certain ideas. Here's a chance to discuss them with remarkable men. That's all."

I ended by accepting. "Madame de Caillavet" was a name not unknown to me. It belonged to Anatole France's elderly friend, the mother of Gaston de Caillavet, co-author with Robert de Flers of *Le Roi, Primerose* and *l'Habit Vert*. I expected to see a domineering old lady. I was delightfully surprised when I entered a ground floor apartment in the Boulevard Malesherbes with Grasset and was presented to a young woman. My hostess was pretty and handsomely dressed in a black and white gown. She knew of my bereavement and talked to me with a compassion that touched me deeply. The Marshal had been detained by some official duty and did not appear, but thanks to Valéry, Robert de Flers, Henri-Robert, Grasset and Madame de Caillavet herself, who knew countless anecdotes and told them wittily, the conversation was sparkling and the luncheon delightful. I left with Grasset:

"Now," I said, "explain this mystery. I expected to see a very old woman . . ."

He burst into laughter:

"You're dreaming! Madame Arman de Caillavet has been dead for fifteen years; this is her granddaughter, Simone de Caillavet."

"Then why is she called *Madame* de Caillavet? Why not *Mademoiselle?*"

"Because she was once married. During the Peace Conference she married a foreign diplomat. After three years the marriage was broken, annulled."

"She is unhappy?"

"I don't know at all . . . Her mother (the widow of Gaston de Caillavet) is remarried, to a cousin of hers and her name is now Madame Maurice Pouquet . . . Robert de Flers, who was Simone's guardian, takes the place of a father . . . Many writers and politicians come to her house, some because she is intelligent, .others to see Robert de Flers."

"Has she any children?"

"A little girl of four."

"Is she a writer?"

"Some time ago she wrote verses and a few articles. I do not know whether she still writes. But she is much interested in literature . . . By the way, you're a great admirer of Proust, you must talk to her about him. She knew him very well."

Madame de Caillavet had asked me to inscribe certain of my books for her. I took them to her myself; she was at home and received me; this was what I had hoped. This time I looked at her apartment more closely; it was darkened by tapestries of somber foliage that were too high and appeared to have been made for a medieval hall; the walls of the drawing-room were lined with mirrors; the floor, covered in large black and white squares, gave the impression of a hotel lobby. Our conversation was animated. Naturally we talked about Proust.

"For my mother," she said, "he had a childhood friendship, intermittent but strong . . . He drew from her (in part at least) the character of Gilberte Swann . . . And as for me, in his book I am Gilberte's daughter Mademoiselle de Saint-Loup."

She told me how Proust had come, after twelve or thirteen years, to call on the Gaston de Caillavets one evening at midnight and had asked to see their daughter.

"But she's been in bed for a long time!" Madame de Caillavet said.

"Have her get up, I beg you," Proust said.

"He insisted so successfully," Simone de Caillavet went on, "that they got me out of bed . . . And possibly you remember the imaginary character that was born of that visit?"

She went to find a copy of *The Past Recaptured* and showed me the passage about Mademoiselle de Saint-Loup which ends with these sentences: "I found her very beautiful: still full of hope. Laughing, shaped by the very years that I had lost, she resembled my youth."

I looked with emotion at the living woman who was Mademoiselle de Saint-Loup.

"Would you like to see Proust's letters?" she asked.

"He wrote to you?"

"Often."

From a box she produced pages covered with that rapid handwriting which I knew well.

Marcel Proust to Madame de Caillavet: "I found your hanging gardens, your antique columns and even, despite my pretended disdain, the signature of Napoleon, I found all this most agreeable. But even more, I like your daughter and the prodigious wealth of intelligence in a glance or exclamation of hers. 'I do all I can!' (to be nice to you) was sublime . . ." *Marcel Proust to Simone de Caillavet:* "I was disappointed after your last *Dear friend* to read *Dear Monsieur Marcel.* That's the way officers in the army are reduced in rank . . . Have you read *The Mill on the Floss?* If not, I beg you to read it . . . How can you possibly write, or rather draw, whole pages of those little Chinese wands? You seem to produce a sort of strange painting in place of letters. It's delightful, it's more like water color painting or gardening than writing."

I asked to see this writing that resembled a Chinese garden, and like Proust I found it surprising. It had a deliberate, restrained grace.

Marcel Proust to Madame de Caillavet: "Strange that one can love opposite physical types. For here am I in love with your daughter. How naughty she is to be agreeable, for it is her smile that has made me fall in love and that gives meaning to her whole person. If she had frowned, how completely at peace I should be. I am searching for the species of flower whose petals are exactly like her cheeks when she laughs . . . I should like to see her laugh again."

Bernard Grasset let me read a preface, that Anatole France had written, for a volume of verse *Les Heures Latines* published in 1918 by Simone de Caillavet when she was quite young. France had drawn a curious portrait of her. He represented her as a girl who was "mysterious, haughty, a little wild."

"At five years of age Simone was writing novels in a firm hand in school note books. One is surprised that she undertook them; the admirable thing is that she completed them . . : One cannot will to will. Simone could use her will. She was born resolute. That can be seen from her firm little mouth, her determined chin, the way she carries her head and from her whole purposeful manner . . . There is something predestined about a child whom a familiar spirit inspires, contending for attention with her dolls."

He found that resolute soul again in the form and substance of her verses: "Stubborn, attracted by obstacles, she instinctively chose a difficult art. She liked to find resistance in the medium. She is, in the noblest sense of the word, a young craftsman. May she proudly accept this name. *Minerva the Craftsman,* thus the Athenians called their goddess."

Proust himself has shown how all a man's tastes enter into the composition of his loves and how Swann who was mad about painting was captivated by Odette on the day when he found a resemblance between her and one Zephora, daughter of Jethro, as painted by Botticelli. I knew hardly anything about Madame de Caillavet; I was ignorant of all the details of her life, of her tastes, of her character; but a young woman who, as a child, had strolled through the museums of Paris with Anatole France and, as a girl, had been admired by Marcel Proust, seemed to me framed in precious imagery, adorned with rare and luminous words, and clothed in noble prose and wondrous legends. For the first time in a year I felt keen interest in a woman's presence, curiosity, perhaps hope. I asked her if her little daughter, who was of the age of my sons, would like to come and play with them, and I took my leave.

Françoise came to see Gerald and Olivier. She was a delicate child, overly intelligent, restless and sensitive. Her mother came to my apart-

ment to take her home. By an extraordinary coincidence Madame de
Caillavet was wearing on that day a last year's dress, the same model
that Janine had worn a few days before her death. It was a shock, both
painful and sweet. She must have found a tragic atmosphere in those
rooms filled with portraits in front of which stood arrangements of
white flowers. Arnold Bennett, who came to see me about that time,
noted in his journal that the air of this house seemed charged with an
almost morbid mystery. Once more on this occasion we talked about
poets and musicians. Next day I sent her *The Etruscan Vase* by
Mérimée and Heine's *Intermezzo*. She expected flowers and was surprised, but I continued to be the man I had been at eighteen who
delivered commentaries on the *Tractatus Politicus* to young girls.

I had promised for a long time to go to Italy to see friends, and I
left in January 1925. I was withdrawing more and more from the mill,
and my cousins seeing my indifference had brought their sons-in-law
into the business. I was still on the board but I planned to hand in my
resignation as soon as the "duck's eggs" had hatched. In Rome, Signora
Paolo Orano (she was a French woman, Camille Mallarmé, niece of
the poet and author of a good novel, *Casa Seca*, whom I had met
during the war) asked me if I wanted to meet Mussolini who was at
the threshold of his power. I was taken to the Chigi Palace by
Orano. I can still see that long feudal gallery, the little desk and
the man with the out-thrust jaw who talked to me about the *Divine
Comedy*. Next day I went to place violets near the Pyramid of Cestius
on the tomb of Shelley. From the gardens of the Palatine I gazed at the
Forum bathed in a light of dusty gold. I wandered through the Roman
Campagna in pursuit of Chateaubriand and the night. In the shadow
of the Coliseum I evoked the shade of Byron. A crowd of phantoms
accompanied me, thronging so close that I hardly saw the living.

When I returned the time of the first anniversary of Janine's death
was approaching. I had an anniversary mass celebrated at Saint-Pierre
de Neuilly; they played the same music as at her funeral. Fauré,
Händel and the harmonious voices of the choir reawakened and then
assuaged my grief. Madame de Caillavet attended this mass, together

with my friends of Pontigny, my friends of the war and a few of my literary friends.

Through Grasset I had become acquainted with Paul Morand, François Mauriac and Jean Giraudoux. At the Du Bos' I had met Jean-Louis Vaudoyer and Jacques Chardonne. Edmond Jaloux and his wife Germaine had become delightful friends. Germaine Jaloux, an excellent pianist, taught me at that time to love Wagner. In this field I once more encountered Simone de Caillavet, who was a devoted Wagnerian. She invited me to her home rather often, and there I saw Henri de Regnier, Gabriel Hanotaux, Paul Valéry and the dear Abbé Mugnier, an indulgent and romantic priest who was the first to make me love and understand Chateaubriand. Each time he saw me he would recite some beautiful phrases:

"Oh, Monsieur Maurois!" he would say to me . . . "Do you remember the moon of Combourg and 'that majestic secret of melancholy which it loves to impart to the ancient oaks and to the antique shores of the sea'? . . . How beautiful it is!"

And his eyes would sparkle with enthusiasm, his white hair would form a hazy and poetic nimbus about his head. I loved him very much.

Simone de Caillavet's mother, Madame Maurice Pouquet—who was still young, celebrated for her beauty and possessed of a redoubtable and mordant wit—had revived in her mansion in the Avenue Hoche the tradition of her mother-in-law Madame Arman de Caillavet, and in her home I found the Poincarés, great friends of the family, Professor Dumas, General Weygand, Admiral Lacaze, Anna de Noailles, Paul Souday, Henri-Robert, Paul Valéry and many writers of my generation. I was timid and rarely spoke in these assemblies, still being bewildered by the rapidity of Paris conversations. I preferred to see Simone de Caillavet alone and have her describe for me, with her relentless memory, this Parisian world of which I knew so little. From my province I had little realized the secret bonds that unite the political, the financial, the literary and social worlds. The role of an institution like the Académie Française had completely escaped me. I had never imagined the slow conquest of radical politicians from the province by the Parisian drawing-rooms. Madame de Caillavet clarified these pictures for me. But at the same time this young woman, who was so brilliant, let me catch sight occasionally of her own humility and this moved me.

It was evident that her marriage had counted for little in her life. She talked about it without bitterness. On the other hand she had retained, I know not why, a dull memory of her childhood. She had been brought up by Miss Varley, an English governess, who still lived with her mother and to whom she was very much attached. From her she had gained a knowledge of the English language and literature which was another bond between us. Through the efforts of Miss Varley she had learned Shakespeare by heart before the nursery rhymes and recited: *"Most friendship is feigning, most loving mere folly"* at an age when she would have done better to be at play. Even her games had been Shakespearean. Her mother told me that as a child Simone had played at the "marching forest" and had gravely made a circuit of the walks in their park at Perigord carrying an oak branch. When her parents, in order to strengthen her, had made her take baths in the river, the child had replied that she would only consent on condition that she be crowned with flowers and be allowed to wear a white night-gown "to play the death of Ophelia." Once when she was sent to wash ink stains from her hands she cried: "All the perfumes of Arabia will not sweeten this little hand!" These stories could not but charm me.

.   .   .   .

In March 1925 I was due to leave Paris for a trip to Morocco. Marshal Lyautey, with whom I had remained in correspondence since *Bramble,* had invited me to attend the inauguration of the first railroad in Morocco which ran from Casablanca to Rabat. I went with my friend Emile Henriot of the Paris *Temps.* In Casablanca Lyautey himself was waiting for us on the pier. There for the first time I saw his bold and tormented face, his warlike mustache (his teeth had been smashed by a horse's hoof), his hair that bristled straight up, his rapid stride, his explosive, prancing and fruitful impatience.

"Will you walk back with me?" he asked the moment we stepped on Moroccan soil. "I should like to show you the city."

"We shall be delighted, *Monsieur le Maréchal.*"

"Well then . . ."

He led us at a run among the cubical Arab houses of rough stucco covered with pink geraniums and violet-colored bougainvillea blossoms. Sometimes to make his plans clear to us he would leap upon the pedestal of some statue and with a sweeping gesture of his cane would indicate future edifices. Finally he brought us back to the harbor. We were having trouble to keep up.

"Come on, come on!" he cried to us. "Good Lord, how slow you walk! In an action time is everything . . . All right. Here we are. Now listen . . . Monsieur Delandres, engineer in charge of the harbor, is going to explain the progress of operations . . . And you, Delandres, above all, put it in logical order."

Monsieur Delandres told us how it had been necessary, since the Port of Casablanca was blocked by a bar, to extend the breakwater far enough to break up the bar; he explained the facilities provided for the export of phosphates.

"Very good," the Marshal said. "Now in my turn I am going to explain the philosophy of the thing . . . When I began this harbor everyone said: 'Lyautey is planning on too large a scale. He is mad!' But that made no difference to me. I thought: 'This is a great country. The demands will come. I must be ready . . .' Good . . . You know that quite near here at Kouriga they found deposits of phosphates which are the best in the world. This year we will produce six hundred thousand tons; next year we will reach a million . . . Now these phosphates by themselves would justify the importance given to the harbor . . . Very good . . . You say to me: 'And if there hadn't been any phosphates?' . . . Yes . . . But my reply is that there are always phosphates . . . When one does something, he must have confidence in what he's doing."

One can easily imagine how this wonderful success, this intelligent activity, this rational exercise of authority would fill with enthusiasm the author of *Dialogues on Leadership*. In Lyautey I found the best traits of the man of action whom I had tried to portray. In the following days he took us to see Rabat, Marrakesh and Meknès. The more

I saw the extent of his work, the more I admired its perfection. Under the convenient fiction of the Protectorate, this great leader had freed Frenchmen from the tyranny of bureaucracy and, behold, the French in a few years had established a model country.

In Rabat he took us to see the Sultan, accompanied by a superb mounted troop whose red coats streamed in the wind. A negro guard playing flutes and tambourines received us in the courtyard of a palace out of *The Thousand and One Nights* where visitors and beggars along the walls formed a frieze worthy of a palace in Susa. The Sultan swathed in veils was seated on his throne. The Marshal bowed very low and said to the interpreter:

"Tell Sidna (His Majesty) that I felicitate him on having constructed so fine a railroad in his possessions."

The interpreter murmured a few words in Arabic; the Sultan replied.

"Sidna says," the interpreter translated, "that he would never have accomplished it without the Marshal's support."

Such indeed was our impression as well.

"Say to Sidna," the Marshal went on, "that his subjects like the new railroad and that many of them are already traveling on the sections that are now open."

Translation . . . Reply:

"Sidna says that even more would do so if it were less expensive."

When the audience ended the Marshal made us walk out backward. He imposed on all, and on himself as well, the respect required by imperial protocol, for by maintaining the prestige of the Sultan he strengthened his own power.

In Fez we lodged in the beautiful palace of Bou Jeloud in rooms paneled in cedarwood with high sculptured doors. In the morning we would go out barefooted into a courtyard paved with sun-warmed tiles of white and blue faïence. Orange trees, planted amid the flagging perfumed the warm air and a gentle Arabic fountain played in a faïence basin. The officer in command of Fez was General de Chambrun, whom I had known in Paris, and whose wife (née Clara Longworth) was an erudite Shakespearean. With them I went up on the hills beyond the gates of the city to see the evening shadows invade the white terraces and a little later to hear the shrill, sad singing of the women.

In the evening Henriot and I dined with General de Chambrun. Our host and his wife showed a forced gaiety and we noticed strange, secret conferences, military messengers came in during the meal and whispered incomprehensible news in an atmosphere of apprehension and expectancy.

"Haven't you a feeling," I said to Henriot, "that we are in a house where someone is very sick and where, through courtesy, an attempt is being made to keep the news from the guests?"

"Yes," Henriot said, "there's certainly something wrong . . . I heard one of the officers say: 'Is the post going to hold?' "

Next day as we were sitting down to dinner, General Heusch, the Marshal's chief of staff, arrived. He was a witty Alsatian and was the life of the party. But the moment the last bite had been swallowed he shut himself up with General de Chambrun. Since they did not reappear, we took leave of Madame de Chambrun and toward midnight returned to our beautiful courtyard with its orange trees. At three o'clock in the morning we were abruptly awakened by dark silhouettes. We saw an adjutant and some soldiers:

"Messieurs, the General begs you to leave at once for Oudjda. The car is at the door."

"A car? . . . But why?"

"The General desires you to reach Oran as quickly as possible. He has had rifles placed in the car."

"Rifles? What sort of joke is this?"

We got dressed grumbling. There were indeed three rifles in the car and a box of cartridges. Our chauffeur was a little soldier from the Midi, resourceful and intelligent. We got him to talk.

"What?" said he. "You don't know? Why, it's war. Abd-el-Krim, the fellow who beat the Spaniards, has started an uprising in the Rif . . . All the tribes are revolting and going to join him . . . Look there . . ."

We were crossing a desert of white sand and we could see, riding along the crest of the dunes, handsome Arab warriors, with their long rifles slung over their backs. They were setting out for the Holy War.

"Do you think they are going to attack us?"

"As to that," he said, "I don't know any more than you do . . . But I'll be glad when we get within reach of Oudjda."

As a matter of fact, we arrived in Oudjda without being forced to defend ourselves. The French Consul, Monsieur de Witasse and his wife, a cultured pair, gave us tea, comfortable chairs and *La Nouvelle Revue Française.*

"Ah!" they said. "We were certainly glad to see you arrive. The General telephoned us three times from Fez about you. He was worried."

When I saw General de Chambrun in Paris some time later he said to me laughingly:

"Well, well! You know, when I made you leave Fez I wondered whether you were going to get through . . ."

"But why then did you take the risk, General?"

"Because Fez might have been surrounded or even taken the following day . . . I gave you a chance to escape . . . But it was a relief to hear you had arrived."

Just as I owe a group of friends to Pontigny, I owe another to Morocco. Commandant Cellier, Pierre Viénot and Lieutenant Blacque-Belair belonged to both groups. But this trip, and reunions later on in the Rue Bonaparte, introduced me to the whole crowd who had worked with the man they affectionately called the "Chief." Among them were Pierre Lyautey, nephew of the Chief, Wladimir d'Ormesson, Félix de Vogüé, Cénival and Captain Durozoy. When at the end of the year the Chief returned to Paris, he often invited me to his house. I liked the spirit of his staff. These were men who thought of their work and of their duty ahead of themselves or of any party. In France, which was so badly divided, Lyautey was one of those rare leaders who knew how to make use of men of all opinions and all faiths and make them work together for the glory of their country. He was a monarchist, but he got on well with Herriot, the radical, because Herriot was a patriot. He was an ardent Catholic, but he had among his intimate friends

Protestants, Israelites, Mohammedans and free thinkers. When Millerand, then President of France, came to Morocco, the Marshal said to him:

"Monsieur the President, I know that in Paris you do not go to Mass, but here I request you to go every Sunday because the Arabs are a religious people and they would not understand . . . "

And the free-thinking President respectfully accompanied the Catholic Resident to church.

"The Marshal, mighty ruler," the natives said to me in Rabat or Marrakesh as they saw the Chief's car flash by at full speed. I thought so too.

CHAPTER XVI

The Walkyrie

O N MY return from Morocco I found my father about to undergo a serious operation. For two years he had been suffering from disease of the prostate gland. A first operation had made it possible for him to go on living but at a reduced rate and with constant care, which irritated him. Although the doctors themselves had told him his general condition was not good and he would do better to wait, he decided to take the risk and be done with it.

"Dying doesn't frighten me," he said, "and living this way is unbearable."

And so he entered the clinic of the Brothers Saint-Jean de Dieu in Paris and resigned himself to Fate. On the day before the operation I went to see him and had a long conversation with him. He seemed happy and in good spirits.

"Whatever happens now," he said, "at the end of my life I have seen the thing I hoped for more than anything else in the world: the return of Alsace to France."

Alas, from the first day after the operation it was clear that it had not been successful. He was seized by vomitings, complained of frightful suffering and little by little fell into a lethargy which was the result of uremia. The following day the surgeon admitted to us that there was no longer any hope. A few seconds before the end Papa opened his eyes and called me:

"You are there?" he said in a barely audible voice. "Then it's all right . . ."

After that he drew two or three breaths and appeared to fall asleep.

The nurse held a mirror to his lips. He was dead. Never did purer heart cease to beat. For my mother, who had brought him there with so much confidence, it was a terrible blow and the end of her real life. But she showed great courage. The burial, which took place at Elbeuf, was just as he had wished. From the cemetery, on the side of a hill overlooking the town, one could see the long orange roofs and the high chimneys of the mill to which he had dedicated his life. The workers all came. Many of the old Alsatian women wept. Bellouin, a weaver who had been one of his most loyal friends, gave a simple and moving discourse. From Le Havre Monseigneur Alleaume wrote me: "Your father was one of the most thoroughly noble men I have ever met. At the time when I was living in Elbeuf he did not have a single enemy." This was the exact truth.

.   .   .   .

His death severed the last bond between the mill and me. I continued to go there, but each week I abandoned more of my prerogatives. Even when I was at La Saussaye I devoted almost all my time to writing. I had begun two books. One of them, *Bernard Quesnay,* was a novel of industrial life, an elaboration of the long short story I had published under the title of *Prosperity and Depression.* As Veronese did in certain of his pictures, I put myself in it twice: under the name of Bernard and under the name of Antoine Quesnay. Bernard was what I might have been if I had tried to live the *Dialogues on Leadership;* Antoine what I might perhaps have been if Janine had lived. *Bernard Quesnay* is not a "great" novel, far from it, but it is an honest book, much truer in its description of the industrial world than those pamphlets published under the name of novels by men who have only seen that life from the outside and through the distorting medium of their own prejudices. My other and more important work was a *Life of Disraeli.*

Where had I come upon that idea? First in a comment by Barrès: "The three most interesting men of the Nineteenth Century are Byron, Disraeli and Rossetti." This gave me the idea of reading the life and works of Disraeli. They filled me with enthusiasm. In him I found a hero after my own heart: "I am," he said, "a radical in order to uproot what is bad; a conservative in order to preserve what is good." And also: "To conserve is to maintain and to reform." This was the political philosophy that experience had taught me. The more I studied both history and men, the clearer it became to me that civilizations, as Valéry says, are "edifices of enchantment." The acceptance of conventions gives rise to a reign of order, and under the shelter of these conventions liberty flourishes. British conventions were perhaps the most amazing of all, but because they were respected the country had been preserved from brutal shocks and, without a revolution, had become one of the freest in the world.

Since the war I had shared Disraeli's admiration for British tradition. Like him I believed that a man born a Jew, if he is intelligent and honest, should understand and respect the Christian tradition as much as, if not more than, anyone else. Many of Disraeli's sayings pleased me by their form and content. *"Never explain, never complain." "Or perfect solitude, or perfect sympathy."* Phrases like these awoke an instant response in me. His long devotion to his wife was the perfect image of the life I had hoped for and that had been denied me. His influence on world affairs, to me who had no such influence (nor wished to have), was a vicarious compensation. I had never written a book with greater pleasure.

In July I interrupted this work to go and spend some days in Périgord with the family of Madame de Caillavet's mother, the Pouquets. (The Caillavets themselves were from Bordeaux.) The Pouquets owned the little château of Essendiéras between Périgueux and Limoges. This ancient dwelling, adorned with feudal turrets, had been bought by Maître Antoine-Chéri Pouquet, a lawyer in Angoisse, at the time of the Revolution. Beside it on the same hill a new house, more comfortable but without beauty, had been built by Simone's grandfather, a stock broker in Paris, during the period of prosperity and bad taste. The tapestries, the overstuffed furniture, the thick curtains, the innumerable portraits and knickknacks gave Essendiéras an air of Louis-Philippe. To find there the same bronzes as at Elbeuf amused me. The employees of the Pouquet office had given Simone's grandfather, just as the workmen had given my father, a bronze representing *Work* by Barbedienne, with this inscription: "On the battlefields of labor victory is fruitful . . ." But the photographs which covered the tables at Essendiéras, just as in Elbeuf, were more interesting here. You saw Anatole France, now leaning against the shaft of an antique column, now in contemplation of the pyramids. An adolescent Proust with velvety eyes; a Victorien Sardou wearing a beret; innumerable pictures of Robert de Flers and Gaston de Caillavet with arms linked in friendship; and actresses: the exuberant Jeanne Granier; the beautiful and tragic Lantelme; the humorous and subtle Marie Leconte with her tiptilted nose; and above all Eve Lavalliére, an acidulous Miquette, who was to become a saint.

The view across the valley of the Isle was beautiful, embracing a region of tenant farms with lovely names: Brouillac, la Guichardie, la Cerise. Two long converging alleys, one of oaks, the other of chestnut trees, led from the road up to the château. A rushing stream, the Loue (or Louve), ran along the foot of the hills and nibbled at the banks of the Essendiéras fields.

In addition to Madame de Caillavet and Madame Pouquet, I found there the latter's husband, a mining engineer whose alert and precise intelligence I quickly learned to value; Simone's grandmother, a fine old lady, but a little confused; and Miss Varley, a super-English Englishwoman and passionate Victorian. To be honest, during these ten days, I saw hardly anyone but Simone de Caillavet, for she had undertaken to show me Périgord and we were on the go from morning till night. At Essendiéras I fell in love simultaneously with the landscapes of Périgord and with the woman who showed them to me. She passionately loved her province and talked about it with a profound and living knowledge of its ways that I found attractive. Each village had its château, each château its legend. My companion told me the story of *La Fileuse* of Jumilhac and that of the châtelaine of Montal, the story of the château of Biron and of the château of Hautefort. She took me on literary pilgrimages in honor of Montaigne, Brantôme, Fénelon —and to Montignac where Joubert and Eugène Le Roy had lived. She knew all about these men and their works, and I was struck by the seriousness and soundness of her mind.

I went down into the chasm of Padirac; I climbed with her by precipitous roads to the tableland of Domme, whence one can see the lovely valley of the Dordogne framed by graceful fortresses and by serried rows of poplars. If she had been a coquette, she would have found a hundred occasions, during these many difficult passages, to fall into my arms, but I found her timid, apprehensive, reserved, almost unsociable. Although she had been married, she retained some of the qualities of a young girl. She had been raised most religiously, with a horror of sin and a fear of profane love. "Apt at suffering and more fearful of joy than of sorrow," Anatole France had written of her. When she talked about love it was in an heroic, Wagnerian sense. Valkyrie surrounded with thorns and flames, she awaited Siegfried, but with a strange dread. In the course of my life I had known bold virgins, passionate girl students and idle women of Paris; I was ill prepared to understand a puritan who could not enter upon passion except after a long stage of tenderness.

Later she admitted to me that she had been obsessed by the romance of her grandmother with Anatole France, and she had always hoped to devote herself, heart and mind, to an artist's work. She talked of "going into literature as one goes into religion." One evening as a result of a breakdown of the car which obliged the chauffeur to go back for repairs, we remained alone for an hour in the forest. The air was mild and caressing, the rays of the moon through the trees lighted the path we were following; the earth, covered with pine needles, moss and dry leaves, was springy beneath our feet. The simple beauty of sleeping nature put an end to our resistance. I dared say to her that I loved her. But I did not know how to reconcile this feeling which was young, ardent and new with a past whose funereal shadows still completely enveloped me.

The following winter in Paris I saw Simone almost every day. Together we went to the theater and to concerts. Ardent admirer of Wagner that she was, she determined to make me love and understand him. In this she succeeded all the more easily because I myself was trying earnestly to understand her, and her Wagnerian reveries illuminated her character, which was far more that of Brünnhilde than of Isolde. She believed in the superhuman power of Parsifal because he was chaste; she felt a horror of the Magic Maidens, a physical horror that was almost hatred.

"Woe unto them through whom the offense cometh," she would say when I reproached her for her extreme severity toward other women.

The music brought us together. Simone found in Wagner the symbol and perhaps the solution of her problems. And I, in turn, discovered profound lessons for the writer. The themes that illuminated and rendered intelligible that enormous cataract of sound seemed to me also appropriate to light up and arrange the confused masses of fact in a biography or history. In Siegfried's Funeral March, in the conclusion of the *Twilight of the Gods,* I saw the inimitable model of what the end of a great book should be. I endeavored to explain this to my beautiful concert companion and I led her by the paths of music to understand what in my eyes was the art of writing.

There was another bond which united us closely: that of work. She had told me at Essendiéras that her father had had her learn typewriting and that nothing would interest her more than to copy manuscripts for me. I had not taken her offer seriously. Nevertheless, as she continually talked about it, I gave her the manuscript of the beginning of *Bernard Quesnay.* I was stupefied when, after a period that was so short she must have worked all night, she brought me an impeccable text. The perfection of the margins recalled the amazing garden of little Chinese wands that was her handwriting. I entrusted her with other work. Then one day I said to her jokingly that if she also knew shorthand I would never want any other secretary. Without saying a word to me she took lessons in shorthand and a few months later asked me to dictate letters to her. Due to hard work and determination she had become in record time the best stenographer I had ever had. Anatole France had well described her as "Minerva the craftsman," who performed her tasks with singular and meticulous perfection.

We found so much pleasure in being together that we paid no heed to the reactions of our families and our friends, who complained that they never found us free any more. Many of those around us under stood more clearly than we ourselves that we were drifting toward marriage. At one of Madame Pouquet's "Sundays" in the Avenue Hoche, Marshal Pétain found me sitting with Simone on a sofa and asked smilingly:

"When will it be proper to congratulate you?"

Rumors in the little newspapers predicted our marriage. Even my mother said to me:

"How can you live without a woman in your house? . . . Who will bring up your children? . . ."

Yes, it seemed wise for me to marry again, and if I should do so, Simone was a companion after my own heart who was capable of taking a living part in my work and whom I loved. But her friends, like mine, tried to dissuade us from the idea. In the eyes of Pontigny, an alliance with the world of *Figaro* and *l'Habit Vert* seemed a frivolous contract and a danger to my work. Charles Du Bos, with his kind and touching gravity, put me on my guard against "the salons." Ah, if he had only known how little I liked them! To Simone people said:

"Marry a widower with three children, what a mistake! You will have endless conflicts with grandmothers and governesses!"

Moreover she had always said that she would never remarry. She had had brilliant opportunities more than once and had rejected them. In the independent life, which her inheritance from her father assured her, she had found peace, a little dull perhaps, but such as marriage had not afforded her. Her instinct prompted her to preserve it.

Nevertheless when it became evident that the manners and customs of our two families were such that the passionate friendship that united us could not continue except in marriage, our feelings were stronger than the objections of our friends. One evening we had a long conversation which lasted until dawn and in the course of which we decided to be married the following summer. Françoise was of the same age as my sons and got along well with them. Why not bring together the raveled threads of two families torn by destiny and weave from them a single happiness? When we went to Elbeuf to announce this news to my mother, she received it with joy. It was decided that the wedding should take place in Périgord and that only the official witnesses were to be present.

I did not wish Pontigny to be sacrificed to Essendiéras, and at the end of August I went to Burgundy to attend a *"decade"* and there encountered again, as of old, Gide, Charles Du Bos and Martin du Gard. Then on the fourth of September 1926 I left for Périgord. There I found the Abbé Mugnier who had promised to marry us (he had married my mother-in-law and was to marry my daughter), Gabriel Hanotaux and Robert de Flers who were to be our witnesses. I had also asked Aimery Blacque-Belair, the lieutenant of the *Dialogues on Leadership* and his wife, a pair for whom I felt a brother's affection, to come and join us.

For a year I had known Simone's family. Her mother, a vivacious and passionate woman, had a true talent as a comedienne which appeared in her way of telling stories. An excellent friend to those whom she liked, she was a redoubtable enemy to those she hated. She loved to be obeyed, but in exchange for submission she offered limitless devotion. Moreover this authoritarian person recognized one authority herself, that of her husband Maurice Pouquet. It was easy to understand why she respected him. A native of Périgord, brought up on a country estate, graduate in engineering from the School of Mines, he combined the shrewd wisdom of the peasant with an astonishing and varied culture. He knew the most unexpected things, from the technique of industry to that of the fine arts, from the history of Egypt to that of Sweden; from the geology of Paraguay to the physiology of truffles. He was capable of managing a country estate, an industry, a bank, or of telling a story with a precision of detail that enchanted a writer, and during the war of 1914 he had systematized the technique of aerial photography for the French Army. Distrustful and even hostile as long as he did not know you well, he was a most loyal and dependable friend to those whom he had adopted. How many happy evenings I have spent listening to him on the terrace of Essendiéras while the constellations rose slowly above the cedars, the shooting stars streaked the summer sky with their long trails of fire, the familiar owl quitted her tower to go hunting, and in the immense sleeping plain at our feet the night mists prowled.

It was a country wedding, intimate and charming. In the little town hall of the village my wife's uncle Pierre Pouquet, who was mayor of the district, asked us the conventional questions. Robert de Flers made a lively and emotional speech in his best manner. He spoke very nicely of my parents whose life Simone had described to him; of Simone herself who was so well prepared for the difficult task of being a writer's wife; then he said to me that he hoped some day to receive me in the French Academy and, after having called me for several years "my dear André," to refer to me for an hour as "Monsieur." The church was tiny. Abbé Mugnier officiated there and said sweet and beautiful things to us about love, fidelity, and the relation between art and religion. Gabriel Hanotaux, a retired statesman and an active historian, astonishingly vigorous in mind and body, was the wit of the wedding breakfast which, as is customary in Périgord, was abundant and savory. The omelette with truffles, the preserved goose and the cherry tarts, together with the maxims of Monsieur Hanotaux, made a thoroughly French mixture. "If everyone knew what everyone says about everyone," Monsieur Hanotaux said, "no one would speak to anyone . . ." Abbé Mugnier quoted Chateaubriand and Joubert as well as Goethe and Shakespeare. Simone, pretty and animated, sparkled, and I was proud of her. Yes, it was a very nice wedding.

In the journal of Mary Shelley one may read between two notes on her reading for the day, "A wedding took place . . ." This dry discretion pleased me, and it seems that I had formed the strange project of making my second marriage slip into my daily life without causing any change in the arrangement of the latter. Simone, like every young woman, would have liked a wedding trip, a few weeks of solitude for two, in classical Italy or voluptuous Morocco. In this she was right, for the first adjustment of two lives is easier in a foreign environment which relaxes former ties. By a strange aberration I decided that we would do nothing of the sort but on the following day would join my three children and the nurse at the seashore at Hendaye. This is the explanation, though not a justification, of this absurd plan: I believe

I had unconsciously found a somber and bitter joy in being, in my own eyes and in those of my friends, the Inconsolable, and I had ended by indulging in a sentimental fetishism which was neither reasonable nor generous. Perhaps it had some obscure connection with the ancient cult of the dead and the need of appeasing their shades, which is as old as human society. Perhaps my white flowers, my sacred images and my commemorative services were nothing but attenuated forms of very ancient sacrifices.

At first this sentimentality had been the quite natural expression of an immense sorrow; now it was no longer healthy. The living should live with the living and for the living, and if it is laudable and pious to respect the dead, it is cruel to offer them human sacrifices. Worried, torn by memory and tormented by the chimera of an impossible post-humous loyalty, I had tried to make of my second marriage as small an event as possible with the obscure and naïve hope, no doubt, that the news, hushed, compressed into three words, would not penetrate as far as the dismal realms. For the same reasons, or rather the same super-stitions, I refused under thin pretexts, to use the familiar *"tu"* with my wife, though she wished it; I made her live in Neuilly in an apartment filled with memories of another woman, and when she tried to make my children hers, I rendered her attempted contacts with them more difficult by scruples and reservations which no reasonable being would have put in her way. But on this subject I was not a reasonable being.

The magic hold of the dead is strong and fearful. *"Tel qu'en lui-même enfin l'éternité le change,"* the dead escape all accidents, temp-tations and errors. Like the King, the dead *"can do no wrong."* For two years I had been shaping a superhuman figure, retouching memo-ries of the past, orchestrating a funeral hymn. I committed the error of trying to associate with me in this cult the woman I now loved. She was willing, but she suffered from it. The servants and the children's nurse contradicted her decisions with the wishes of "Madame," and "Madame" was a beautiful, impalpable phantom. The transfer of authority was accomplished with difficulty. The cook, the chauffeur, the latter's wife whom the children called "Mammy Georges," stood upon privileges which they maintained they had received from the departed.

I knew a long time later from Simone's confidences that during that first year she had been unhappy to the point of desperation. I did not notice it. We are all blind when it is only the feelings of others that are at stake.

The adjustment of friendships in a newly formed household is also a delicate matter. My friends of Pontigny, the Desjardins, Charles Du Bos, continued with affectionate persistence to put me on my guard against the people of society and their enchantments. I confess I did not on that subject agree with them. Society, in its best aspects, taught me a great deal, and in the time of my misfortunes I found it, on the whole, steadfast and dependable.

One of my great discoveries at that time was men of state. In my province of Normandy I had known the small fry of local political workers; party leaders, ministers and presidents retained in my eyes a legendary quality. I should have been as dumbfounded as Dr. Cottard if Swann had said to me, as he did to him: "I had lunch at the home of the President of France." Now at my mother-in-law's home Monsieur Raymond Poincaré, former President of the Republic and present Premier, was a guest like any other, human, ready to answer questions (like Monsieur de Norpois at the home of Madame de Villeparisis), and even strangely anxious to explain the part he was playing and to win approval. One day when an American magazine had asked me for an article about him, Simone begged him to tell us his early life. He did so with an obliging, meticulous wealth of detail, constantly turning to his wife whom he treated with touching tenderness and attention:

"Isn't that so, Henriette? Surely it was in 1897? . . ."

That day I learned it was entirely by accident that he had got into politics and that he had not planned to. A surprising characteristic was that he continued to be shy, and this resulted in a certain brusqueness:

"Don't go abroad too much," he said to me. "As soon as one leaves the Place de la Concorde one ceases to make sense . . ."

His honesty and patriotism inspired respect. He had been ready to collaborate with Briand or Clemenceau, neither of whom he liked, whenever the safety of France demanded it. From the moment I met him I sent him every one of my books. He replied, with an almost unique courtesy, by long letters in his own hand in which the book was analyzed and praised with intelligence, precision and terseness.

Briand had long been a frequenter of the Avenue Hoche, but he never came there at the same time as Poincaré. The two men were too different to understand each other or to take pleasure in meeting. Poincaré was a lawyer; Briand a poet. Poincaré loved the farmlands of his native Lorraine; Briand the seascapes of his native Brittany. Poincaré felt a need of facts and figures; Briand had a horror of figures, and if some inept person provided him with them he forgot them as soon as possible. Poincaré wrote out his speeches from the first line to the last in a neat, small, sloping hand and thereafter knew them by heart; Briand would prepare his while rolling one cigarette after another and trying out his arguments on whatever audience chance provided, and would then create his best effects from the reactions of these listeners. Poincaré's files were impeccable, aligned like the battalion of *chasseurs* he had formerly commanded; in the hands of Briand a file soon became so confused that he would discard it in disgust. Poincaré governed through bureaus, Briand through hearts. Poincaré from Lorraine and hence a neighbor of the Germans feared them; Briand, a Breton, did not fear them enough. Poincaré was painfully sensitive to everything people said about him; Briand did not read what was written about him and would cheerfully have said with Queen Victoria: "The important thing is not what they think of me, it is what I think of them." A wit declared that Poincaré knew everything and understood nothing, while Briand knew nothing and understood everything; but this was not true, for Poincaré understood a great many things and Briand knew and read much more than he admitted.

Both were great servants of the State and of irreproachable honesty. When Poincaré would ask Ribière, his righthand man, to send some proofs to his publisher Plon, he would call him back and say:

"Don't forget this is a private errand. It must not be done by one of the doormen of the Ministry. Send a messenger boy; here's five francs."

Briand when he was Minister of Foreign Affairs and had control of

thirty million francs in secret funds, handed them on almost untouched
to Tardieu, his successor.

"One can say what he likes about Aristide," Tardieu said to me one
day, "and I myself have often opposed his policies, but he was damnably
honest. For if he had been willing to spend a small part of that thirty
million on newspaper campaigns he could have been President of
France!"

But their honesty was of different sorts. When Briand was assailed in
the Chamber by cries of: "Renegade!" he replied proudly: "Present!"
and he added:

"In my native Brittany at low tide you find little fish caught in the
hollows of the rocks and wriggling about in the seawater. Round about
them, stuck to the rocks, are the mussels. Let a tide pass and come back:
Your little fish will have disappeared; the mussels will still be there.
Mussels are steadfast, but in the scale of being fish stand higher than
mussels."

Such remarks shocked Poincaré. He for his part was proud of sticking
tenaciously to signed contracts and to engagements he had made,
and it must be admitted that if all European statesmen had had the
same exacting respect for contracts, perhaps Europe today would not
be consumed with misery and sorrow. But in Briand's character there
were large elements of kindness and charity, virtues seldom found
among politicians.

Clemenceau, the remaining one of the three giants of the epoch,
never came to the Avenue Hoche; nevertheless I was slightly acquainted
with him. He had written me a lively and penetrating note about *The
Dialogues*. I went to thank him and found him in his little apartment
in the Rue Franklin seated in front of a semicircular desk and wearing
a forage cap on one side of his head and black gloves on his aged hands.
His doctor was with him.

"The doctor here," he said to me, "has been assuring me that I have
only a few months left to live."

"They've said that to me a number of times, *Monsieur le Président*,
and I'm still here."

"Ah, you are young . . . What are you going to give us next?"

"I'm thinking of writing a Life of Wilson, *Monsieur le Président* . . ."

"Don't do it," he said vehemently. "That man has done us a great deal of harm."

Behind him was a canvas by Claude Monet depicting a landscape in la Creuse.

"Nice, isn't it?" he said . . . "Those stones, I always have a feeling that if I struck them with my cane sparks would fly out . . ."

He himself, so it seemed to me, was charged with sparks of genius.

. . . .

With a better knowledge of these great men, I felt a growing desire to write the lives of illustrious Frenchmen. I found them quite different from the picture that rumor had drawn, and more human, infinitely more human, than the shadows they had thrown on the walls of my cave of Elbeuf. "Hell must exist," Abbé Mugnier used to say, "since they teach us to believe in it; very well, Hell exists, but there is no one in it . . ." And Alain: "As for Hell, the only people you consign to it are the people you don't know." And so I welcomed the masters of France into the Purgatory of my judgments and, like Marcel Proust in his childhood before the belfries of Martinville, I felt growing within me the obscure, obsessing, unexpected but imperious desire to paint them.

CHAPTER XVII

Climates

PERSONAL friendships and reading, war and travels, had given me some knowledge of England, in so far as one can know a people, which is, alas, very little. Of America I knew nothing. It remained for me what it had been in my childhood, a mixture of Jules Verne and Mark Twain, to which there was now added Charlie Chaplin, André Siegfried and Theodore Dreiser. But in 1927 James Hazen Hyde, who was the Founder of the Alliance Française in the United States, proposed to me that I should be the official lecturer of the Alliance for that year. He explained the reasons for his choice. I was becoming, he told me, a pretty well known writer in America. *Bramble* had not been published in the United States but *Ariel* had had thousands of readers there; *Disraeli* had just been chosen by the Book-of-the-Month Club. In addition, I was now getting my start as a lecturer in Paris. I have told how at twenty I delivered lectures at the People's Universities in Normandy and how I misguidedly gave it up as the result of unimportant attacks. Nevertheless, I had acquired a taste for public speaking and the knowledge that this form of activity was easier for me than any other.

About 1925 a string of accidents had thrust me into this new career. The *Vieux-Colombier* was arranging a series of lectures on the cinema and, because I had written an article on the subject, asked me to deliver one of them. Madame Adolphe Brisson (Yvonne Sarcey) who was president of the *"Annales"* Lectures, heard me and decided to give me a try. She proposed that I give one of a series of talks on the Eighteenth Century for her Society, a lecture on Horace Walpole and Madame du Deffand. And so began with generous, enthusiastic and motherly Madame Brisson and with her son Pierre, an inflexible critic, an exacting and loyal friend, a relationship which nothing has ever altered. The other important Lecture Association in Paris (*Société des Conférences*) was presided over by Monsieur René Doumic, Permanent Secretary of the Académie Française and editor of the *Revue des Deux Mondes,* an all-powerful authoritarian, feudal baron of the realm of letters. He summoned me to the office of the *Revue des Deux Mondes* in the Rue de l'Université and received me with his legs wrapped in blankets and seated behind a desk that had belonged to Brunetière and Buloz; he offered to let me give a "little course" of four lectures in the Lecture Association in the spring of 1927. The "big course" (of ten lectures) was, he told me, too heavy a responsibility for a beginner. Even the "little course," he gave me to understand, was an honor of which I had still to prove myself worthy.

I accepted. There remained the problem of choosing a subject. Here Monsieur Doumic had very determined ideas. Sometimes they shocked authors and orators, but I think one could say of him what Lord Salisbury said of Queen Victoria, to wit, that it was enough to know his opinion on any subject to know that of the general public as well. Monsieur René Doumic had studied the reactions of his subscribers. When he said: "For the French public there are only four English writers: Shakespeare, Byron, Dickens and Kipling," he might dismay a lecturer who wanted to talk about John Donne, Keats or Swinburne; actually he was right, and the faithfulness of his subscribers testified to the accuracy of his judgments. For my first course he chose Dickens, a great subject which my four lectures could no more than skim over. My course was mediocre. But Monsieur Doumic continued to treat me with a mixture of esteem and brutal frankness, for which I am grateful to him. The esteem was proved by his confiding one of his precious courses to me; the frankness permitted him to tell me after the first lecture that I articulated badly, that the back rows had not heard me, and that I must not let my voice drop at the end of a sentence. I took this very seriously and with good results, I trust, for he said no more about it.

.   .   .   .

My trip to America was an important initiation. I made it alone, being too uncertain of the difficulties and fatigues to take my wife with me. On the *Paris* I learned about life on shipboard for the first time, the ephemeral intimacies it can create, the bracing air of the decks; the women stretched out on deck chairs with their legs wrapped up in blankets by deck stewards as a grocer wraps up a package; and the nightly conversations without end and without subject beneath the stars, amid which a reddish moon comes up, leaving a long luminous track upon the surface of the waters. For the first time I saw, on arrival in New York, the airplanes and the birds wheeling about the ship, the fishermen's boats, the noisy launches of the Health Department, the fortified hills which on nearer approach became skyscrapers, the pleasure resorts crowded with quaintly decorated buildings, the picturesque and singular animation of the Hudson River, then Pier 57 of the French Line, waving handkerchiefs, the mad confusion of the customs shed and finally the city, the city massive and geometrical and nevertheless monstrous, the city that is gigantic and yet human.

At the end of a few days I wrote to a friend: "Come. Nothing gives one more of a zest for life than a morning on Fifth Avenue. Come. The atmosphere is young, the pedestrians hurry along. The crowds enslaved by the red and green lights, surge forward in waves like the sea. The churches have the appearance of children which other buildings lead by the hand. Come. The locomotives have little bells around their necks like the cows in Switzerland, and the negro porters wear tortoise-shell glasses like young French women. Come. The valley through which the train is running is called the Naugatuck. It winds among the cliffs like the valley of St. Moritz. From each of the wooden stations one expects to see Charlot emerge dressed as a clergyman. Close to the tracks hundreds of cars are parked in a semi-circle. Come. America is a vast desert interspersed with oases of Fords. Come, ready to believe in life and perhaps even in humanity. Come and try, for a few months, being younger by several centuries."

Just what was it that I had loved so much? Everything—beautiful valleys, stately rivers, the sharp and bracing air of the American autumn, the blazing colors of the trees, the grace of New England villages. And then the youth and confidence. America in 1927 was not doubtful and cynical as it became after the Great Depression. In the universities, the ardor, the desire to learn and the faith in the future of humanity rested me after so much European negativism. Most of all I had loved the atmosphere of goodwill and comradeship in which the social life moved. No doubt there were there, as elsewhere, the hardheartedness of the wealthy, the enviousness of the unfortunate and the often sterile criticism of the intellectuals. But these reactions, which are native to every society, seemed to me tempered by a real desire not to inflict pain needlessly and by an absence of maliciousness which, to a European, seemed marvelous.

When I was about to leave, Paul Claudel, who was then our Ambassador to Washington, said to me in a frankly humorous tone:

"No doubt you are now going to write a book about the United States like everyone else?"

"Certainly not," I said. "My visit has only lasted a few weeks."

"Quite right," he said, "that's much too long."

On the *Ile-de-France* which took me back to Europe I made this note: "What have I gained from these two months? Is my memory of them pleasant or unpleasant? Pleasant, without question. I loved this country . . . Henceforth I shall remember that over there—quite close to us, only six days at sea away—there is an immense reservoir of strength and friendship . . . I myself, who am nervous and easily tired, have been healthy, alert and happy for two months, despite a frantic schedule. I felt younger in America. There was a youthful vigor in that fine autumn air that took me out of myself . . ."

.   .   .   .

From then on I was never to forget the existence beyond the seas of that "reservoir of strength and friendship." And a short time after my return to France I was to have need of this memory, for I suddenly found myself—I who in my provincial naïveté had believed I had no enemies—the object of an absurd and brutal attack which, however, was contrived with Machiavellian cunning. Who was the instigator?

A young Egyptian, who had no qualification for this task, whom I did not know but who seems to have felt for me a hatred that was as violent as it was unexplainable. What charges did he bring against me? The charge of having plagiarized certain English writers in *Ariel* and *Disraeli*! What proof did he give? None, except quotations whose choice was ridiculous, for every time he found in my book and in earlier English works a fact such as: "Little Ianthe, Shelley's daughter, had blue eyes," he was noisily triumphant. Every aspect of this attack was puerile, but it had been published in a magazine that had a reputation for seriousness and for this reason it made something of a stir. Being perfectly sure of my good faith I went to see Alfred Vallette, the editor of this magazine, who, I was told by his authors, was an honest man, and I reproached him for the irresponsibility with which he had accepted a defamatory article.

"None of this will hold water," I said. "If you had sent me a proof, which would have been the decent and courteous thing to do, I would immediately have shown you the baselessness of this accusation."

He replied that it was customary for his magazine to welcome "campaigns" of this sort, and that he would be equally happy to publish my reply if I thought I ought to make one. My literary friends, who had had more experience than I, begged me not to reply:

"You're just playing these people's game," they said. "What do they want? Free copy, noise and publicity . . . Don't help them."

But I was too sure of being right to keep quiet. I replied at length. The greatest of the English critics, Edmund Gosse and Arnold Bennett, took up the question and wrote that they were unreservedly on my side. The campaign collapsed. It left me with the strange sensation of having been, without realizing it, for a long time the object of furious hatred on the part of a group whom I did not know.

Before this incident I had little idea of hatred because I had never felt it toward anyone. I was not jealous of my fellow writers, a fact for which I deserve no credit since I had always found the literary world cordial and on the whole fair. When Robert de Flers had said to me: "I am going to have the French Academy award you the *Grand Prix* for novels," I pointed out to him a novelist I thought more worthy, and he was given the award. But our best actions gain us fewer friends than our omissions and forgetfulness earn us enemies. Without knowing it I had offended certain writers by not naming them in a list of my spiritual mentors, others by neglecting to invite them to my house or thank them for an article or for sending me a book. Completely wrapped up in my work I had disregarded public opinion. This was a mistake. Moreover, Grasset's publicity, which was ingenious, brilliant and spectacular, and the sudden rise of his firm which had become one of the foremost in France had exasperated certain other publishers, and Vallette was not sorry to punish one of Grasset's "youngsters," for an ascent he considered too rapid.

It may be that since my residence in Paris I had committed errors of tact and judgment in surroundings that were new to me. But I was conscious of my own good will, of the pleasure I derived from the success of writers whom I admired and of a sincere modesty in respect to my own work. Hence my amazement when faced with the hideous portrait of me drawn by this Zoïle. It was because I had forgotten the Personage who had been constantly growing at my side from the instant I began to lead a public life and who had been generously fed by jealous and unfriendly hearts. What could this Personage be? A writer sprung from the business world who was interested solely in large sales (when, to the contrary, in writing the Life of Shelley I had thought, and my publisher had agreed, that I was giving up all hope of large sales and that this book composed for myself would attract only a limited audience); a rich man surrounded by a crowd of secretaries who did his research for him (when I had no other secretary than my wife and my greatest pleasure was in doing my own research work); a man who was always in a rush and who dictated his books and threw them together hastily (when I wrote them all by hand, beginning them over again five or six times). If I had met this Personage no one would have detested him more than I. The Real Man was so passionately devoted to his work, he had so great a desire not to injure others, to be just, honest and as Proust would have said *"gentil,"* that I believe Zoïle himself, if he had known him, would have judged him inoffensive and perhaps likable.

But Zoïle knew him only as the Personage and that's why Zoïle was Zoïle.

When everything is taken into account, there is something to be said for enemies; they produce friendships by reaction. Writers who had become irritated by this too easy career and by sales that seemed to them (as to me) out of proportion to the importance of my works, suddenly became sympathetically inclined toward me because I had been unjustly attacked. Young men with more radical sympathies than mine, but of great talent, who had hitherto ignored me, expressed their sympathy: "And so," wrote Jean Prévost, the socialist, "the most evident professional conscientiousness, the most perfect honesty of judgment do not make a writer secure from calumny." This defense gave me more pleasure than the attack had given me pain. The appearance of my next book, which was a novel, *Atmosphere of Love,* was greeted by all the critics with a cordiality and a unanimous warmth that reconciled me to life.

The story of this book was strange, for I had produced it in spite of myself. The *Revue de Paris* had asked me for a story of four or five thousand words, and it occurred to me to recount an adventure I had heard about by accident. One of my friends while in Morocco had had a cardiac syncope and a doctor had brutally announced that the sick man had only a few hours more to live. Feeling himself condemned to death, he had summoned some of his intimate friends about his bed and had told them that he did not wish to die without leaving a true account of his life. Thereupon he had launched into a long public confession after the fashion of Russian novels. Emotion. Tears. Farewells. Then the vain wait for death. Death did not come, and the unfortunate man had to begin to live again among friends who now knew all about him and who henceforth refused to accept him as the Personage he had played all his life. I called the story *Moroccan Night* or *The Death and Resurrection of Philippe.* Philippe's confession was the story of his love for three successive women and the harm he had done to all of them because of his weaknesses.

When Simone had copied the story and I had reread it, I observed that two of the three women (the first and the third) were very much alive, but the middle one, Jenny Sorbier, an actress, was completely unreal. The Moroccan setting of the beginning and the epilogue had not turned out very well either. By abolishing it, together with Jenny Sorbier, there remained the framework of a novel. Almost unconsciously I began to develop it and it "came" with extraordinary ease. Was it because it was close to my life? Actually it was rather far removed, and those who read both *Atmosphere* and the present account, will see that in many points the divergence is great. But I was able to nourish my imaginary characters on real emotions, hence the ease of composition.

Heroes in novels sometimes escape from the novelist's control. In my first version of *Atmosphere* Philippe Marcenat after the death of Odile made up his mind to take measures against romantic love by entering upon a conventional marriage. He married his own cousin Renée Marcenat, a mature young woman of sound character but no beauty. When I reread the book, however, I found strange discords. My Philippe of the first part who had found in Odile the incarnate Enchantress of his dreams could not have agreed to the sensible marriage I planned to impose upon him. To induce Philippe to remarry it was necessary to give him the illusion of an Enchantress lost and found again, to put him in the presence of a woman close enough to "his type" for him honestly to believe that it was the reincarnation of Odile. Isabelle was born of the impossibility I encountered of making Philippe marry Renée, and Isabelle in essence is Philippe himself transmuted into a woman, just as Stendhal's Lamiel is the female counterpart of Julien Sorel. What Isabelle brings to Philippe is less the image of Odile than the reflection of his own youth.

When this new version was finished I realized that the first part was moving; the second, painful. Why? Because in the first part the hero kept saying: "I am in love and am not loved in return"; in the second: "I am loved, I do not love," which seemed insupportably fatuous. I decided to recast the second half of the book and to turn it into a confession by Isabelle. It was thus, and not by deliberate design, that *Atmosphere* acquired that appearance of a diptych which some have praised for its originality and others criticized for its artificial symmetry. *Atmosphere* is, of all my books, the one that has had the greatest number of readers, not in the Anglo-Saxon countries but in France, in Germany, in Italy, in Spain, in Poland. Is this right? Is it the best? Is it a true picture of love? "I leave the decision to a lover and make no judgment."

.   .   .   .

I finished *Atmosphere* at Shalford Park in Surrey where we had spent the summer. In the spring of that year (1928) I had gone to Cambridge to deliver the Clark Lectures, an annual series of literary talks, which had been given in the preceding year by E. M. Forster and were given the year following by Desmond MacCarthy. Forster had chosen for his subject: *Aspects of the Novel*; I chose: *Aspects of Biography*, and I tried to give some idea of the biographer's technique. The series lasted for six weeks and during that time the lecturer lived in the Harcourt Rooms in Trinity College, imposing chambers, heavy with history, and took his meals at the High Table in the Hall beside the Master of Trinity who was the great physicist Sir Joseph Thomson.

I liked Cambridge very much, the ancient colleges of gray stone scattered along the river, the tender greensward of the banks, the willow trees leaning over the Cam, the old bridges beneath which passed the students' punts, and the room centuries old in which I spoke beneath the jovial but stern eye of Henry the Eighth painted by Holbein. Besides Sir Joseph, two other famous professors attended my lectures: the poet Housman and the historian Trevelyan. It was the latter who said to me one day when I had been talking about Lytton Strachey:

"The most important event in the history of English biography in the Twentieth Century is not the portrait of Queen Victoria by Strachey, it is the conquest of Strachey by Queen Victoria."

Trinity College where I was living had been Byron's college, and I often went to the little pool at a bend in the river into which he loved to dive and cling to a rotten log on the bottom. I was gathering notes at that time to write a life of Byron. In *Ariel* I had sketched his portrait but I was not pleased with it. It seemed to me that I had been somewhat unjust to Byron and that perhaps his apparent cynicism was more generous than the sensual idealism of Shelley. His correspondence, which I annotated carefully, charmed me by its brusque and vigorous way of juxtaposing naked facts, just as certain painters juxtapose pure colors. In the course of the summer I made a pilgrimage to Harrow where I saw Byron's name carved by him in the woodwork, the tomb of Peachey to which he used to come limping in order to meditate there, and the rosebush planted above the ashes of his daughter Allegra. Then I went to the far north of England to visit Newstead Abbey, Byron's family seat. The monks' church was in ruins, the residential buildings, imposing and noble; and seeing these Gothic arches, these cloisters, these forests and this lake, one could understand the feelings of the small boy who, after the meanness of Aberdeen, suddenly found himself lord and master of this magnificent estate. Rarely have I seen clearer proof of the necessity for a biographer to see with his own eyes the surroundings in which his heroes have lived. Newstead gave me the key to Byron's childhood: what the poet's enemies were later to call snobbery was the tumultuous surprise of the penniless little Byron of Aberdeen faced by Lord Byron of Newstead.

At Annesley Hall, not far from Newstead, there still lived descendants of Mary Chaworth who had been Byron's first love. I asked to see the stairs, at the foot of which he had heard the girl say: "How could I be interested in that lame boy?" and the door he had riddled with bullets when he practiced pistol shooting. The owners of Annesley, Mr. and Mrs. Musters, did not know much about their ancestress. This was not the case with Lady Lovelace, widow of Byron's grandson, who guarded the family papers with vigilant piety. I knew that she owned countless precious documents and among them the Journal of Lady Byron which contained the answer to the difficult question of incest. It was impossible to write the book without seeing this Journal. Thanks to a mutual fried, Lady George Hamilton, I obtained permission to read it and went to spend two days at Ockham Park which was the manor house of Lady Lovelace. There, straight through the night, by the light of two candles I passionately deciphered this extraordinary document, the memoirs of a puritan who had been bold to the point of brazenness; they were so filled with life that I believed that I could see Byron walking with jerky steps and crying aloud between those walls of gray stone. After this reading it was no longer possible to doubt the incest. When I returned to London I went to see old Lord Ernle who (under his original name of Rowland Edmund Prothero) had published Byron's correspondence and whose labors had greatly aided me in my Byronian studies.

"I am much embarrassed, Lord Ernle," I said . . . "You have always maintained that incest did not take place between Byron and Augusta. I have proof to the contrary and I have serious scruples in contradicting you . . . What am I to do?"

He laughed gaily:

"What are you to do?" he said. "That's very simple. If incest took place, say so . . . As for me, I am almost eighty years old and at my age I am certainly not going to alter my opinion . . ."

To complete my Byronian researches I had to make Childe Harold's pilgrimage and go to see Missolonghi. During the years 1928-1930 this was an agreeable excuse for long trips across Europe. I lectured in Vienna, Berlin, Bucharest, Constantinople and Athens. My wife accompanied me; we went from embassies to ministries, from the charming women of Austria to the beautiful women of Greece, from the marshy pine forests of Ravenna to the glorious palaces of Venice, from the Pariser Platz to Saint Sophia, from the Acropolis to the lagoons of Missolonghi. We little thought that ten years later this hospitable and diversified Europe was to become the domain of a single tenant, sown with hatred and misery.

When I returned Harold Nicolson, author of the excellent book *Byron: the Last Phase*, entrusted me with a precious document,— Tom Moore's book about Byron annotated by Hobhouse; and Lady Lovelace with numerous letters, among them those by Byron's father which were surprising by reason of the quality of style, reminiscent of that of the poet, and also for the very exact idea they gave of the pair who had been Byron's parents. Rarely has a biographer had at his disposal so many unpublished documents. Perhaps the book suffered from this, artistically speaking. I did not want to sacrifice anything.

Hence the length of the work, which is a defect. But I think the picture of Byron is true in so far as a portrait can be.

Some critics found fault with me for having written, not a living biography like that of Disraeli, but a thesis for the Sorbonne. I have not reread the book recently and I myself no longer know its worth. Be that as it may, so far as I was concerned, it produced one useful result: it killed the myth of romanticized biography. Good or bad, this *Byron* represented an enormous amount of work. "It must not be forgotten," wrote the English critic Desmond MacCarthy, "that this book is the most serious and most complete work we have on Byron." This biography set the seal on my reconciliation with the scholars. Entrenched behind formidable parapets of notes and references I could henceforth await them without fear. They came, not as foes, but as friends. There, as elsewhere, preparedness assured peace.

I corrected the last proofs of *Byron* at Villard-de-Lans in the Alps at Christmas time, 1929. We had gone there to join my wife's daughter Françoise who, on doctor's orders, was obliged to live in the mountains. In the story of Byron there had been a person who had touched me very much; this was Allegra, daughter of Byron and Claire, who died alone and miserable in an Italian convent. Much against our will, for we loved her tenderly, little Françoise had somewhat the fate of Allegra. At an early age she had suffered from the results of being born in a broken home. She would have liked to grow up in the company of happy parents and to play with brothers and sisters. When she saw normal families she experienced a vague feeling of inferiority.

Our marriage filled her with joy. "The good Lord is going to send me a big sister, two little brothers and a papa," she announced proudly in the Parc Monceau. But she was not able to enjoy this new family. She had suffered from typhoid fever with hepatic complications and soon the doctors diagnosed a sclerosis of the liver. They did not conceal from us the extreme gravity of this disease. Only a sojourn at high altitude offered some small hope. And so Françoise spent the last two years of her life in the mountains and far from us. She did not

suffer, but her extreme weakness and her little waxen face filled us
with pity. Since violent games were forbidden, she read from morning
till night and, at nine years of age, kept a diary. "If God were really
so powerful," she wrote, "there would not be any unhappy people.
. . . I have done nothing wrong; why am I being punished? Why have
they sent me away from home where I was so happy with my brothers?"
When her nurse read *Oliver Twist* aloud to her, she said: "I do not
understand everything but I like it . . ."

The most tragic thing was that, not knowing she was seriously ill,
she believed herself unjustly exiled by us. Her grandmother Pouquet,
who adored her, made her long visits; we all went there as often as
we could. But she suffered from that life and her mother suffered as
well. Simone, a great reader of novels, had sworn to herself when she
married me, that she would be careful not to play either of two characters who inspired her with a particular horror: that of a woman
more interested in love than in her children, and that of the harsh
stepmother, Mrs. Murdstone. Like her little daughter she dreamed of
a fictitious family that would be just as united as if it were bound together by ties of blood. But she found herself, much against her will,
forced by circumstances not exactly into these characters, but into a
semblance of them. My foolish and obstinate refusal to allow my
children to call her *Maman* had created a permanent embarrassment
between them and her, a wall of words transparent but unbreakable;
whereas Françoise, alone and miserable, thought her *Maman* belonged
to her more than to anyone and should remain near her.

But on this Christmas in 1929 we had the feeling of having solved
this insoluble problem. Françoise, touchingly delighted to see Gerald
and Olivier again, was for some days exuberant with joy. I spent
much time with the children and I wrote a story for them, *Patapoufs
and Filifers*. This reunion of a family that was too often separated gave
us great pleasure. One of our friends in that region, Monsieur Pierre
Chabert, a descendant of the Gagnons who were the family of Stendhal's mother, arranged a Christmas tree for the children in our hotel
and after that a book party with tableaus and charades. I remember
that Françoise, Gerald, Olivier and I played *Recherche du Temps*

rdu. I was reading the newspaper *Temps,* then I let it fall between
‛o pieces of furniture and set the children on a search for the lost
emps. These are very little things, but moments of unmixed happi-
:ss are rare and it is sweet to record them.

When Twelfth Night came we had to leave the mountains. Gerald
ιd Olivier were to return to the Pasteur Lycée at Neuilly and I had
cture engagements to fulfill. In despair Françoise saw the beautiful
yth of her family vanish once more. She clung to her mother's coat:
ξtay, *Maman,* stay!" Then she grew serious and brave. While we got
ιto the car she stood stoically on the hotel steps. I looked at her white
ress, her thin little arms and her eyes that were so intelligent and so
nder, and I admired her silent courage. Poor Françoise! In her were
ιe qualities of a charming and heroic woman which she was destined
ever to become.

We had barely returned to Paris when my wife had to undergo
n operation. I had just left the hospital where I had spent two hours
t her bedside when the doctor called me by telephone from Villard-
e-Lans: Françoise had had a severe hemorrhage; she had lost con-
:iousness. An oxygen tent and camphorated oil had been of no avail;
ιere was no more hope. Toward eleven o'clock that evening he called
ιe again to say that Françoise was dead. When they had put her to
ed she had said: "I want the photograph of my brothers . . ." The
urse had given her a little snapshot of Gerald and Olivier laughing,
ressed in gray coats and shorts. Then the oxygen had produced a
ɔrt of intoxication and she had died without suffering.

One can imagine how painful and difficult it was to communicate
his frightful news to Simone who had not yet recovered from the
hock of the operation. Naturally she was too weak to travel. I went
lone to the burial which took place in Périgord. With my mother-
n-law and father-in-law I escorted the little coffin to the tiny church
vhere Abbé Mugnier had married us. The countryside, which I re-
ιembered bathed in sunlight and laden with the harvest, was wrapped
n dismal fog. In the little village cemetery the tenant farmers filed
•ast the opening of the great vault where reposed four generations
•f Pouquets as well as Gaston de Caillavet. I thought of the little girl

in the white dress whom I had seen for the last time standing on the snow-covered steps bravely trying to smile.

To add to Simone's despair, our surgeon Dr. de Martel disclosed to her that she could have no more children. For this reason she passionately desired to adopt mine and consulted Maître Wateau, our legal advisor and one of our most faithful friends.

"French law," he told us, "allows adoption in only three circumstances: One must have saved the child from a fire, a shipwreck or have given it maternal care . . ."

"The last is my case," said Simone.

"Yes," replied Wateau, "but in addition it is necessary to be forty years old."

And so my wife had to wait seven years before achieving a desire that lay so close to her heart.

. . . .

So many losses and misfortunes in the space of a few years had profoundly altered my outlook on life. I have shown how the easy successes of my early years, followed by authority over a huge factory, had made me dangerously sure of myself. Until I was thirty years old I had not known failure in any sphere. For this reason I suffered from serious gaps in the training of my character, an unintentional harshness, and a surprising lack of maturity. "The feeling of awe is the best part of man," Goethe said. I had lived too long unacquainted with awe. But the war, anguish, illness and death had given me an apprenticeship in sorrow. It was also an apprenticeship in patience and pity.

CHAPTER XVIII

The Twilight of the Gods

O F ALL my ports of call during my first voyage to America my favorite had been Princeton. That American university I found was not very unlike Oxford or Cambridge. No doubt there was a difference of four or five centuries in age and only the English Gothic was authentic, but Princeton could show very graceful Eighteenth Century buildings, fine old lawns and a preceptorial system that recalled the Oxonian tutors. I had formed friendships: President Hibben, Dean Gauss; a young professor, Percy Chapman, one of the most cultivated Americans I have ever met; a charming Frenchman, Maurice Coindreau, were among them. When I received a letter from President Hibben in 1930 announcing the endowment of a new chair in French to be called the Meredith Howland Pyne chair, in memory of a Princeton student killed in the war, and asking me if I would be the first incumbent, I accepted with joy. In my youth it had been my ambition to teach; in maturity, I was to have the opportunity; I was delighted.

As it was to be a long stay, Simone accompanied me and we decided to bring with us Emilie and Gaston Wolff, a young French Alsatian couple who had been in our home for a number of years and whose devotion and intelligence made them much more our friends than our servants. The university rented us a house that belonged to a professor who was taking his "sabbatical year," an excellent American custom which consists in giving professors every seven years an entire year's vacation, thus allowing them to read, to refurbish and enrich their minds and to escape from routine. It was a frame house, surrounded by maples and sycamores which the American autumn soon clothed in brilliant reds and yellows. Our lawn adjoined those of our neighbors; this country ignores the enclosures that are so dear to ours. Squirrels played beneath our windows. Our street, where only professors lived, was silent and provincial. My wife and I have retained the most tender memories of that semester spent at Princeton. We found a full and tranquil happiness there which neither Neuilly nor the country, nor our hectic trips had ever been able to give us because we had everywhere encountered excitement, professional duties or ties with the past. In that house in Broadmead we were alone together, bound to the world by no other tie than the work we had in common and that we both loved. Nothing spoiled these happy hours. My colleagues were courteous, helpful and agreeable companions, but they did not claim the confidential intimacy of our European friends. Almost every day we had at least one meal alone together.

"At last!" Simone said. "I am having my wedding trip . . ."

In Paris those who did not know her well had believed she was infatuated with social life, formal dinners and receptions at the embassies, and she had played the role expected of her. In Princeton she took pleasure in living a life of complete simplicity, doing her own marketing, going to the butcher and to the confectioner and serving tea to the students. In addition, eight hours of typing a day.

"I have never been so happy," she said to me in rapture.

We began a new life, and it was the life both of us had always longed for.

As for me, I was at length engaged in the calling of professor which, together with that of writer, was that for which I had been born. My course was called: "The French Novel from the *Princess of Clèves* to *Remembrance of Things Past.*" Fifty students had been admitted after an examination which had shown that their knowledge of French was adequate. Twice a week I gave a public lecture. On the other days students came to my house in groups of seven or eight, sat on the floor, smoked cigarettes and discussed with me the books of Balzac or Stendhal, of Flaubert or Anatole France that I had asked them to read. These conversations were pleasant, free and without strain. We talked about literary technique but also about the social life of France and about history, morals and philosophy. I found a wholly new pleasure in being intimately associated with the life of the young and in becoming once more a student myself.

My pupils told me about their traditional jokes, the cruel treatment they inflicted on the statue of the *Christian Student*, the campus scapegoat, and the difficulties they encountered in stealing the clapper of the bell which seemed to be an inescapable moral obligation. On Saturday I attended football games. At the Lycée of Rouen I had become an expert in rugby. At first American football seemed incomprehensible, brutal and slow, but very soon I acquired a taste for it to such an extent that I would sit in an open stadium on a cold day and give voice to cries of enthusiasm or rage. It was a bad year for Princeton and the disconsolate alumni said to the President:

"Mr. President, less scholarship and more victories, please!"

Since then the Tiger has had his revenge.

At the end of the semester President Hibben said to me:

"Your course has been a success; your students have made notable progress; would you like to stay with us and occupy this chair permanently? You would have to spend eight months of the year in the United States but you would have four months of vacation in France . . ."

I was sorely tempted, asked for time to discuss it with my wife and we hesitated a long while. We liked Princeton; we had been happy there; the life of a professor delighted me. Moreover, we realized that the Old World was heading toward shipwreck and that it would be wise to provide a refuge for ourselves elsewhere. But to accept meant to leave France, to lose touch with our friends, to bring up our children in a foreign land. We believed we had no right to make that decision. I refused. Was it a mistake? It seems to me if I had said yes that day my life would have been much easier. Would it have been as full and as exciting? No one will ever know and I have formed the habit of considering that "what did not take place was, so far as I am concerned, absolutely impossible."

This long stay in Princeton, and my intimacy with Percy Chapman, helped me to understand America better than my earlier trip had done. When I returned I wrote an article in which I said that I had encountered everywhere three phantoms: the Puritan, the Pioneer and the Feudal Lord. It was an accurate description. Even today my three specters continue to haunt many sections of America. But I had then, and still have, confidence in the future of the United States because I find here more numerous elements of social understanding than in any other country. As I have already noted in connection with my first trip, maliciousness is not an American vice. Why this remission of original sin? Perhaps because the dangers are less and the blessings more abundant. Fear engenders cruelty, and hitherto the Americans have hardly known fear. Misery gives birth to envy, and misery, although it exists in America, is less irremediable there than in the old countries.

In England the solidity of the institutions had seemed to me based on the solidity of traditions. "England is a democracy because it is an aristocracy," Professor Barker used to say, and it was true. America shares with England, and unhappily not with France, the good fortune of not being a country divided by history. It went through the Civil War, but the South as well as the North accepts the regime without reservation. Of course we shall see social revolution in America, but only the perpetration of very serious blunders could dig "the bloody ditch" of a Terror between the classes here. As to the relations between France and the United States, though they were at that time poisoned by the absurd question of the debts, I did not find the future disturbing. French culture in all forms found a public in the United States ready to understand it. England, resting on its long past, felt sufficient unto itself; America, a mixture of races in search of a culture, found in France a common denominator and a universal thought.

.   .   .   .

And so I returned from the United States certain that there was a duty to be discharged by a French writer who could speak English, which was to maintain, on every opportunity offered, a spiritual bond between France and America. This was certainly no reason to neglect my English friends, but the task with them had become more difficult and perhaps the key to these difficulties lay in Washington. During the war when I had talked to the French about the English and to the English about the French I had found sympathetic auditors because their interests were identical. After the war these interests had diverged. France had asked for guaranties of security and, not receiving them, had carried on alone the policy of the Ruhr and that of Eastern alliances. England, frightened by old Napoleonic memories and disturbed by American public opinion, had thereupon fallen back on an outmoded doctrine, that of the balance of power. Through fear of too strong a France she had favored the rearmament of Germany. I had done my best to point out, in articles in the English newspapers and in lectures, the danger of a rupture and even of a permanent disagreement between the two powers interested in maintaining the peace of Europe. But I had found in each of the two countries a profound distrust of the other.

"We English," Lord Tyrrell, the new Ambassador to Paris, said to me, "made two mistakes after the war: we thought that the French, because they had been victorious, had become Germans; and we thought that the Germans, because they had been defeated, had become Englishmen . . ."

I had met Lord Tyrrell (then Sir William Tyrrell) in London at the home of Lady Colefax. He was an Irish Catholic and less impermeable to French reactions than are many English Protestants. He had directed the Foreign Office for a long time as Permanent Secretary and he had appointed himself ambassador to Paris. Subtle, witty and adroit, he was successful there in so far as that was possible. To my great surprise he did me the honor of inviting me to the first formal dinner he gave. It was a strange occasion. Ramsay MacDonald, the Labor leader, was about to come into power, and Lord Tyrrell thought it would be useful to bring him into contact with some of the leaders of the French Left. So he had invited the two Sarraut brothers, Painlevé and Léon Blum. But since Ramsay MacDonald knew no French, the rest of the party was made up of bilingual Frenchmen and Englishmen who were to serve as interpreters. Hence my presence and, if my memory is accurate, that of André Siegfried.

The thing that struck me in these conversations was a difference so profound in character between the English Left and the French Left that they had almost nothing in common. Ramsay MacDonald was a Puritan whose ideology and morals remained religious. His French interlocutors were anticlerical. Ramsay MacDonald was a socialistic reformer who above all did not want to alarm the English conservatives; Léon Blum, the only socialist present, belonged to a party which called itself Marxist and revolutionary. I saw at once there was no remedy for this misunderstanding. English conservatives and French conservatives had not understood each other because there had been fear on both sides for the security of their respective countries; the English laborites and French socialists were to understand each other even less because their philosophies were opposed. A little later one was to see with surprise the British conservatives seeking support from the French Left and thus losing in France their natural allies. Lord Tyrrell's task was not easy; indeed it was almost impossible.

As a matter of fact, one of the greatest dangers to Franco-English relations came from these meetings between statesmen who could not understand one another. France liked precise engagements. The English had a horror of them. Poincaré had irritated the English by his inflexibility. Curzon exasperated the French by his arrogance. The English loved Herriot because they found him like the traditional Frenchman and also because he was very well educated and could talk to them about their history. The French liked Austen Chamberlain because he said: "I love France like a mistress," but this imprudent remark cost him the prime ministry. Briand and Austen Chamberlain were great friends. Both were men of good will but both collided with the prejudices of their country. I remember hearing Briand tell with amused patience about that conference at the Hague at which Snowden had insulted Chéron, French Minister of Finance, by describing him as "grotesque and ridiculous."

"After that," Briand said, "Snowden was worried . . . The two delegations no longer spoke to each other . . . National honor did not allow either side to take the first step . . . Luckily I met Mrs. Snowden and we threshed the matter out . . . I said to her: 'Why all

this fuss? . . . It's perfectly simple . . . Your husband wants a reconciliation but he cannot give in? . . . Is that it? Well then! Ask Adatci,
the Japanese, to entertain us together . . . We will accept and no
one will have taken the first step.' "

But even Briand had some difficulty in adapting himself to British
customs. One day before a luncheon at the British Embassy he took
me into a corner of the drawing-room: "I'm counting on you," he said,
"to help me and to toss the conversation my way . . . These Englishmen don't know what general conversation is . . . And if I take the
trouble to tell stories I want people to listen to me and not whisper
to their neighbors."

On many occasions I saw him in Geneva at the League of Nations.
He had great oratorical success there and this pleased him, but contrary to the legend he saw without illusion the weaknesses of the
League. When he tried to create the European Confederation it was
to remedy them:

"People make fun of me . . . 'Ah! this is Briand,' they say, 'with
his everlasting nebulous projects!' But this isn't true at all. What I am
trying to do is to put a little realism into the League of Nations by
eliminating from the discussions of European problems all those distant countries that talk, vote, constitute a majority and are never
willing to act."

He knew that he was unpopular in many quarters in France, where
neither his seriousness nor his patriotism was understood.

"I entertain you," he said. "You listen to my stories . . . But when
you leave me you think: 'This is Briand, he is not serious . . .' No.
I shall never succeed in inspiring confidence in my own country because France loves solemn men who carry their heads like the Holy
Sacrament."

Briand was in favor of a limited revision of the Treaty of Versailles
and of financial aid to the German government. He hoped thus to
bring about a reconciliation between the two countries. I was in the
Chamber on the day when he said to Franklin-Bouillon:

"You say you have no confidence in the men who are governing
Germany . . . Formerly I heard you say that you had no confidence in

Stresemann and he died in harness . . . I heard you say in days past that you had no confidence in Rathenau and he was assassinated for his ideas . . . Does a man have to be dead in order to be trusted by you?"

It was a nice piece of oratory in the manner of the Ancients. Toward the end of his life he no longer had any hope:

"It's not enough," he said, "for the French Minister of Foreign Affairs to put in an appearance in Berlin with an engaging smile. He must be free to negotiate, and this right is refused me."

In 1931 even his friends were deserting him, with the exception of certain faithful men like Alexis Léger, and after his defeat for the Presidency of the Republic his face took on a pathetic expression. Hurt and ill, he slept through the Council meetings. After he had retired to Cocherel, a friend who went to see him found him alone in an easy chair playing with a little mechanical mouse which he wound up and let run across the floor.

"You see," he said with a melancholy smile, "to what the Republic reduces its servants."

But he said it without bitterness. He knew men, even his enemies, too well to hate them.

It has been said that ingratitude is the mark of strong nations, but that is false. Post-war France (I mean official France) was not strong but she was ungrateful. Who gave a thought to Poincaré, that great servant of his country, at the time when he was dying, poor and paralyzed, tenderly watched over by his wife in a villa in the Midi? Who rendered thanks to Lyautey who had given France an empire? No one save a small band of faithful friends to which I was proud to belong. I used to go sometimes and spend several days at his home at Thorey in Lorraine. The Marshal's deafness made conversation difficult. But I loved to hear him tell of the great things he had done or to see him in his garden laying out a path with the same pains that he had formerly given to planning a city or mapping the course of a railroad.

Little by little, as a result of listening to him, the idea dawned upon me that there could be no healthier reading for the bewildered youth

of France than a Life of Lyautey. I was very familiar with it. He had
given me a memoir about his youth which he had written himself with
distinction, for he had the style of a gentleman and cavalier which was
in the grand tradition of France. For the rest of his life I had his
letters, his stories and many witnesses. The only obstacle was the difficulty I should encounter in writing for the first time the biography
of a living man. Would the Marshal respect a writer's liberty? I believed he would and I was right. From the moment I first spoke to
him about this project he became fired with enthusiasm and gave me
all his documents. When I commenced to write, he offered to read
each chapter, and for two years was a most active and, on the whole,
most reasonable collaborator. He asked me to suppress certain anecdotes; they were of no importance. He made me work at hours which
were not natural to me, for he liked the night and hardly slept at all.
But he allowed me free exercise of my judgment and he helped me
generously.

His circle was full of men of talent who were friendly but exacting
critics in anything that had to do with their Chief. Several of them
read my proofs. Their conclusion was that of Alain about *Bramble*:
"It is not the *whole* truth, and just now it would be hard to tell
that, but it is nothing but the truth . . ."

That's all I asked. Up to that time many Frenchmen had not
known what a great figure Lyautey was. The book earned him new
admirers. "You have invented me," he wrote. That was only a witticism,
but it showed that he was pleased. After that I was often asked to go
and speak about him to groups of young people. It became the bond
in common between me and Robert Garric's *Equipes Sociales,* a movement of young intellectuals who were missionaries of culture among
the French people, no longer in the too oratorical form of the People's
Universities, but in the more human fashion of little circles of ten or
twelve members which reminded me of my "preceptorials" in Princeton. "Not a day passes," Lyautey wrote me again, "when I do not
receive from some stranger a letter that I owe to you." If by this book
I helped, however little, however inadequately, in surrounding his

retirement with the thanks and the glory he had so amply earned, there is no work I am prouder of.

Often he was sad. He had sudden lapses of memory which were frightening to his friends and which they tried conscientiously to hide from him. One evening when I was alone with him in his study in the Rue Bonaparte, he suddenly fell into a terrifying state of speechlessness and rigidity. I dared not say anything for fear of provoking an attack and I stayed close by, affectionately watching over him, for a period that seemed very long. Suddenly he looked at me and said:

"You are Poeymirau, aren't you?"

General de Poeymirau had been one of his adjutants in Morocco twenty years earlier. I did not contradict him, and little by little he emerged from his dream. One day I heard the present Queen of England very charmingly draw him out of a similar reverie. It was at the Colonial Exposition at Vincennes over which he had presided with his customary skill and which he had made one of the last French successes. The Duke and Duchess of York had come to see it. He had taken them walking from the Pagoda of Ankor to the Algerian village and from Tahiti to Djibuti, and then had given them tea on the shore of the lake. Little tables for three had been set up. The Marshal, tired by this long walk, was a little somber. He invited the Duchess to sit down at his table and then asked:

"To whom does your Royal Highness wish to give the honor of occupying the third place?"

The Duchess who knew me and had asked me to speak for her charities in London, happened to notice me in the crowd.

"Mr. Maurois," she said.

And so I was summoned, feeling much embarrassment at being chosen. The young princess addressed several remarks to me, and then turning to the Marshal:

"*Monsieur le Maréchal*," she said, "you are so powerful, you created the beautiful country of Morocco and you have made this fine exposition, would you do something for me?"

"For you, Madame?" Lyautey said in surprise. "But what can I do for your Royal Highness?"

"Why this," she said. "The sun is in my eyes, *Monsieur le Maréchal.* Will you make it disappear?"

The Marshal was looking at her in stupefaction when suddenly the sun went behind a cloud.

"Thank you, *Monsieur le Maréchal*," said the Duchess with perfect equanimity. "I knew that you could do anything, even control the sun."

He laughed and relaxed. In lowered voice the Duchess said to me: "I saw the cloud coming . . ."

On that day she gave him one of his last moments of happiness. After the conclusion of the Colonial Exposition he suffered from the lack of an outlet for his energy which remained intact and young. For the man of action, as for the Don Juan, old age is terrible. Born to create and to command, in the little Lorraine village of Thorey he was like the sovereign of a tiny kingdom.

"But good Lord," he said to me, "can't they see that I am champing at the bit with impatience? Can't I still serve? Won't they give me some work to do? . . . No! . . . They think I am no longer good for anything . . . I have been written off as dead."

"*Monsieur le Maréchal,* they can't leave a man like you inactive . . . The government will find something."

"*Will find,* my friend! . . . *Will find!* . . . That's all very well, but I am almost eighty years old . . . If I am to make a career it's time for me to get started."

When he died in 1934 I was in England. I returned immediately and rushed to Thorey, too late to attend his funeral. But he remains present among us and there are some of us Frenchmen on the earth who, in our days of despair and loneliness, feel ourselves united in hope by the memory of Lyautey.

CHAPTER XIX

My Dear Time's Waste

ART is long, life is short." For the artist a year without progress is a year wasted. From 1932 to 1937 I wasted five years. Not that I was ever unoccupied. It was during this period that I wrote *The Miracle of England* which Arthème Fayard had commissioned on the advice of Jacques Bainville and which necessitated enormous reading. But aside from this work, which I believe was sound enough, these five years were for me a time of distraction and confusion of mind. The public lectures involved much squandering of time. The lecture trips were a pretext for innumerable changes of scene. The preparation of courses for Monsieur Doumic or Madame Brisson absorbed my energies. From these courses, to be sure, certain books emerged (*Edward VII, Magicians and Logicians, Sentiments and Customs, The Art of Living*) but they no longer answered, as had *Atmosphere of Love, Bernard Quesnay, Ariel* and *Disraeli*, that imperious need for expression which produces original and lasting works.

For some years my wife and I suffered from a dangerous hunger for travel. One winter we spent three months in Egypt because I had promised to give a series of lectures at the French Lycée in Alexandria. Egypt was beautiful and worth seeing; we enjoyed visiting the tombs of Sakkara and the mosque-citadel of Cairo, but beyond that it was necessary to give talks, receive journalists and see various officials, French, English, Egyptian, Syrian, Coptic and Jewish. Time flowed by, irretrievably. In the spring we left for Malta because in a moment of weakness I had promised to write a little book about the island. The English critic Desmond MacCarthy gave us a letter of introduction to his brother-in-law Admiral Sir William Fisher, Commander-in-Chief of the British fleet in the Mediterranean, a great sailor and a great gentleman: suddenly we found ourselves guests of honor who went from party to party and from dockyard to cruiser.

Then, almost as soon as we had returned from our spring trip, we left for England where we spent part of the summer. What beautiful houses we lived in there! Colonel Stirling and his wife, Scotch friends of ours gifted with infallible taste, selected enchanting places for us to stay. It was necessary that our dwellings should be near London because I was working in the libraries there on my History of England. One year we rented Ormeley Lodge on Ham Common, a red brick house which bore, carved in an architrave of white stone as well as in many details of the woodwork, the three plumes of the Prince de Galles, for it had been given by the Regent to his morganatic wife, Maria Fitzherbert. From our garden we could see Richmond Park with its fine oaks and its copses stocked with deer.

"Ah!" we said. "How wonderful it would be to live in Richmond Park!" But the Park contained only three or four houses which belonged to the Crown. In 1934 the invaluable Stirling leased us one of them, Pembroke Lodge in which Lord Russell had lived at the time of the Reform Bill. In our drawing-room a Cabinet Meeting had declared the Crimean War; from a hillock in the rose garden Henry VIII had seen the signal which announced the execution of Anne Boleyn; on our lawn was a little monument erected by Lord Russell to commemorate fifty years of conjugal happiness. At night the whole of Richmond Park was ours and there we met, beneath the great trees, motionless and startled deer whose eyes gleamed in the moonlight.

It was from Pembroke Lodge that I went one fine summer day to receive the Degree of Doctor of Letters *honoris causa* at Oxford. Lord Halifax, Chancellor of the University, had chosen my name together with that of Lord Tyrrell, Sir Samuel Hoare, Arthur Henderson, Sir Maurice Hankey and a few others. In a long robe of black velvet embroidered in gold, his train carried by his son dressed as a page, he nobly presided over the ceremony in the Sheldonian Theater. At the moment when each new doctor was presented to the assembly brief notices in Latin were read by the public orator. He had translated *Les Silences du Colonel Bramble* as *"Vepris illius, tribuni militum silentia."* Arthur Henderson, who was called "Uncle Arthur" by the English workmen, had become: *"Plebi laboriosae quasi avunculus."* These learned jokes amused the English. For my part, as I bent down before Lord Halifax to receive the investiture, I was thinking of her who, twenty-four years before, had for the first time guided me so graciously and gaily among the gray stones of Oxford.

After long hesitation on my part we had left, in 1931, the apartment in the Rue Borghèse in Neuilly, the haunt of beautiful and melancholy memories. My wife on several occasions had suggested houses which I did not like. Finally I had been seduced, not by a lodging but by an address. The new apartment was situated on the Boulevard Maurice Barrès; it was very close to the white house that had belonged to the writer and where his son Philippe now lived. Our windows afforded a sweeping view over the Bois de Boulogne and over Paris; as far as the eye could see stretched green waves of trees; to the left one saw the Arc de Triomphe always bathed in mist, gray or golden according to the weather; to the right, Mont Valérien was like one of the hills of Florence crowned by cypress trees. Soon I was very much attached to this new setting. I loved our white walls, our huge mahogany bookcases, which reminded me of my first house, and our pictures which were not numerous but had been lovingly selected. The decorations were simple, a little bare and severe, but harmonious. We looked forward with pleasure to spending the rest of our lives there.

I had taken an apartment for my mother near ours so that she could spend the winter in Paris. Her own mother and her sisters lived there and they, together with her children, constituted for her the whole world. As formerly, the five sisters dressed in black would meet every afternoon in the Rue de Tocqueville around the armchair of my grandmother, who was ninety years old and who remained as lively in mind, as curious about new books and as reasonable as ever. Simone, like Janine before her, had been surprised at first by these long seances in which gentle black-clothed priestesses intoned in responsive verses, interspersed with religious silences, the daily catalogue of all the deaths, births, cases of scarlatina and chicken pox, degrees, marriages, appendectomies and promotions in the Family. But she quickly accustomed herself to the simple, severe and lovable rule of this house and with her prodigious memory she soon became as learned in the genealogical and pathological mysteries of the clan as the Vestals themselves. She was not unwelcome there and she breathed without boredom that strange, heavy and silent atmosphere which reminded her as it had me of the Brontë sisters' novels.

But in Paris as in London "duties"—articles, lectures, prefaces and talks—devoured my time. The only months of uninterrupted work were those I spent at Essendiéras at the home of my mother-in-law. Périgord had captivated me and had taught me a great deal. In the army, and later at the mill, I had observed the Norman middle class and the workmen; at La Saussaye I had come to know the farmers. In Périgord I had an opportunity of studying the gentry, descendants of the ancient landed aristocracy, a class that played a more important part in the life of France than the people of Paris, London and Washington knew, for it furnished the officers for the armies and the diplomats for the Quai d'Orsay; and on the other hand, I saw the tenants who were hard working, economical, distrustful toward the Church and the Château, desirous of dividing up large estates and protecting small ones, socialists by fits and starts, radicals by inclination, conservatives by heredity and patriots to the core without knowing it. There I recognized, in listening to the stories of political quarrels, the implacable division among Frenchmen and also as I looked at the Monument to the Dead, bearing more names than there were houses in the village, the solid unity of France always ready to arise again in the face of the enemy. Neither the novelist nor the historian can understand France at all unless he has an observation post in Paris *and* in the provinces. My knowledge of my country rested upon Normandy and upon Périgord. They were two strong pillars.

.   .   .   .

Our family life at Essendiéras was studious and intentionally monotonous. At eight o'clock each morning I would sit down to work in front of a window that opened on a wide horizon of hills, streams, villages and woods. No sound but the purring of the threshing machine, the humming of the wasps envious of my flowers, the distant murmur of the Loue rushing over the stones of the valley and the clicking of the typewriter at which Simone in the next room was copying the chapter written the day before. At eleven o'clock I would join her and we would take the Tour of the Two Paths, the classic walk of Essendiéras, leaving by way of the oaks and returning by way of the chestnuts, the itinerary that Simone as a child had followed disguised as the forest in *Macbeth*. At La Guichardie farm we would stop to talk to the tenants about their children and their crops. In the fields or in one of the pastures the overseer Ménicot, a veteran of the wars and an excellent farmer, whose son was a great friend of my sons, would be superintending the work of harvesting, hay making or second planting, according to the season. We would confer with him about the small affairs of the estate.

On our return we would find a typical Périgord luncheon, always delicious and the result of careful thought, which was enlivened by the wit of my mother-in-law and the gaiety of the children. Then Simone and I would go back to work each in our own place. Toward five o'clock we would leave by the Oak Path or the Chestnut Path for a longer walk on which we would sometimes be gone two hours, discussing the progress of the novel. I would tell her about the new chapters. She would approve or criticize my ideas. When it was a question of the conduct of the heroine she would often foresee better than I could myself what that rebellious spirit was going to demand of us. We got to the point, both of us, where we considered these characters real and, as in the time of *Atmosphere*, they acted independently of me and sometimes contrary to my plans. In *The Family Circle* which was finished at Essendiéras during the summer of 1931, I did not wish Denise Herpain to become the mistress of Jacques Pelletot before their marriage. But one day as we were walking along the Oak Path I had to confess the indiscretion they had just committed:

"I did all I could to prevent it . . . But he was a soldier and wounded; he was going away again; she had great need of sacrifice . . . In short what could you expect? There it is!"

"What will Monsieur Doumic think?" my wife asked.

The novel *The Family Circle* was, in fact, intended for the *Revue des Deux Mondes*. When it was finished I was a little anxious about the impression that the sins of my heroine might produce on Monsieur Doumic and I read the beginning of my book to his son-in-law, my very dear friend, Louis Gillet. He encouraged me and I took the manuscript to Monsieur Doumic. A week later the latter summoned me and, in friendly sternness, received me with his legs wrapped up in a blanket.

"I am very sorry," he said. "I am even upset . . . I definitely wanted a novel by you, but the *Revue* cannot publish this one . . . No, indeed it is not possible. Our subscribers would protest."

"But why, Monsieur?"

"Why? You ask that? These successive adulteries . . ."

"But, Monsieur, there is hardly one great French novel without adultery . . . *Madame Bovary* . . . *Le Père Goriot* . . ."

"Oh, to be sure, the *Revue* is obliged to admit adultery. But it only admits it when accompanied by remorse. At no moment does your heroine repent of her misdeeds . . ."

And so my novel was rejected. I felt no rancor toward Monsieur Doumic whose strong character I admired and who, I could not doubt, knew his subscribers better than I did.

The inspiration for *The Family Circle* was a conversation I had with a young woman who described the emotions she had felt as a little girl when she discovered that a man used to come to see her mother without her father's knowledge. Her story was so poignant that I asked her how the incident had turned out. She told me and furnished me with many excellent details, but the actual romance stopped abruptly. I needed a conclusion. And then I remembered another person who might very well represent what Denise Herpain, married and unsatisfactorily married, would become. From a combination of these two characters with certain traits borrowed from other women *The Family Circle* was born. I took pleasure in reviving some of the characters from *Atmosphere of Love* and *Bernard Quesnay*. Then in *A Time for Silence* which I wrote next I made a point of establishing connections between the industrial Normandy of my first books and the agricultural Périgord of this. It was not a bad beginning and perhaps if the times had been different and my life more tranquil I might, in a series of novels, have been able to create a fresco of post-war French Society. This was what Alain advised; he, unlike most of the critics, considered me more of a novelist than an essayist.

"And now," he wrote me after *The Family Circle*, "and now you must create a living world."

.   .   .   .

Events decided otherwise. The political life of Europe was rapidly becoming so disquieting that it was no longer easy to find refuge in the world of fiction. In France Tardieu had been defeated in the election of 1932. We knew him well, for he too had been a frequenter of the Avenue Hoche. He was fond of good living, cultured and cynical, at least in words, for I believe he retained traces of sentimentality. He had kidney trouble and the doctors told him that if he went on eating and drinking so well he would never live to be old.

"I'm not concerned about that," he would say. "Short and sweet!"

After his defeat he went to live in Menton at the Hotel de l'Annonciata, and we went to see him there. He was writing political books and expected to transform France with his pen:

"And then," he said, "I shall come back to power but in a regenerated France . . ."

For a veteran of politics this was an amazingly naïve conception. But poor Tardieu, like all men who are too brilliant and have had an easy success, had astonishing illusions.

While Tardieu was Premier I accidentally witnessed a tragic scene: the assassination of President Paul Doumer by the mad Russian Gorguloff. Every year a charity bazaar was held in Paris for the benefit of the widows and children of writers killed during the war. Many authors used to go there, together with pretty actresses, to autograph their books, and each year the President of the Republic would honor the gathering by a visit. In 1932 I was there as usual seated behind a table covered with my books; I was just signing *Atmosphere* for an old lady when I heard a prolonged uproar. The Chief of State entered. There was the sound of faint reports to which I paid no heed. But running feet, cries, and a sudden silence attracted my attention. I lifted my head and saw the President lying on the ground surrounded by kneeling men. At first I could not believe my eyes.

"What is happening?" I asked.

I left my table to go for news. Claude Farrère, who was then President of our Society and a brave naval officer, had thrown himself in front of Monsieur Doumer and had received a bullet in his arm. A doctor who had been leaning over the body got up saying:

"Messieurs, take off your hats . . . The President is dead."

He was obviously mistaken, for just then the wounded man opened his eyes and moved his lips. The doors of the hall were thrown open. It was Tardieu, wearing a coat with a fur collar and a high hat. I shall never forget the expression of despair and rage on his face.

"But who did it?" he demanded . . . "Why? . . ."

Only then did I think of the assassin and saw a big fellow with the appearance of a stupid brute surrounded by policemen. Someone touched me on the shoulder. It was the old lady.

"Well, Monsieur?" she said . . . "What about my inscription? . . ."

Because Monsieur Doumer had been killed at a meeting of writers, it was decided that writers should stand guard over his body at the Elysée while he lay in state. And so I found myself standing at attention with three other comrades near the funeral bier on which the President lay in full dress with the red grand cordon of the Legion of Honor diagonally across his breast. The crowd filed past, sorrowful and respectful. As one couple was passing I heard the woman say to her husband, after looking for a long time at the President:

"It is indeed he!"

.   .   .   .

After the election of 1932 Herriot, who had come to power, made an attempt at the Lausanne Conference to adjust the question of reparations which was then poisoning France's relations both with Germany and with England. I knew Edouard Herriot only slightly but I had a high regard for his culture and honesty. One morning Jean Giraudoux, who was an attaché in his Cabinet, telephoned me:

"Would you like to come to Lausanne?" he asked. "The Chief has authorized me to take you there."

I accepted and had no cause to regret it, for I saw at very close range how an international conference functions. It was essentially a conflict of prestige between irascible experts whom uninformed but well-intentioned statesmen tried to placate. Herriot, generous and eloquent, rising above clouds of figures, would tell humorous anecdotes about Louis Philippe or discuss music with the Germans. The English delegation, knowing that he had written a *Beethoven*, had prepared themselves brilliantly on this subject, but he held forth on the poetry of jazz and took them by surprise. Ramsay MacDonald was there, accompanied by his daughter Ishbel, the Runcimans and the unfortunate Ralph Wigram who had been stricken by poliomyelitis but continued his work with inspiring abnegation. Every evening Paganon, Minister of the Interior and member of the French Delegation, would receive the journalists:

"Today," he would say, "it would not be correct to say that we have taken a step forward, no, but it would be equally incorrect to say that we have withdrawn . . . If you wish to give the public an exact idea of the situation say that, although we cannot indicate any actual change, the climate, the atmosphere (am I right, Monsieur Maurois?) is better . . . No! . . . Say: *imperceptibly* better . . ."

Positive result: France gave up the reparations without any settlement of the question of the American debts. The delegates took a last dip in Lake Geneva. Giraudoux who, like his hero Jérôme Bardini, had disappeared for almost the whole conference, reappeared on the last day:

"Giraudoux," Herriot said to him, "you are the most detached attaché."

When we left, a Swiss railroad employee at the Ouchy-Lausanne station asked me to point out Herriot.

"Are you interested in politics?" I asked.

"No," he confessed. "It's because I was told he looked like Porter Number Twelve . . ."

A trivial anecdote, but the terrible thing about this post-war world, which for lack of a pilot was drifting toward new and more terrible catastrophes, was that it left behind it nothing except a wake of trivial anecdotes.

Soon the radical party was torn by the War of the Two Edouards, and Daladier replaced Herriot. His desire, it seemed, was to reconcile France first with Italy then with Germany. To Rome he sent as ambassador Henry de Jouvenel, an adroit and brilliant politician who knew how to get along with Mussolini. Over the head of Paul Boncour, who was Minister of Foreign Affairs, Daladier and Jouvenel prepared for signature a Four Power Pact: France—Italy—England—Germany. Jouvenel did not live far from Essendiéras. We often went to see him in his old family mansion at Varetz near Brive in the district from which he was Senator.

"The French Senate," he said to us in his clear, mocking voice, "is a club one has to understand. One is only accepted there slowly. For the first two years it is wise to remain absolutely immobile. Any initiative would give offense. The third year a man of ability may smile once or twice. The fourth year he is allowed to risk a few interruptions. At the end of six years, if you feel the ground has been prepared, deliver a short speech, dull and unimportant. After nine years, when you have been re-elected, you have the right to be eloquent."

But he had not applied these rules himself but had been immediately and successfully eloquent. His premature death was a loss to his country. He was one of those rare men who can deal with foreign affairs realistically and without partisan bias.

.   .   .   .

The enemies of the government had a field day when a large-scale swindle, the *Affaire Stavisky*, was shown to have numerous political ramifications. The *Action Française* and numerous Leagues, formed in imitation of the Fascist countries, began to hold street demonstrations against the deputies. During the winter of 1933-1934 we were at Valescure in the Midi and we used to hear members of the Right and Left shouting insults at one another on the sidewalks of Saint-Raphaël, "just as in Paris." On the seventh of February there was a crowd in the room where the telegraphic bulletins from the *Eclaireur de Nice* were posted: "Riots in Paris . . . Many dead . . ." We had left our children in Neuilly. Ought we to hurry back? Was a revolution beginning? But a few hours later we learned that the Daladier Cabinet had capitulated and that the President of the Republic had summoned Monsieur Doumergue, who in turn had appealed to Marshal Pétain, Barthou, Tardieu and Herriot. It looked as if this were going to be the great coalition ministry desired by those of the French who, like us, had grown tired of the violence of political struggles and desired a period of respite to rebuild the forces of the country.

CHAPTER XX

Brother Against Brother

WHEN we returned to Paris we saw with sorrow that the parties had not disarmed. Monsieur Prince, a magistrate, had been found dead on the railroad tracks at Dijon. The parties of the Right maintained that he had been assassinated by the Free Masons because he knew all about the *Affaire Stavisky*. The parties of the Left said he had committed suicide. The passions of the two sides were stronger than their interest in the truth. Two famous detectives, summoned from London by a great French magazine, came to the conclusion that it was suicide; the results of their investigation were never published. "I should have lost all my readers!" the editor said to me naïvely.

Not being a party man nor acquainted with the facts, I reserved judgment. But one day meeting Georges Mandel, a Cabinet minister, at a friend's house I asked:

"What is one to make of the *Affaire Prince*?"

"That's an odd question!" he replied lifting his chin with a disdainful grimace above his strange high collar of the vintage of 1830. "You're the only one who can answer it . . ."

"I? But I haven't any of the facts in the case."

"It's not a question of facts," Mandel said, shrugging his shoulders. "If you belong to the Right, Prince was assassinated; if you belong to the Left, he killed himself. And so you alone, as I said, can answer your question."

This paradox, unhappily, illustrated only too well the new crisis of delusions and bad faith. Left and Right set out to fight against imaginary monsters and the wild and random swinging of their swords dismembered unhappy France. The Radicals of the sixth of February, tired of being called assassins by their adversaries, prepared for revenge by allying themselves with the Socialists, and also with the Communists. The Doumergue Ministry which could not exist without the Radicals saw itself threatened with dissolution when it had not as yet even begun the reforms that were expected of it.

Certain obstinate doctrinaires maintained that these reforms would endanger the Republic. Actually these reforms alone could have saved it, as events clearly proved. President Doumergue, instead of acting, made speeches over the radio and let the opportune moment slip by. His popularity, which had been tremendous, declined. In order to lighten ship he dismissed Chéron, his Minister of Justice, whom one section of public opinion blamed for not having arrested the murderers of Prince. This ridiculous-looking fat man one day made a profound remark to Henry de Jouvenel who repeated it to me:

"You think me ridiculous, Monsieur?" Chéron said. "I *want* to be ridiculous, Monsieur. And do you know why? It's because in this jealous country being ridiculous is the only form of notoriety that does not kill a politician."

It was Marshal Pétain who, with the brusqueness of a timid man, put an end to Chéron. One day at a Cabinet meeting the Marshal said:

"We are carrying too much dead wood around with us."

"To whom do you refer?" Chéron asked.

"To you, Monsieur," the Marshal said.

Chéron collapsed.

Doumergue's Minister of Foreign Affairs was Louis Barthou, a native of Béarn, who wore a goatee and eyeglasses and was prodigiously pleased with himself. He belonged to Poincaré's generation; both had been ministers at thirty, and at that time had been called "the two babies." A collector of autographs, he had amassed a collection which after his death was sold for seven million francs. I loved to look at his beautiful editions of Hugo, Rimbaud and Verlaine. Pleased by my enthusiasm, he treated me as a young protégé until the day when Marshal Lyautey inadvertently turned him against me. After dinner Lyautey had taken me by the arm and had said, jokingly:

"Look here, Barthou! This is the man who invented me."

I protested, but Barthou, who had himself written a book about Lyautey before I had, never forgave me for this incident. He was a vain man but I respected him all the same because his vanity seemed to me more than balanced by his sincere patriotism. He had just completed a grand tour of Europe to strengthen our alliances when King Alexander I of Yugoslavia came to Marseille. Barthou went there to greet him and both were assassinated. I remember the feeling of disintegration at that time. A film which was suppressed but which I saw at a private showing, revealed the miserable insufficiency of the police protection. One was forced to admit that in France, while the people remained hardworking, sane and courageous, the machine of government had ceased to function.

.   .   .   .

What was the source of the evil? It lay in the violence of political passions adroitly inflamed by foreign propaganda. Since the Revolution France had been a disunited country. "This bloody ditch will never be filled in," Chateaubriand had said of the Terror. That was still true. I felt it very strongly, as I have said, in Périgord where the aristocracy remained loyal to the Old Regime while the peasants voted for the Left. But up to 1918 patriotism had held together Frenchmen who were divided on all other points. After the Russian Revolution the middle class had been terrified by the formation of a strong Communist party and had reacted by rushing to join the Leagues. These in their turn had terrified the Radicals who rushed into the arms of the Socialists. On July Fourteenth you no longer saw a single parade of patriots proceeding toward the tomb of the Unknown Soldier, but two parades, one of the Left, the other of the Right, so hostile to each other that only the presence of the police kept them from coming to blows.

All this would have been less serious had it not been that at this very time Germany was beginning its formidable rearmament. For us to grow disunited as she became unified was folly. I did my best to say so. I made speeches before the *Equipes Sociales*, the Christian

Union of Young People, the Jocistes, gatherings of young workmen toward whom I felt sympathetic, and in the big schools. I invoked the spirit of Lyautey who had united men of all persuasions and had made them work together for the glory of France. This message was well received by the young men to whom I talked, and I am convinced that if more speakers had preached union throughout the country they would have been listened to, but a campaign of this sort when it is not endorsed by any party or supported by the press reaches only very small groups.

Conscious of my weakness and my isolation I remembered sadly that Disraeli at the beginning of his political career had tried to remain independent and had been forced to recognize, after two or three resounding defeats, that action demands intellectual sacrifices, simplifications of thought and a participation in the life of a party. Not being a politician, I did not draw the conclusion from this example that I should affiliate myself with a party, but rather that I should give up action, preserve a writer's freedom of expression and wait for the French to come to understand, as I had done, that by being disunited they were disarmed.

For a time I believed I had found another form of action, that of journalism. The *Figaro*, which had for a while followed a policy contrary to its tradition, had just been bought by Mr. and Mrs. Léon Cotnareanu. It was their intention to bring the paper back to its traditional mission: objectivity in politics and an intelligent leadership in literature and art. Pierre Brisson suggested to Léon Cotnareanu an editorial committee of five, of which I would be a member. Cotnareanu agreed and I was strongly attracted by the idea of working with friends for whose intelligence and honesty I had a high regard. Moreover my wife was delighted to see me join a paper for which her father had written and which had been edited by Robert de Flers. But I was neglecting two important facts. The first was that a committee cannot run anything. In a newspaper, as in a factory or government, there is need of a prime minister.

The second fact was my own character. I have tried a hundred

mes in my life to participate in a committee, a group or a council.
Almost always after a short time I have had to resign because of my
desire to have them act or write otherwise than they did. In my youth
I was efficient as a manufacturer because I was master in my own
domain and responsible for my own decisions; I had been efficient in
various capacities in the army because my situation, though a subor-
dinate one, was perfectly definite; but I am inept at politics and at
collective action. For consolation I tell myself that a writer is a being
who should act alone and not sign anything except what he himself
has written. But I know that lack of aptitude for team work is one
of my weaknesses. After one year I resigned from the editorial committee of *Figaro*: naturally I remained on very intimate terms with the
paper for which I continued to write.

.   .   .   .

Meanwhile the foreign danger was increasing. I was in Paris when
the Hoare-Laval agreement was torpedoed by English public opinion.
There was one man in the British Parliament who emphatically denounced the rashness of a policy that combined intransigent principles
and inefficient armaments. That man was Winston Churchill. And
this is what he said:

> When we think of the great power and influence which this
> country exercises we cannot look back with much pleasure on our
> foreign policy in the last five years. . . . We have pressed upon
> France a policy of sanctions against Italy that is estranging these
> two countries. . . . The friendship between France and Italy was
> vital to the defense and security of every home in France, and
> France out of regard for Britain and out of loyalty to the principle
> of the League of Nations went very far, and considerable injury
> was inevitable in the relations of France and Italy. . . . In this
> island—where we are still blessed by being surrounded by a strip
> of salt water, in spite of the alterations which later developments
> have caused—we ought to be careful that in our interventions in
> the foreign sphere we understand fully the consequences they may
> bring to those who live upon the continent, and the feelings which
> they may create there.

After this the premonitory tremors grew more frequent. When I went to London in February 1936 after the death of George V to deliver his funeral eulogy before a Franco-English Society, the chairman, Sir Austen Chamberlain, expressed his fears to me. They were acute, and Sir Austen clearly saw the danger of the policies his country was following. But next day I met Lord Lothian at the home of Ava Wigram who was trying with great kindness to maintain liaison between the English and French.

"And what will France do," his Lordship asked me, "if the German Army occupies the left bank of the Rhine?"

"I am not in the confidence of our government," I replied, "but I hope the French Army will not permit it."

"And by what right?" he said. "Germany can do what she likes in her own back garden."

A few days later on the seventh of March 1936, while I was delivering a lecture in Basle, the thing Lord Lothian had predicted came to pass. The German Army crossed the Rhine. As I was at the frontier I rushed into Alsace to see how the population would react. They were courageous and ready for anything. But the elections were not far off and we had at that time a Ministry that felt it had no authority. England, although the Treaty of Locarno had been violated, applied the brakes with all her strength. The French Cabinet contented itself with sending a note of protest. Thenceforth Germany could build a line of fortifications to protect her armies in the west; she had her hands free in the East.

The election of 1936 which brought the Popular Front to power upset the French political system. Not because a coalition of the parties of the Left came to power (France had seen this without perturbation in 1924 and 1932) but because the Socialists, a so-called revolutionary party, snatched the leadership of the coalition away from the Radicals, old hands at government, and because the Communists now formed a very powerful group of seventy-two deputies. The French middle class had expected Daladier and were undismayed; they saw the arrival of Léon Blum flanked by Thorez and Duclos.

At first Léon Blum did not terrify them too much. After all, wasn't

e, too, middle class in life and culture? Since by all counts it was
necessary to rejuvenate France, wasn't it better to have the task done
by a man who was intelligent and perhaps moderate? I often heard
reasoning of this sort in May 1936 in strong conservative circles in
Paris. In addition England and America, both capitalist countries,
seemed favorable to this government. The American Club in Paris
held a luncheon in honor of the new Premier. The conservatives in
London hoped to find in him a French Disraeli. The first Blum
Ministry came to power in a favorable atmosphere.

After June 1936 the honeymoon was over. The Communist party
which true to its doctrine wanted, not reforms, but revolution, had
organized "sit-down" strikes with occupation of the factories and
forced Léon Blum to do in four days what he had planned to do in
four years. Paris assumed an air of violence. Bands of lads wandered
down the Champs Elysées hooting at passersby, and the police, lacking
orders, did nothing to stop them. One Sunday, since we were going to
have lunch in the country at the home of a mutual friend, Max
Fischer, Tardieu took us in his car. He considered the suburbs so
unsafe that he had put a policeman in plain clothes beside his chauffeur. Everywhere we saw red flags, parades and deserted streets,
emptied through fear.

The reaction was extremely violent. The middle class had been
frightened. From this time dates the renaissance in France of anti-
Semitism which since the war of 1914, when so many young Jews had
splendidly served their country, had appeared to be if not extinguished
at least greatly diminished. The sit-down strikes had spelled the doom
of the administration. The English theorists of Democracy have
always rightly maintained that the form of government in which a
minority after an election agrees to be governed for a fixed period by
the majority is only possible if that minority is sure their essential
liberties will be respected. It must be admitted that this guarantee
ceased to exist at the moment when the Communist party, openly in
favor of a dictatorship of the proletariat, participated in the majority
and imposed its will on it.

For my own part, I had voted against the Popular Front (which

meant, in my constituency, that I had voted for Henri de Kerillis), bu
at the time it came into power I shared the hopes of those who expecte
Léon Blum to achieve his reforms with order and moderation. Pre
occupied first of all by danger from abroad, I was ready to sacrific
a great deal to bring about a united France. I believed that grea
changes were necessary and that the well-to-do classes in France (aside
from certain very honorable exceptions) were too often selfish, I ha
written a series of articles for *Marianne* on the best aspects of the New
Deal. That is to say, I was not *a priori* hostile to a French New Dea
But I hated lawlessness and I thought that insurrection, which is
legitimate protest against tyranny, is a crime in a free country.

I hardly knew Léon Blum, having met him only once at the hom
of Lord Tyrrell, but the following winter when we were as usual a
Valescure in the south of France, the manager of the hotel informe
us in great secrecy that the Premier, whose wife was very ill, was comin
to spend a short vacation under the same roof with us. When the new
spread it was a shock for the hotel guests who were very conservative

"If you take in people like that," said an irascible old gentleman, "w
are going to leave!"

"But after all," the poor manager replied, "I can't very well refus
to receive the Premier of France."

I cite this little incident because it shows the violence of emotion
at that time.

Then it became known that the Premier was going to occupy th
whole fifth floor and have his meals there and so would not be seen
This calmed people's feelings. Soon gangs of workmen arrived t
install a direct telephone line between the Golf Hotel and the Pre
mier's office in Paris. Finally a group of policemen descended to mak
inquiries about each one of us and established themselves in the lobby
One evening the manager said to us in a hushed voice:

"*They* have arrived."

Next day, I was at work while watching the mistral chase cloud
across the bay, when a chambermaid brought in a bunch of flower
and a letter. The letter was addressed to my wife and was from
Léon Blum. He reminded her that as a young critic he had been

eceived at the Avenue Hoche by Madame Arman de Caillavet and hat he would be happy to meet her granddaughter. He added that it vould be a pleasure to talk to me about England and English states-men. The letter ended with an invitation to have tea on the Fifth 'loor that same day. I found an affable, cultured and sensitive man vho appeared to have courage, generosity and a sincere desire to do vhat was right but whose judgment seemed to me warped on certain)oints by strong prejudices. When I said good-by he asked:

"What are you working on now?"

"I am correcting the proofs of a History of England."

"May I see them? I have nothing to read here and they would interest ne very much."

I sent him a set of proofs and received a kind letter about my book. But I did not see him again except in the hotel lobby on the day of lis departure for Paris. That single interview naturally did not enable ne to form an opinion of him. The course of events proved that he vas not (and did not want to be) a Disraeli. His mistake was not in vanting to achieve certain reforms for the benefit of the workmen, nany of which were useful and some urgent; he erred only through veakness and by allowing a minority to force upon him a rhythm of action which France was not able to endure. It is not possible in a lemocratic regime to govern a country against the wishes of forty per cent of its inhabitants. In particular, it is just as impossible to govern France against a class that produces almost all the leaders in the Army, the Navy and Industry, as it would be to govern it for long against the interests of its civil servants or workers.

Whatever the divisions among Frenchmen, they cannot get along without one another. If the leaders of the Popular Front *and* their opponents had understood this they would have avoided many hatreds.

.   .   .   .

England that year was not less agitated than France, but for wholly different reasons. King Edward VIII who had ascended the throne in January 1936 had abdicated in December. I attended the coronation of his brother in Westminster Abbey. How beautiful that medieval ceremony was! I watched for the oft described moment when the Queen is crowned and the peeresses put their coronets on their own heads, a thousand white arms rising at a single instant. I was not disappointed in that nor in the summons to the people, made to the four points of the compass, by the Archbishop.

The Duke and Duchess of Windsor came to live in France after their wedding and rented a house in Versailles. They invited us there. We were eager to meet the heroine of this great love story. Seeing her helped us a great deal to understand it. She had so much vitality that it seemed natural to be attracted to her. The etiquette of royalty was maintained. Major Metcalfe assembled the guests in the drawing room, then the Duke and Duchess descended the stairs and made the rounds of those present. The Duke wore a kilt of the Stuart tartan with sporran and with a silver dagger in his sock. In this costume he had great charm and appeared extraordinarily young. At table I was seated next to the Duchess; the Duke looked at her constantly. They seemed a much enamored pair. He talked to me about a book he had admired a great deal; it was Guedalla's book on Wellington.

"But I have read very little," he said modestly, "and the principal reason is that we were taught in rooms at Windsor that were so cold we had just enough strength to keep ourselves warm . . . They tell me that you have written a book about my grandfather; I should like very much to read it."

Then he described, without bitterness, the groups that had opposed him; he gave the impression of having wanted to be King of the little people as opposed to an aristocratic clique. His deepest rancor was against Mr. Baldwin.

After that we saw the Windsors often. They invited us to spend Christmas of 1938 at their house at Cap d'Antibes and gave us a real English Christmas dinner to which the Duchess added smoked turkey from Virginia. In Paris they took us to a concert by Stokowski, the Duke much embarrassed because he had orchestra seats and had never been in the theater before except in a royal box. They came a number of times to have dinner with us, and to please the Duke I invited the politicians whom he wished to meet, among others Monsieur Hanotaux who had been Minister of Foreign Affairs during the reign of his great-grandmother. One felt that he would have liked to be active, to remain in contact with the affairs of the world:

"Why don't they send me to South America?" he said. "Wasn't I once a good traveling salesman for the Empire?"

When my wife was forty-three years old, since her birthday coincided with the seventy-seventh birthday of our friend Abel Hermant, we invited a few friends and had a birthday cake decorated with a hundred and twenty candles. At dessert the Duke of Windsor got up and made a charming little speech.

"How strange life is!" Simone said to me after our guests had left . . . "I never dreamed that my birthday toast would ever be given by a former King of England."

"You wouldn't have guessed either that one day, as happened in Malta, a former King of Spain would come himself to open the door for you."

"Nor," said she, "that the Emperor of Austria would be living in a students' hotel in the Latin Quarter."

"All this," I said, "reminds one of that inn in Venice where Candide found six strangers who were all dethroned monarchs. Like Voltaire we are witnessing the end of a world. That is always a melancholy spectacle."

"What will our revolution be?" she asked. "Fascist? Communist?"

"That all depends on forces it is impossible to gauge and over which, alas, we have no control."

"And what must we do?"

"We must," I told her, "cultivate our garden."

CHAPTER XXI

The Capitol

THE garden I had to cultivate was a course of lectures on Chateau-briand I had promised in 1937 to give the following year for the Lecture Society.

My relations with Monsieur Doumic from the day when he had rejected *The Family Circle* had become, little by little, very friendly. He had confidence in me because he knew I would do, not always well, but at least as well as I could, whatever I agreed to undertake; I had confidence in him because, again and again, I had found him fair, exacting and courageous. It was the third time he had asked me to give his "big course" of ten lectures. In the office of the *Revue* together we had settled upon the subject. He had suggested Shakespeare. I had replied: "*Domine, non sum dignus,*" and I had proposed Chateaubriand who had interested me for a long time. The Abbé Mugnier had been the first to reveal to me the human being in Chateaubriand beneath the theatrical Personage. I had devoted much study to him and I hoped to make him live again.

"I see only one objection," Monsieur Doumic said, wrapping his legs in his blanket, "that is we have already presented a course on Chateaubriand at the Lecture Society by Jules Lemaitre, but that is not a serious objection because Lemaitre who was excellent on Racine and fairly good on Rousseau did a *Chateaubriand* that was unworthy of him . . . And of Chateaubriand . . . And so—go ahead . . ."

Thereupon he added of his own accord that if the course was a success a membership in the French Academy might be my reward. I thanked him without placing too much faith in what he said, for he had already on several occasions made similar remarks. It was the harmless, amiable and centuries-old custom of the Academicians to dangle this bait in front of their ambitious juniors. Barthou at the time when I was still his protégé had advised me, although I was very young, to present myself as a candidate for the chair of Anatole France because he wanted a candidate against Léon Bérard.

As a studious child, raised in the shadow of the classics, the Academy had inspired me with the same sentiments and ambitions that the English Parliament inspires in the students of Oxford and Cambridge. To be chosen by one's elders and one's peers to sit in the company to which Corneille and Racine, Voltaire and Victor Hugo, Taine and Renan had belonged, seemed to me a consummation devoutly to be wished. But at the time when I received Barthou's letter I had published only a few books which were not of sufficient importance to justify my being chosen. I replied that there were a number of very talented writers who had the indisputable right to be admitted before me, and despite his insistence I persisted in my refusal. Eight years later Paul Valéry asked me: "You or Mauriac?" I replied: "Mauriac," and to my great joy François Mauriac, who had a much greater title and a much greater chance than I, was elected.

I had great affection and esteem for him, sentiments which in the course of fifteen years have constantly increased. At the time when I began my career in the literary world certain people took pleasure in opposing us to each other. Base minds believe they see baseness everywhere, and some sought in Mauriac and in me ground favorable for the cultivation of jealousy. They failed. At first we studied each other with the anxiety one feels before the unknown, then a friendship sprang up, soon to be reinforced by that of our children. Mauriac spent some weeks with us at Essendiéras during the autumn of 1934 and in the course of our walks we had long and intimate conversations. After Mauriac, many of my friends had been elected to the French Academy. Then in 1936 Monsieur Doumic for the first time said to me:

"Your turn has come."

I listened to the Sirens and for some weeks I thought, to my great surprise, that I, although I was neither a Marshal nor a Cardinal nor dying, was going to be successful in this first candidacy, which would have been contrary to the wise traditions of the institution. But Joseph de Pesquidoux, a good regional writer and an old contributor to the *Revue*, presented himself against me and Monsieur Doumic abandoned me, which immediately spelled my doom. When I next saw him he said to me, stroking his beard:

"Don't complain . . . Victor Hugo had three defeats . . . Besides out of thirty-one votes you got eleven . . . That's a good trial gallop."

This was the traditional consolation.

.   .   .   .

But it was not the mirage of the Cupola that inspired me with the desire to write a *Chateaubriand*. My hero intrigued me: the women who surrounded him—Pauline de Beaumont, Delphine de Custine, Nathalie de Noailles, Juliette Récamier and Céleste de Chateaubriand herself—were a delight to draw; the epoch was one of the most dramatic in history and permitted me to sketch a picture of France; finally to live in intimate association with the beautiful *Mémoires d'Outre-Tombe* was enchanting. I went to Brittany and from St. Malo to Combourg, from Fougères to Grand-Bé, I tried to become thoroughly acquainted with the scenes in which Chateaubriand had passed his youth. Few writers today have so many faithful followers as he. The Chateaubriand Society helped me and protected me from errors. Countess de Durfort, née Sibylle de Chateaubriand, opened the Combourg archives to me. If my wife and irreplaceable collaborator had not been painfully ill I should have been happy in my work. But all that year was saddened by the dangers to Simone caused by a malady which was ill-defined but terrifying in its ravages.

The final touches on *Chateaubriand* had almost been completed, and with Monsieur Doumic I was searching for a title for the ten lectures, when he was taken ill with pneumonia. For a long time he had seemed to be growing feebler; it was a shock and a sorrow when I learned on the second of December that he was dead.

At this time I often saw Marshal Pétain, who was President of the

French Information Center for the United States, of which I had been named administrator. At the meetings of the Council he was friendly, exacting, punctual and precise. One evening as we were leaving a meeting he said to me:

"Why don't you present yourself as a candidate for Doumic's chair?"

I was astonished.

"I had not thought of it, *Monsieur le Maréchal* . . . And then a second defeat would give me more pain than success would give me pleasure."

"I shall give you my support."

I consulted some of my friends and then sent off my letter of candidacy. It was addressed to the Permanent Secretary, and one had to weigh each word, for it was read aloud before the Academy and judged by severe critics. Austerity, simplicity, brevity are the rules. Then begins the period of visits. Many candidates retain a poisoned memory of this time. This is not true of me. To pay calls on thirty-nine men who are all, or almost all, very remarkable, some as writers, others as generals, prelates, admirals, scientists, ambassadors, is far from boring. Quite the contrary. Those who intend to vote for you say so, which immediately makes the visit happy and intimate; those who are against you have recourse to various tactics which are amusing to observe and which vary from brutal frankness to complete abstention. If a general talks to you for an hour about Frederick II or an archaeologist about cathedrals, you know that their votes have been promised elsewhere, but you have heard two brilliant lectures delivered to you alone by two eminent authorities. That's not time wasted.

My shortest visit was the one I paid to Marshal Franchet d'Esperey. I knew him and relished his military brusqueness.

"I know what brings you here," he said. "You want to belong to the French Academy . . . That's perfectly reasonable . . . Only I've made out a table of promotion . . . You are Number Two . . . Number One is Jérôme Tharaud . . . And so if Tharaud presents himself against you I shall vote for him . . . If he does not present himself I shall vote for you . . . *Au revoir,* my friend."

Tharaud did not present himself against me; my competitor was Paul Hazard, whose courtesy and perfect honesty guaranteed a chivalrous combat. We emerged from it closer to each other than ever. We had many friends in common so that certain men—such as Admiral Lacaze, Joseph Bédier, Louis Madelin—who would have voted for me against anyone else very loyally told me that they would begin by voting for Hazard. And so I did not count them in the score I was keeping, but even without them it seemed to me that I should have a majority in my favor.

"Don't have any illusions," old experts like Abel Hermant told me, "we've seen candidates whose reckoning gave them twenty-seven votes, unconditional promises, and who at the time of balloting received three."

Hermant had had a great deal of experience in campaigns for the Academy, having had to present himself six times before being elected, a fact which he used to recount with much humor. Although well along in years he retained his youthfulness of spirit.

"The Institute preserves you," he would say. "So many candidates are hoping for your death that you go on living to spite them."

When he was forced to undergo a painful and dangerous operation he showed the courage and resiliency of a young man. Before going into the operating room he wrote his weekly articles for the *Temps*, the *Figaro* and *Paris-Midi*. Within a week he was at work in his hospital bed. With him I followed the fluctuations of my chances and the strange maneuvers of the last hour. There is a legend that the Academy is divided into Right and Left. In my case the dividing line in the voting was not at all political. On my side were the Permanent Secretary Goyau, the Marshal, many writers, the two scientists (the Duc de Broglie and Monsieur Emile Picard); against me the Ecole Normale, which is very powerful in the Academy and which naturally supported its graduate Paul Hazard. "Oh, if only the dead could vote," I thought in moments of anxiety, "without doubt I should have the support of Lyautey, Cambon, Poincaré; and Robert de Flers would campaign for me." For the charming Robert de Flers had died in 1927 while still quite young.

Bergson, who kept me for more than two hours, said he would have liked to vote for me, but for several years had not been attending meetings of the Academy. He was in fact paralyzed by arthritis deformans, and a meeting would have been torture. When I went to see him I knew he took no part in the elections and my visit was a pure matter of form. It turned out to be a delightful experience because of the importance of the subjects he discussed and the beauty of his language. Another memory left with me by that campaign was of the courage of Georges Lecomte, who was very ill and was supposed to enter a hospital but put off the day of the operation, against the advice of his doctors, in order to be able to vote. There is an academic heroism.

The day of the election, Thursday the 23rd of June 1938, I went for a walk in the Bois with my three children. Simone, who was passionately interested in my success, had asked a friend to telephone her the results of the balloting and waited anxiously beside the instrument. The sky was clear, the air mild and our walk was delightful. We talked gaily of a thousand things and almost forgot the hour. At the exact moment of our return the telephone rang. It was a reporter:

"Please get off the line, Monsieur," Simone said in exasperation. "I am expecting an important communication."

"Certainly, Madame," he replied. "I simply wanted to tell you that your husband has been elected to the French Academy."

My wife emitted a cry of joy and dropped the receiver. The noise attracted our attention. It was a happy moment. Five minutes later the first friends arrived. The election had been quick and had been completed on the second ballot by nineteen to thirteen. I was, as Disraeli said, "at the top of the greasy pole."

That evening we kept with us for dinner some of our dearest friends. Their presence, their obvious pleasure, were sweeter to me than the victory itself. Not only were they my friends but they were all men I loved and admired. "Oh, my friends," I thought, "how I thank you, being what you are, for being also my friends!" I had a fugitive impression, on that twenty-third of June 1938, that I had won my place in the world and that my old age would be, as befits that time of life, tranquil, respected, honored. But in the far depths of my mind I heard, as in the *Ring*, the rumble and roar of the Theme of Destiny. Never in my experience had happiness been lasting or unmixed. In 1918 the joy of victory was blended with the anguish of illness. In 1924 at the moment when I believed that my household had been restored, death wiped it out. In 1930 a delightful and tender Christmas was followed by the death of little Françoise. In this year of 1938 the Academy had crowned the most daring ambitions of my youth; my wife who had been ill for two years began to recover; my enemies seemed disarmed; my charming and dearly beloved daughter was engaged; my sons were becoming fine young men; my life seemed like one of those fairy stories in which a benevolent magician lavishes his gifts upon the possessor of some talisman, but I told myself with anxiety, as I watched the golden champagne froth within my cup, that the Gods are jealous and that the hour had come to cast into the waves the Ring of Polycrates.

.   .   .   .

There was one man I especially wanted to see after the election. That was Alain. I knew he had often attacked the Academy in his *Comments*. For my part I saw nothing but good in this institution, which was one of the very few that had bridged the gap between the French Monarchy and the regimes that followed the Revolution. But I cared a great deal about my master's esteem and I wished to know how he felt. He had retired some years before and had left the Lycée Henri IV. For several winters he had continued giving an open course at the Collège Sévigné and this I had attended, happy to be a student once more, to sit at his feet and to listen to those splendid, those unique lectures. I knew that later on the rheumatism he had contracted in the damp dug-outs in 1914 had paralyzed him completely, like Bergson, François Porché, who had gone to see him, had described him as "a lightning-stricken oak."

I found him in a little house at Vésinet, watched over by a faithful woman friend. His inability to move his limbs made him a child so far as physical life was concerned. His immobility had resulted in an increase of weight, and the contrast between his huge body and his extreme feebleness was poignant. But his face and head remained quite unaltered, and as soon as he spoke I recognized my master.

"Not only do I not blame you," he said smiling, "but if I hadn't been so ill I should have written you after your election. I'm pleased that you should have had this joy . . ."

And he repeated an affectionate phrase he had used before:

"I know you well. You are a tender-hearted boy."

But the "boy" was now fifty-three.

Then we talked about Chateaubriand. I had brought him my book which was just out, and I had written in the front of it as we used to do in his classes: "*Lege quaeso.*" Alain knew the *Mémoires d'Outre-Tombe* as well as I did; it was one of "his" books. We had a happy hour together.

The summer of 1938, which I spent as usual in Périgord, was devoted to my Speech of Reception at the French Academy. It was my duty to deliver a eulogy of Monsieur Doumic. His son Jacques Doumic and his son-in-law, Louis Gillet, had loaned me his private papers and his Journal; the man who emerged was a living being and, for all his eccentricity, lovable. Having known him well myself and having worked with him helped me, and I tried to draw a true picture of him. I was just finishing it when the first rumblings of an international storm were heard. Berlin was threatening Prague. The French government mobilized several classes. We returned to Paris and went straight to the *Figaro* to see Lucien Romier whose intelligence I trusted.

"I don't think there will be war," he told us.

I had confidence in his judgment and was not surprised when Neville Chamberlain flew first to Berchtesgaden, then to Godesberg, and when Munich established a precarious peace. The truth was that we were not ready and England even less than we. This was the opinion of my friend Eric Phipps, British Ambassador to Paris. For a long time I had been acquainted with Sir Eric and Lady Phipps. I had met them after the war when Phipps had been appointed for the first time to Paris. Later he had been made Minister to Vienna, then Ambassador to Berlin; but when he spent his vacations in England I used to go and see him in his country house in Wiltshire. In the course of my life I have never met a woman more completely kind than Lady Phipps. A convert to Catholicism and very religious, she unostentatiously scattered about her material and moral good deeds which have saved many unfortunates from misery and despair.

She made the British Embassy in Paris the scene of amicable and intimate reunions. Throughout all that year a great effort was made by both governments to strengthen the Franco-English ties which, because of the policy of Sanctions, had become much weakened in the French middle class. In July the King and Queen had come to France and had seemed to conquer Paris as his grandfather Edward VII had done before them. In November Neville Chamberlain was officially received in his turn. We dined with him at the Quai d'Orsay and later heard him, while dominating the group with his little birdlike head, tell of the interviews at Berchtesgaden and Godesberg.

On the fifth of November my daughter Michelle was married. This great happiness was tempered by painful anxiety about the future of Europe and the future of so many French couples. In the excitement of these beclouded festivities Simone lost a family ring which she valued highly. Was this the ring of Polycrates? No fisherman brought it back but an insurance company, modern incarnation of Destiny, reimbursed my wife for her loss. The Gods were not disarmed.

.   .   .   .   .   .

We were to leave in February 1939 for America where I had promised to make a long lecture tour. When we left Le Havre on the fifteenth of February, Franco-Italian relations were strained. Were we going to be called back as soon as we landed? On the day of our arrival in New York the newspapers carried huge headlines: "SIXTY-FOUR ITALIANS AND TWELVE FRENCHMEN KILLED ON THE BORDER OF TUNIS." Next day the news was denied. I found America irritated at France and England. All my American friends criticized the Munich agreement.

"But," I said to them, "what would you have done to help us?"

"Nothing," they replied with candor.

The truth is that the Americans' principal preoccupation in 1939 was not the European situation but the presidential election of 1940. The business world which was hostile to the President was isolationist at that time through fear of a third term. Meanwhile Roosevelt's partisans were behaving cautiously in order not to compromise his chances. This was a situation very favorable to Germany's plans. I was surprised by the violence of feeling. To an old lady who sat beside me at dinner I said:

"Would you go so far, Madame, as to sacrifice your country and mine to your resentment against the New Deal?"

"Mr. Maurois," she replied, "I should rather see this planet blown into small pieces than have Roosevelt elected a third time . . ."

This seemed to me a perfect example of *dementia politica*. My excellent manager Harold Peat had arranged a long trip for me: Philadelphia, Boston, Cincinnati, Columbus, Minneapolis, Detroit, Omaha, Tulsa, Chicago. In the last named city friends had me to dinner with ex-President Hoover. He humorously described the amazement of men who in two or three thousand years would study our economy and discover that we had dug holes at great expense in Africa, found an ore there from which we extracted gold, transported this metal to America, dug holes at great expense in Kentucky and buried the gold there. Despite all our follies he retained his faith in democratic institutions:

"It's the only form of government," he said, "that makes it possible when things go badly to change leadership without violence. But for it to work, liberties must be respected, not only in theory but in fact."

A little later I had lunch at the White House with a group of writers and was introduced to President Roosevelt whose lofty and gracious manner I admired. A patrician Whig and a plebeian Tory at the time of the Reform Bill, such were my impressions of Roosevelt and Hoover.

On the fifteenth of March when I was in Dallas, Texas, the Germans marched into Prague. Was this war? Many Americans seemed to hope so. But were they ready to fight? Quite the contrary; they were voting at that time for rigorous neutrality laws. Were we and England alone strong enough to win? I did not think so, and so it seemed to me my duty to counsel moderation at the Congress of Pen Clubs which was held in New York during the World's Fair. I have always had great respect for soldiers who sacrifice their lives, and little sympathy for bards who urge them on from afar with their songs. I made a point of saying this, although such a thesis cannot be very popular in a congress of writers:

> "If men had a greater consciousness of the dangers that go with the use of certain words, every dictionary in the book shops would be wrapped with a scarlet band on which one could read: 'High explosives. Handle with care.' Military experts tell us of incendiary bombs which can set fire to whole towns, but we know of words which have set fire to an entire continent . . . We have anti-aircraft guns; we need anti-wordcraft batteries . . . Novelists, biographers, historians, it is our duty to draw of our little world, as exact a representation as lies within our power. We have no axes to grind, no theses to prove, no election to win. Looking out upon the universe, we should be like the painter before his model; we should try to transfer to our canvas what we see, and only what we see . . . During this difficult and perilous period, the greatest service we, writers, can render to the cause of peace is to hold explosive words under lock and key, to maintain a strict control over our emotions, and to tell our readers the truth, the whole truth, and nothing but the truth. So help us God . . ."

The return trip aboard the *Normandie* over a sunny ocean with the slight feverishness of sleepless nights, the long political conversations, the sentimental badinage on deck, was a mixture of Watteau, Marivaux and Pontigny. I find this note which I made and published at that time: "What will the United States do if we go to war? Nothing for a year. After that it will give financial and industrial assistance. It will be at war at the end of two years . . ." I was not far from the truth. As we entered the port of Le Havre we saw with sorrow the wreck of the *Paris*, capsized and showing only her swollen belly. A mysterious fire had destroyed the beautiful ship on which I made my first crossing. Wasn't this, even now, the work of an enemy who chose this way of attacking our fleet?

We arrived just in time for my reception at the French Academy. But before that ceremony there was another that moved me deeply. The headmaster of the Lycée of Rouen had asked me to come and dedicate a new statue of Corneille in the Court of Honor. I had been overcome to learn that my dear old plaster Corneille, that of David d'Angers, past which I had so often marched, had been washed away by the Norman rains. The young cavalier who took his place on the pedestal disconcerted me. But it was a great pleasure to deliver a eulogy of Corneille in this setting where forty years before I had commenced to read him. Beside me on the platform was General de La Laurencie who was in command of the Third Army Corps; I did not think at that time that I was soon to see him again on the northern frontier in tragic circumstances. During the reception which followed, my old schoolmates presented me with a bronze plaque, the work of one of them who was a sculptor; it represented the Seine with the Pont Boïeldieu, which I had crossed every morning in Rouen on my way to the Lycée, and the Pont des Arts, in Paris which is dominated by the cupola of the Institute.

To find my old friends of Rouen white-haired, some of them fat, and nevertheless so similar to the young men I had known, gave me much the same feelings that Proust experienced at the ball of the Prince de Guermantes. Yes, all these boys with whom I had played seemed disguised as old men. One was a prefect, another a senator, another a colonel of constabulary. Many had already retired. The elder Dupré, who had first taught me to love music, dragged himself about with the aid of two canes. My mother, who had come from Elbeuf as she used to do formerly "for the prizes" was touched by the affectionate speeches in which reference was made to the child she had raised. I thought: "The evening of a fair day . . ." Alas, the evening had barely begun and storm was gathering on the horizon.

A reception at the Academy is one of the beautiful French ceremonies. Everything contributes to its grandeur: the antiquity of the building, the strangeness of the procedure, the narrowness of the room, the quality of the audience, the prestige of the members, the military trappings, the traditional vocabulary and often the quality of the eloquence. Before being read at a public session, the speeches have to be accepted by a committee. I appeared before the latter and passed, with kind praises, this last examination of my life. The Duke de La Force said to me:

"You must remove the word *inlassablement* (indefatigably) which is not in the Dictionary of the Academy."

He was right.

After this test the newly elected member takes his seat. At the moment he enters, the whole Academy rises as a mark of courtesy; he bows, seats himself and takes part for the first time in the work on the Dictionary. The contrast between the simplicity of this ceremony and the majesty of the institution is not without grandeur and charm.

The following Thursday, the twenty-second of June 1939, the public session took place. The Secretary of the Academy gives only twenty seats to the newly elected member. I could only provide places in the Center for my mother, my wife, my children, my mother- and father-in-law and a few of my intimates. But many of my friends had obtained tickets by courtesy of other academicians, and as I entered I saw the faces of all those who were dear to me. This entrance is made to the sound of rolling drums while the guards present arms and their officer salutes with his sword. For the man who is going to speak it is a thrilling moment. Seated between my two sponsors, somewhat stifled by my green uniform, uncomfortable in my plumed bicorn hat, I looked at the two statues that stood on either side of the Desk, those of Bossuet and Fénelon. Seated exactly below were General Weygand and Ambassador Paléologue; one of my great anxieties throughout my whole speech was the glass of water resting on the narrow shelf, which I feared I might upset upon those illustrious heads.

"Monsieur André Maurois has the floor for the reading of his speech of thanks . . ."

My heart pounded, but when I got to my feet the reception was such that I felt reassured. I do not know whether the heart of Paris has changed; I do not think so; however that may be, the Parisian public that day gave me one of the great joys of my life.

Monsieur André Chevrillon, who replied, graciously spared me the customary strictures so that no bitterness spoiled that enchanted hour for me. As I listened to him, I looked at the attentive and crowded heads of the onlookers. At the foot of the Desk, perched on high stools, sat some of the beautiful women of Paris: Edmée de La Rochefoucauld, Marthe de Fels, Henriette de Martel. In the center I discovered the sweet face of Frances Phipps; then the bright eyes of Anne Desjardins which brought back the walks beneath the cloisters and the beautiful evenings at Pontigny; Jeanne Mauriac and her daughters; Blanche Duhamel and her sons; higher up the fourteen grandchildren of Monsieur Doumic, a group of Norman students from the Lycée, comrades of war and a few old friends from Elbeuf who evoked the pounding of the looms and the high chimneys with their tufts of smoke. It was sweet on such a day to find this cluster of friends come together from all the stages of my life . . . But while André Chevrillon talked about Byron, Disraeli and Lyautey, why should a Greek verse, unsummoned, echo ceaselessly in my mind, lugubrious and prophetic? Why should the sublime and bleeding face of Mounet-Sully in *Œdipus Rex* haunt me on this day of triumph? Why should I think so forcibly, the while a thousand faces smiled, that Destiny remains as redoubtable as it was in the most ancient times, that the sad wisdom of Sophocles is still true and that "no man may be called happy before his death"?

CHAPTER XXII

Sitzkrieg

THE vales of Périgord, lined with poplars and willows, were more beautiful and peaceful than ever in that month of July 1939. The purple roofs of the tenant farm of Brouillac in the evening sunlight stood in soft contrast to the green of the fields. Only the wasps, jealous of my flowers, in the mornings still disturbed my tranquil solitude. But this enchanted silence, this prodigious immobility of nature seemed to me, as in July 1914, charged with mysterious menace. Each day when we opened the newspaper we expected to see in it the death warrant of our happiness. Poland, Dantzig, the Corridor . . . When the terms of the Treaty of Versailles had become known persons of intelligence had believed that from this bizarre map, from these impacted countries, the next war one day would come. After a thousand diverse feints it was at this vulnerable point that Mars once more spied his prey.

At the beginning of August we learned of the death of Charles Du Bos. My sorrow was all the more acute because I had not seen him again. He had just spent two years teaching at the University of Notre Dame in Indiana. The tempo of American life had been too rapid for his feeble strength. In him I lost a friend who had guided me, uplifted me and often forced me to live, as he would say, "at the extreme point of myself." I, like all his friends, had often laughed at his gravity, at his masses of pencils, at his long quotations, at his carefully cherished maladies. Like so many supposed hypochondriacs, he had given irrefutable disproof to our skepticism by his death, and now we remembered nothing except his virtues. I saw again the affectionate

softness of his eyes, the excited trembling of his long mustache, the
thick coats which swathed his martyred body. From now on who
would talk to me as he had done of Benjamin Constant or of Sainte-
Beuve? From now on who would talk to me with so much penetrating
affection about myself? We were told by those who had been present
at his end that he had died peacefully as a saint and a poet. Poor
Charlie! For twenty years he had suffered, but he had been able to
extract from the sufferings of the body the salvation of the soul. Might
not the day come when we ourselves would need to remember his
example?

About the twentieth of August the political news became worse.
Worried, we decided not to stay in Essendiéras through September
but to return to Paris by way of Malagar in order to pay a visit there
to François Mauriac.

The house was just as we had expected and as he had often described it, a sunbaked white house, surrounded on all sides as far as the
eye could reach by pale green vines dusted with blue sulphate; it had
the fine, secret and intimate savor of an old liqueur. François and
Jeanne were there, as well as their children and the Abbé Mauriac.
As so often happens in the Bordelais, there was a storm in the air. The
flies stuck to us persistently. We took a long, melancholy walk beneath
a violently hot sun and we talked about the dangers that threatened
us all. At that time the peace depended on Russia, and England and
France were negotiating with her. That evening after dinner, François read us his play *Les Mal Aimées*. He read well in his hurt, muffled
voice that added its own pathos to that of the characters. The play
was a fine one; it had the same atmosphere of moral uneasiness and
of restrained violence as *Asmodée*. Between the second and third acts
we listened to the news over the radio:

"Moscow announces a non-aggression pact with Berlin . . ."
One of the children asked:
"What does that mean?"
I replied:
"It means war."
We returned to Paris next day. Already troop transports were crawl-

ing along the railroads beside which we drove. When we arrived we hurried, as we had done the year before, to Lucien Romier's office, but this time our prophet did not reassure us. For several days we spent all our time hanging over the radio. The grave, sad speeches of Daladier were in consonance with the French people's desire for peace. But many were exasperated by the constantly renewed alarms.

"After all, *il faut en finir!*" said my barber who was leaving for the Maginot Line.

Almost every evening we dined with Pierre Brisson at some restaurant in the Bois, and then returned with him to the *Figaro* office to get the news. On Thursday August 31st we thought the game had been won. It appeared that honorable terms had been offered to Poland. We returned home mad with joy. Next day the report was denied and Poland was invaded. Once more it was war, but war without Russia, with an America hobbled by neutrality, with an England ill-prepared, and against a formidable German air force. All intelligent Frenchmen were desperate and, to add a crowning touch to their suffering, they could not say so publicly.

Although for a number of years I had not been of military age, I had made application to remain an officer in the reserves. And so, on the second of September, I presented myself at the *Place de Paris* where I was informed that I had been attached, by the Ministry of War, to a Committee on Information of which Jean Giraudoux was to be the head and which was to be installed at the Hotel Continental on the Rue de Rivoli. I went there. *Gardes Mobiles* were guarding the doors. The corridors were full of superannuated colonels, retired ambassadors and professors from the Collège de France. The conversation was brilliant, the disorder terrifying. The unfortunate Giraudoux had found himself suddenly, when war had already begun, forced to improvise a service of almost infinite complexity which, in Germany, had been functioning for years and for which his government gave him at first ridiculous appropriations. It was an impossible undertaking.

As his second in command he had chosen an energetic and devoted man, André Morize, professor at Harvard and a friend of his. The work that Morize succeeded in accomplishing in that year of war, the amount of courage and intelligence he expended on a hopeless task, should be counted to his credit on that day when a liberated France shall take a census of those who were good servants in her time of misfortune. I was in Morize's office at the Prime Ministry on Sunday, the third of September, at five o'clock when the ultimatum expired and the war began. When the five strokes rang out we clasped each other's hands in silence.

A little later I went into Giraudoux's office and he asked me what I wanted to do.

"It seems to me," I said, "that I might usefully maintain liaison with England, explain our needs to the English, urge them to increase their efforts and keep the French informed of this effort."

He approved at once, but he was submerged by the multiplicity of services to be established, and when the list was posted I found myself an assistant to Monsieur Laroche, former French Ambassador to Warsaw, in an office charged with the duty of seeing that articles were written for the French newspapers.

Rarely in the course of my life have I felt such discouragement and sadness as in the few days I spent at the General Commissariat of Information. As in 1914, I arrived bursting with good will, ready to rush across continents and kill myself with work. They said to me:

"See that articles are written."

"Articles? But by whom?"

"By anyone you like."

"But what about?"

"About anything you choose."

"For what newspapers?"

"For all the newspapers that will take them."

"And who will pay for these articles?"

"Oh, don't ask us for money; we haven't a franc."

The most incredible thing was that the General Commissariat of Information of the French Republic in time of war actually had no funds. Also this organization, like the others, was immediately torn by political passions. The people of the Right said that it was the resort of Communists; the people of the Left that it was a den of Reactionaries. The Collège de France felt that there were too many diplomats; the Quai d'Orsay that there were too many professors; the Rue St. Dominique that there were not enough Army men. For me, who hated quarrels, these discussions rapidly became so intolerable that I begged General Chardigny, who was in charge of the Army contingent at the Commissariat of Information, to send me somewhere else.

"I am not afraid of danger, *mon Général*," I said to him, "but I cannot stand inaction and disorder."

"And where would you like to go?" this worthy man asked. "There's no real war, you know."

Unexpectedly, just at the moment when I had given up hope, I received one morning a letter bearing the imprint of the British War Office. Here it is:

> Sir,
>
> I am commanded by the Army Council to convey to you a most cordial invitation to act as French Official Eye-Witness at General Headquarters of the British Field Force, which has now arrived in France.
>
> I am to inform you that, in the event of your accepting this invitation, our Military Attaché in Paris, Lieutenant-Colonel the Hon. W. Fraser, has been instructed to make all the necessary arrangements for your reception with the Commander-in-Chief.
>
> Finally I am to say that the Army Council fully appreciates the great service which a writer of your distinguished attainment and profound knowledge of the British character could render in maintaining these happy relations which have so long existed between the French people and the British soldiers, and to which your own writing has so largely contributed.
>
> I hope you will find it possible to honour us by accepting our invitation.
>
> I am, Sir, your obedient servant,
>
> > H.-J. CREED
> > *Permanent Undersecretary for War.*

It is easy to understand that this letter gave me great pleasure. Not only did I appreciate its warmth and its friendly tone, but I saw in it

my salvation and the possibility of following the war despite my age.
I rushed to show it to General Chardigny and to André Morize, who
both advised me to accept. They saw very clearly that at the Commissariat of Information I was in a blind alley and quite useless. I
called upon Colonel Fraser, the English military Attaché, and he told
me that the British General Headquarters was located at Arras, that
I was expected there and that I should ask for Colonel Reynolds. My
wife, who was now my chauffeur as well as my secretary, drove me to
Arras. During the preceding war I had known that beautiful Hispano-
Flemish city. I found it full of soldiers in khaki, and I seemed to be
witnessing again the scenes in Rouen twenty-five years before.

. . . .

The Official Eye Witness . . . Such was my title. The duties seemed
ill-defined. Colonel Reynolds to whom the Embassy had sent me was
in charge of Public Relations and had his headquarters at a hotel in
Arras; his duties included the press, censorship, cinema and radio. He
was an agreeable but absent-minded Englishman, who would listen
politely to what you had to say, throw himself back in his chair, roar
with laughter and immediately forget all about it. In his world I was
a new and disturbing species . . . the Official Eye Witness . . .
"Witness of what?" he asked me, laughing. "Nothing ever happens."
I paid a visit to General Gort who received me in the Château
d'Habarcq; he assigned me a car for transportation and an officer to
accompany me. It happened that this officer, Captain Grant, was an
old friend from peace time and had been the English publisher of my
little *Voltaire*. Grant was an old cavalry officer, but his regiment had
been motorized and he himself had been classified as: "Non-motorizable
cavalryman," which made him very proud. He did not know exactly
what he could show me but he was an agreeable companion and I
liked him very much. We stayed together from then on.
I needed lodgings. The Château d'Habarcq was full. The hotels of
Arras seemed noisy and mediocre. Grant and his friends did not have
a mess. Just as I was beginning to despair a miracle occurred. I had
gone to present myself, as was my duty, to the French general com-

manding the Arras subdivision. Colonel Gillot, substituting for him,
received me with great courtesy. Commander Poumier, of the Engineers, who was Chief of Staff, talked to me about my books, about
Mauriac and about Julien Green with obvious culture and then invited me to lunch.

"With the Colonel and Captain Puthomme, another engineer," he
said, "we have a little mess in the Rue des Capucins."

I found their little mess very well ordered, the conversation good and
the spirits high. When they asked me after lunch if I should like to
live with them I accepted with enthusiasm. Before long Colonel Gillot
was retired and left us. His successor, General Hémelot, a married man,
lived with his family, and "the Capucins" were reduced to three, but
they kept open house. With Robert Poumier and Raymond Puthomme
I enjoyed, for several months, a delightful and candid friendship. How
many charming boys—Pierre Lyautey, Jean Fayard, Simon de Peyerim-
hoff—were frequent visitors at our mess! Coming from regiments or
staffs near Arras, they would ask us if they could lunch or dine with us.
We were on excellent terms with the French Mission of Liaison attached to the British Army. General Voruz and Colonel de Cardes
would meet, at the Capucins' table, Lord Munster and Gordon, aides-
de-camp of General Gort. If it can ever be said that military co-opera-
tion is assured through personal friendships, then the Capucins of
Arras were good liaison agents.

But this liaison was not always easy. I found Franco-British relations in this war very different from what they had been in 1914. So
far as the work of the general staffs was concerned understanding on
the whole was better. But among the people distrust and sometimes
even hostility were constantly inflamed by German propaganda, which
was insistent, insinuating, sarcastic, tenacious, ingenious, and helped
by the old grievances of the French.

"England will fight to the last Frenchman!" the Stuttgart radio
announced.

The smallest difficulty between British soldiers and French villagers
was exploited by the Germans who would find out about it, I do not
know how, and give it vast publicity. General Brownrigg, Adjutant

General of the British Army, an excellent and very shrewd man, was sincerely distressed by these difficulties. He asked me to draw up the Ten Commandments of the British Soldier in France, had an enormous number of copies printed and distributed them to the troops. So this of all my works is the one that has had the largest printing:

I. Remember that in the eyes of the French who are watching you, you represent England. It is by your appearance, your conduct and your discipline that they will judge our country.

II. Remember that the farm which is only a temporary billet for your battalion is home for some French soldier and that he is attached by memories to every object it contains. Ask yourself: "If the war were being waged on our soil and the French were occupying my home, how should I wish them to behave?"

III. If you have come to France for the first time be careful not to judge the French too hastily. Their customs are different from yours; that is no reason to think them inferior. Remember the last war and the part the French Army played in it.

IV. Tell yourself that behavior which seems natural to you because it is in conformity with British usage, may, without your knowing it, shock or even wound the French. You like human beings to treat each other with a certain amount of indifference; your allies expect more than that. Always show a French friend more consideration than you would an English friend.

V. The women in the houses in which you are living will be under your sole protection. Treat them as you would like your own wives and daughters to be treated in your absence. You will see them in the French country districts engaged in very heavy work and doing their best to replace their men. As far as your military duties allow you, help them.

VI. Strive to become good soldiers. Our enemy is trying by this long respite and these false alarms to lull us to sleep and tire us out. Make use of this period of waiting and turn the false alarms into opportunities for maneuvers. Familiarize yourself more thoroughly with your weapons. Endeavor to make your battalion, your battery or your squadron a crack unit. What time and tradition have done for famous regiments you now have the opportunity and leisure to do for yours. Attach great importance to the details of your clothing and your discipline. The value of an army depends on its habits.

VII. France is entrusting to your guardianship a sector of her frontier, which is now your own. It is a great honor. Never yield an inch of French soil.

VIII. Take care never to spread or listen to rumors. The object of enemy propaganda is to sow unrest and panic. Only repeat what you are certain of. Whoever says: "I haven't seen it myself, but I've heard about it," may become, without realizing it, an agent of the enemy. Be an example of coolness. Yours is supposed to be a phlegmatic race. It is a fine reputation. Deserve it.

IX. Study the French language while you are in France. Help your hosts to learn English. The task of our two countries is not only to win the war but to win the peace afterward. This they will only be able to do if they remain united. They will only remain united if they understand each other.

X. The alliance of France and England has been a political and military necessity. It must become a human reality. These two countries which need each other must hold each other in unreserved esteem. It is within your power to make ten, twenty, a hundred Frenchmen regard England as an ally worthy of trust and affection.

Today I cannot read that text without anguish of heart . . . Meanwhile General Voruz, Commandant of the French Mission of Liaison, had charged me with an analogous and complementary task, that of giving lectures to his liaison agents about the English people and the British Army. He had organized a Liaison School at Auxi-le-Château and I went there from time to time to speak. Colonel de Cardes, Chief of Staff of the Mission, usually accompanied me. He was a native of Béarn, fiendishly clever, an unmerciful mimic and an excellent leader. I loved to see him giving orders and straightening out a situation. Precision, rapidity, authority; he had the best qualities of the professional soldier. But at the meetings of the Franco-British General Staff which he attended he was struck by the incoherence of the plans. They were going into Finland; they were not going into Finland. They were not going into Norway; they were once more planning to go into Norway. No master mind seemed to be guiding the coalition.

I got no better impression from my observations on the Belgian frontier. The line was terrifyingly weak. The French Engineers, to be sure, had in 1937 built little concrete casemates which were supposed to be connected by an anti-tank ditch. But these casemates were few in number and the ditch would be effective only if it were commanded by anti-tank guns. Only the emplacements existed, however, not the guns. To complete the defenses the English dug trenches of the 1914 type, but in the mud of Flanders the parapets collapsed; and moreover what use were these miserable entrenchments against giant tanks or concentrated bombardment? My friends, the correspondents of American, English and French papers, many of whom had fought in the last war, saw with great anxiety the weakness of our defenses. But what could they say? The censorship did not allow them nor me to voice any criticism. Nevertheless the facts were indisputable and certainly known to the enemy! On the frontier a thin line without density and lacking indispensable weapons; behind this line, nothing, no reserves, no mass of maneuver. Such was the terrifying picture.

.   .   .   .

My impression changed in December 1939 when I visited the Maginot Line.

"I wish each British brigade," General Gort said to me, "to spend several weeks in Lorraine to get actual war experience."

And so I went to see the Scotsmen in front of Metz. The French Officer of Liaison was Captain de Chambrun, son of the General who had entertained me in Fez. He gave himself heart and soul to his work and achieved good results. Attached to the Infantry of the Fortress he had served in one of the forts of the Line and took me there for lunch. I saw fine soldiers who inspired confidence. The armament of the forts, the perfection of the firing plans, the multiple observation posts, the large guns that flanked the anti-tank ditches, everything in Lorraine seemed as formidable as the line in Flanders seemed the reverse.

"On this side at least," I said to my guide, "they shall not pass."

But I did not stop to consider that if they broke through elsewhere all this force would become useless and this magnificent army would be imprisoned. On Christmas day Chambrun took me on a tour of the forts and villages of the front lines. It was bitter cold. Snow and frost had enveloped the war in a glistening mantle. No countryside of Dickens was ever a more perfect Christmas setting than the one in which Lorraine entertained our allies that year. It was beautiful to the point of unreality. A vaporous mist wrapped our countryside and clothed it in mystery. One could see barely fifty meters, but this narrow circle was a fairyland. Every tree, every frost-covered bush was transformed into a bouquet of sparkling crystals. The barbed wire entanglements, like monsters touched by one of Shakespeare's fairies, resembled in their white sheaths the silver tinsel that gleams amid the branches of a Christmas tree.

In the evacuated villages the snow had brought the dead houses back to life. Two laurel bushes in front of an empty inn, decorated with luminous crystal, looked like chandeliers, each garden bush became a crèche, every forest glade a church of white marble. On the roads French and English soldiers, invigorated by the cold, slithered over the thin coating of ice and exchanged joyful greetings. Then as one approached the front line the silence became intense: no gun spoke, no voice or cry broke the enchantment. On the deserted farms no dog barked, no cattle lowed. The mist enclosed each outpost, each watcher, in a silver bubble adorned with sparkling branches.

"There are mines all around here," the Scotch Colonel who accompanied us said candidly, "but I don't know exactly where."

This speech made me think of my old Bramble, whom I had vainly sought in this new army.

On the day after Christmas I took my leave and went straight from Lorraine to Périgord. The old house at Essendiéras had been occupied by more than sixty Alsatian refugees. They came from my father's country around Strasbourg, Bischwiller and Haguenau, and I listened with delight to their songs which reminded me of the old workmen in our mill.

Simone and her mother had arranged a Christmas tree for the children and had postponed the distribution of presents until my arrival. I found once more, not without emotion, the pink, blue and green candles, the tinsel and the gilded chestnuts of Pastor Roerich. As in the time of my childhood, the little Alsatians sang:

> Mon beau sapin, roi des forêts,
> Que j'aime ta verdu-re . . .[1]

A few weeks later I saw my son Gerald in uniform for the first time. He had just enlisted in the aviation, at nineteen, and promised to become, so his superiors wrote me, an excellent pilot, though something of a daredevil.

[1] Oh beautiful fir tree, king of the forests, how I love your greenery . . .

CHAPTER XXIII

Blitzkrieg

MANY war correspondents had, like me, visited the French provinces at Christmas and all were worried when they came back.

"The people want to know what the British are doing. A great many listen to the German radio. They must be answered by precise facts, not by mere words. Why not send us to England?" they said. "Why not show us the English effort, if it exists?"

Blaise Cendrars, a journalist and novelist of great talent whom the English adored because of his picturesque, piratical air, his missing arm, his brick red face, his military medal, talked of this project to the D.M.I. (Director of Military Intelligence). The D.M.I., General MacFarlane, was as picturesque and mysterious as he. He was thoroughly acquainted with the German Army, admired it and feared it. Constantly followed by an enormous bulldog, who lay down at his master's feet whenever the latter was talking, he used to come and deliver somberly humorous lectures to the correspondents, and his remarks were often prophetic. He thought the idea was excellent:

"I shall arrange the trip," he said.

And so some ten correspondents, whom I accompanied, crossed the Channel one sad January day on a darkened boat with all lights extinguished. Boulogne enshrouded in snow was sinister. On the other side we were welcomed at the dock by General Beith; it was my old friend Ian Hay of the preceding war, author of *The First Hundred Thousand*. He was now covered with red and gold and laden with honors and just as kindly and humorous as ever, but like myself he had lost his youth. In London the Ministry of Information gave us a huge motor coach and we began to travel all over England in the bitter cold. The method of training pilots, the manufacture of artillery and the building of airplanes seemed to us marvelously well organized. But all my journalist friends who were old soldiers themselves looked at one another sadly each evening:

"The terrifying thing," said the charming Lefèvre, "is that all this is only a sample . . . The materials are good, the methods intelligent, but the quantities are inadequate . . . There are no men, no tanks, no airplanes. Tell me, *mon Capitaine*, have we so much as once seen more than a thousand men in a single group?"

"Just once," I told him . . . "The Canadian Division."

"Yes, that's true. But it's the only case . . . As for tanks, they haven't even enough for purposes of instruction . . . Have you heard anyone talk about combined maneuvers—infantry, tanks and bombers? . . . Not a word! No, *mon Capitaine*, all this cannot be taken seriously. It is nice and well done, but when it is a question of stopping the most formidable war machine they are not ready . . . No more than we are."

My impression was the same. I tried to reassure myself by remembering that "the English lose all the battles except the last one," that they never really go to work until their backs are to the wall, that perhaps they were not showing us their large units. At the bottom of my heart I knew very well that the English effort, like ours, was tragically insufficient. I found once more the qualities that I had always loved in this country: a sense of humor, discipline and courage, but I saw no trace of that enthusiastic, desperate and fanatical state of mind which should have been called forth at such a moment in the face of such an enemy. Nevertheless, I had one consolation: that was the old chauffeur who drove our car. Over icy roads, through ditches filled with snow, plunged from four o'clock on in the opaque darkness of a blackout, this little white-haired man had no easy task. Twenty times I have seen him covered with mud, lost and numb. Never did he lose his courage:

"Don't you worry," he would say to us, "it will be all right in the end."

And in the end it always was all right as a result of tenacity, good humor and patience. I thought then that he was a picture of England; that she also would see herself more than once in the course of that war bogged down and apparently hopeless, and perhaps like him she would get out of her difficulties and end by leading us to the Inn of Victory.

On the boat that carried me from Southampton to Le Havre, and which took twenty-four hours to cross because it had to zig-zag to avoid submarines, I found Professor Langevin and a whole committee of French scientists who had just been conferring with English scientists about technical aspects of the war. From them I heard comforting news:

"What the English physicists have done since the beginning of this campaign," Langevin told me, "is splendid. They have worked out a procedure for detecting airplanes at a distance and a hundred other ingenious methods of defense . . . Just see how fast they have been in the matter of magnetic mines. In two weeks they analyzed the nature of the mines, found a way of countering them and suggested simple and inexpensive means of protecting their ships. There you have efficient work . . . For my own part I am doing research work on two or three fairly important matters . . ."

Talking to these scientists gave me keen pleasure. Deafened by propaganda I had become unused to this precise and detached way of thinking.

·   ·   ·   ·   ·   ·   ·

As soon as I returned to Arras, I was called upon by Captain Georges de Castellane who belonged to the General Staff of the First Army Group and who came on behalf of General Billotte to ask me to give lectures to all the armies of the group. The first was to be delivered at General Billotte's own Headquarters. I was well acquainted with the General, who had been Military Governor of Paris. He was a brusque and brilliant man, competent in every way to command the best of the French armies. Unfortunately he was destined to be killed in an automobile accident at the beginning of the German offensive.

"I'm going to send you around among my armies," he said. "Talk to them about the British Army and also about England in general . . . I myself know the English well; they are slow, terribly slow, but in the end they get things done . . . And then they hold on. That's what you must explain to the French."

Then began for me several strange and exciting weeks. Each morning a French military car would come to get me and take me to a new staff headquarters. I would have lunch with the general, and in the evening my lecture would be delivered before a gathering of two thousand officers, non-coms and soldiers. Thus I saw a large number of our leaders. With the First Army at Bohain I found General Blanchard, a smart and expert soldier, surrounded by enthusiastic officers who planned and replanned the entrance into Belgium in order to save a half hour on the time table. He sent me to see a military review held by General Bougrain and there I saw, with admiration, superb regiments. The motorized cavalry division, the bands, the flourish of trumpets, the brilliant flags, the perfection of the parade, all this gave the impression of a well disciplined group. In the following days I went to speak at General Altmayer's Headquarters at Valenciennes, to General Dame's, the youngest of our divisional commanders; then to General de La Laurencie, whom I had seen at Rouen just before the war and whose reasonable mind and courteous hospitality I enjoyed; to General Prioux and to General Janssen, who were both to become heroes of the defense of Dunkirk (General Janssen, a man of dry humor adored by his officers, met his death after giving the order: "Die where you stand").

It was hard in March 1940, while you were lunching and dining so gaily in the various messes, to imagine that danger was so close. Nevertheless some of the generals saw it and when you were alone with them talked about it with anguish:

"My men are bravery itself," one of them said to me, "but they can't stop tanks with their bare bodies. Unless they are given anti-tank guns I won't answer for what may happen."

In April I went on with my tour. I saw the brilliant General Fagalde, crackling with energy, and, with the Seventh Army, the one holding the left flank along the sea, General Giraud, who made a great impression on me. In physical aspect, in strength of character and in moral worth he seemed a leader after my own heart, a leader for the Lieutenant of my *Dialogues*, a leader for the heroes of Kipling. He was bitter about the inadequacy of our preparations.

"We shall not be ready before 1941," he said. "Do you know how many airplanes I have at my disposal, I, the Commander of an Army? Eight! . . . And how many flying officers for these eight planes? Thirty! . . . There's our aviation."

Despite this terrifying insufficiency of matériel, I took courage again when I saw men like General Giraud and Admiral Abrial, with whom I spent two days at Dunkirk. "No country," I said to myself, "can produce better leaders." It was true, but what can the greatest soldier do if he is completely crippled by total lack of armament?

About the lack of preparation on the part of the Allies, the most clear-sighted of the British commanders were in accord with General Giraud. Vice-Air-Marshal Blount, who was in command of the Component Air Force and whose melancholy distinction I admired, did not hide his anxiety:

"If we only had two hundred more bombers," he said, "I should feel a little more comfortable."

Paul Reynaud was now in power. For a long time I had admired his intelligence and his courage, but what could he do? He said himself that he had found a horrifying situation: no tanks, no airplanes. Raoul Dautry, Minister of Armaments, a stout-hearted man and a patriot, worked unremittingly, but one felt that he too was desperate.

"We shall begin to produce in 1941," Dautry said, "and we shall really be in full production in 1942. But what will happen before 1942?"

By nature I was so optimistic that these views expressed by well-informed men slid off my ill-founded confidence. Nevertheless at the end of April when I went to speak before the Ninth Army, Corap's Army, before Sedan, I experienced once more the feeling of anguish which the weakness of our fortified line in the North had given me. The number of troops seemed insufficient, the entrenchments mediocre.

But the officers were in good spirits and did not seem to have any grave anxieties.

I returned to Paris at the beginning of May, and had lunch at the home of Paul Reynaud in the Place du Palais-Bourbon. Huge maps painted on his walls took the place of wallpaper. As always Reynaud was brilliant, dynamic. But one felt he was nervous. He was in conflict with Daladier on the subject of General Gamelin. His friend Bullitt, Ambassador from the United States, came to dine with us at Neuilly and brought Laurence Steinhardt, Ambassador to Moscow, who was passing through Paris. Both said that America blamed us for not acting:

"You always leave the initiative to the enemy."

"Because the enemy can act without regard for international law . . . We are obliged to pay attention to public opinion and in particular to yours."

"Public opinion in our country," one of them said, "like all public opinion, is just waiting to be violated."

During this same leave in Paris I received a visit from Dorothy Thompson. She arrived from a tour of Europe, overwhelmed by the power of the Axis:

"All Eastern Europe," she said to me, "except Turkey, is in the hands of Germany."

To find so many intelligent men and women depressed and gloomy made me begin to lose my naïve and absurd peace of mind.

I was to spend the end of my leave in Périgord, and it had been agreed that we should start by car on the tenth of May. That morning before setting out I turned on the radio to listen to the news. I heard:

"*Monsieur Frossard, Minister of Information, is about to speak to you . . .*"

It was a bad sign; at that time our Ministers never spoke to us except to announce catastrophes or to ask for money.

"Last night," Frossard said, "the Germans invaded Belgium, Luxembourg and the Low Countries . . . All officers on leave must rejoin their units immediately . . ."

It was the great offensive, predicted long ago by General MacFarlane. I had to return at once to Arras. Simone came with me to the Gare du Nord. There were so many officers on the platform that the trains had to be first doubled, then tripled. My comrades seemed gay and confident:

At last, they said, "we shall have a chance to win this war . . ."

On that morning in a train full of military men I did not hear a single pessimistic comment.

Captain Grant was waiting for me on the station platform in Arras.

"We are leaving for Belgium," he told me.

"What direction?"

"Brussels, Louvain . . . The Dyle line . . . We're taking a correspondent with us: Lefèvre."

"An excellent choice!"

It was exciting to cross the Belgian frontier which we had looked at for so long from a distance. All along the route the British Army advanced in admirable order. The trucks were camouflaged with branches. Women and children along the road held out flowers to the soldiers. At the entrance to Brussels the columns moved off obliquely and swung around the city. Our car went straight in. To our great surprise when we stopped in front of the Hôtel Métropole we were surrounded by an immense crowd which cried: "Long live France! . . . Long live England! . . ." What was there in the presence of two gray-haired captains to warrant all this attention?

At the French Embassy, where I went to see Monsieur Bergeton, the mystery was explained. Brussels had been declared an open city. There was a prohibition against troops entering it, so that Grant and I were among the first men in Allied uniforms that the crowd had seen. Naturally we escaped in haste from this illicit and unearned glory and continued on our way toward the front. That evening our orders were to return to Lille. I spent part of the night there in the high tower of the *Echo du Nord* with Audra, Dean of the Faculty of Letters, and his wife, watching the bombardment of the suburbs. The German airplanes seemed to be everywhere, and high flames encircled the city.

Next day we returned to Belgium. Everything was changed. No more offerings of flowers. No more cheers. Women and old men on their doorsteps were looking in dread toward the sky.

"But what's the matter with them?" Lefèvre asked. "They look as though they had been *struck*."

They had in fact been *struck*. All along the road we found traces of German bombs. It was not especially terrible. Here two houses had been blown up, there a railroad had been wrecked, a little farther on a road had been blasted and a car reduced to fragments. But each village had had its bomb and that was enough to terrify the inhabitants. One little girl killed made all the mothers decide to take their children away. Very soon we saw the first refugees. I have described elsewhere these successive zones in which one encountered first the automobiles of the rich driven by impeccable chauffeurs; then the cars of the poor stuffed with provisions and made ungainly by mattresses tied over the roofs; then the villagers on bicycles, with the curé at their head; then the sad procession of those afoot followed by a few barefooted loafers. A whole country was in exodus and this human wave, when it reached a village or city, swept its population along with it.

Finally we reached the deserted region. Houses were closed, shutters barred; only the animals remained, barking or lowing. In the plain some factories and convents were burning, as red as stage fires. We were at the scene of the Battle of Waterloo. Leaving our car in the sunken road of Ohain we went on foot as far as the Dyle Line which the British Army was to hold. Aside from occasional artillery fire this line was quiet; but one asked oneself why we had left entrenchments that had been prepared with so much labor during a period of eight months in order to come out and await the German tanks in the open field.

Two more days passed, then I noticed grim faces among the Englishmen around me. I heard murmurs, reluctant phrases, and finally I learned of the rupture of the French Front at Sedan. After that our life followed a disordered and unintelligible course. We received orders to return in the direction of Arras. The roads were now so choked with refugees that we could only advance slowly. The approach to Arras was barred by barricades of sandbags. The Hôtel de l'Univers had been destroyed by a bomb. Part of the city had been burned. My friends Poumier and Puthomme of the "Capucins" were still energetic and gay. I went to bed in our house which was still intact, and all night I heard sirens and then the drone of German airplanes; this evoked in my mind the nights in Abbeville twenty-two years before and the wild cries of Childe Douglas.

On the sixteenth of May I wrote this letter to Simone:

> My dearest one, we are living through days of terrible anguish. One must be calm and hopeful. Whatever happens we love each other and that is indestructible. But we must foresee everything, the better as well as the worse. Here are my instructions for you:
>
> a) It is impossible for you to come here again. That is completely out of the question. Moreover I myself am ordered to leave.
>
> b) If things go well it is possible that I shall be sent to Paris in the course of next week, but naturally I shall have neither time nor means of letting you know in advance.
>
> c) If things clearly go worse I wish you to go to Essendiéras. I ardently hope that this will not be necessary, but I wish to have the assurance that you will be wise enough to make this essential retreat in time. Families are like armies; they can be saved by a prudent maneuver.
>
> Since the beginning of this hard period your wisdom and your tenderness have been my only reasons for continuing to live . . .

In the north unverifiable rumors circulated: "The Germans are in Cambrai!" And the French Mission decided to withdraw taking me with it. Then it was learned that the news was false and we returned to Arras. "The Germans are at Bapaume!" And Colonel Medlicott, who was now Chief of Public Relations, said to us:

"Reassemble at Amiens."

On the twentieth of May we found the city of Amiens overrun by refugees and stripped of its substance like a field ravaged by grasshoppers. No beds available. I rolled myself in a blanket. In the night Colonel Medlicott had me awakened:

"We are leaving for Boulogne," I was told by an English officer he had sent, "but two of our cars have been destroyed; we no longer have

room for you or the correspondents . . . The Germans are coming
. . . Return to Paris."

"And how?"

"By railroad."

"There are no more trains . . ."

"Then anyway you can . . ."

He disappeared into the night. There were a dozen of us Frenchmen
there, our baggage lost. We had no orders for transportation. Were we
going to be stupidly taken prisoner? We hurried to the station. It was
packed with refugees. An intelligent and kindly military commissioner
understood our situation:

"There's only one way I can get you away from here," he said.
"There is a baggage car full of gold I am sending to Paris. You can get
in it. Will that do?"

"Yes indeed!"

It was a nightmare trip. German airplanes followed us and tried to
destroy the tracks; we had nothing to eat. The engine proceeded at a
walking pace, and at each grade crossing we found again the sad, rose-
colored tide of refugees which spread out over the tracks and kept us
motionless for hours.

Finally after an interminable journey we arrived in Paris. We were
surprised to find the city little changed. The shock of defeat had been
so sudden and so violent that France, stunned into semi-consciousness
by the blow, had not yet understood what had happened to her. My wife
cried out when she saw me enter. Having had no news from me since
the sixteenth of May she thought I was missing, a prisoner. She told
me what was being said in Paris: Weygand now commanded our
armies, the public was optimistic, hoping for a Battle of the Marne.
Next morning I went to see my chief, Colonel Schiffer, and asked him
what I should do. It was no longer possible to join General Gort.
Couldn't I go to the Royal Air Force which had a base in the East?
He gave me his authorization for a few days and I left for Troyes.
There I found Vice-Air-Marshal Playfair and visited his squadrons.
The pilots were courageous, the planes excellent, but in the air as on
the ground we were overwhelmed by the numbers of the Germans. It

was at Troyes on the twenty-eighth of May in a café that I heard over the radio:

"Monsieur Paul Reynaud, Premier of France, is about to speak to you . . ."

"Here we go," said the man next to me, "another catastrophe!"

And, in fact, Reynaud sorrowfully announced the capitulation of the Belgian Army. I thought: "It's the end."

Returning to Paris, I went to report to Colonel Schiffer and found him with Captain Max Hermant of Weygand's General Staff.

"Why don't you go to London," the latter said to me, "and explain our situation to the English people?"

"I am under the orders of General Headquarters. I have already promised, at the request of our ambassador, to give a talk in London on the twenty-fifth of June; all that's necessary is to send me a little sooner."

"I will talk to Vincennes about it," he said.

On the third of June Paris was bombed by three hundred German airplanes. Despite the large number of dead and wounded this raid made little impression. On the fifth of June the second German offensive began against our new lines along the Somme and the Aisne. At first the news seemed fairly good. At the Ministry of Information it was said that "the line was holding," that the airplane cannon were doing wonders against the tanks and that "the enemy aviation seemed out of breath." But on the evening of the eighth the communiqué was execrable. There began to be talk of Forges-les-Eaux, of the region around Rouen. Would we have to submit to the Germans' entrance into Paris? And would the city be defended? There were already a number of signs indicating that the government was thinking of withdrawing. In front of the Ministry of the Navy and in the courtyard of the Ministry of War trucks were being loaded with the archives.

"The heavy elements are being evacuated," was the noncommittal explanation at the offices.

On Sunday the ninth Colonel Schiffer told me that Captain Hermant had telephoned from General Headquarters that I was to leave immediately for London. He gave me an order, with which I was to secure a place in an English military plane. I went to see the British Air Attaché and he said to me:

"Be at the Buc Airdrome tomorrow at noon."

Would it still be possible at noon on the tenth of June to get to Buc? I began to doubt it. Already it was said that German motorized divisions had reached Vernon, Mantes . . . Tanks had been seen at Isle-Adam. That was in the suburbs of Paris. I begged Simone to leave for Essendiéras with my son Gerald, who had not yet recovered from an appendix operation he had recently undergone at the American Hospital in Neuilly.

"If the Germans, after crossing the Seine, cut the roads to Chartres and Orléans, you will be a prisoner."

"I am not afraid," she said.

"That's all very well for you, but what about the others? . . . There is Gerald who is a soldier and ill and whose incision has not yet healed . . . Emilie whose husband is in the army . . . When the city is taken if you are here, you will have no way of communicating with me and we may be without word of each other for months."

Finally she consented. We spent our last evening sorting out the things she should take with her. She had so little space and we had so many souvenirs we wanted to keep safe that the choice was distressing. From time to time we listened to the radio:

"The enemy is showing less initiative," said the communiqué. *"We are detaining him at many points."*

But the names of the places mentioned proved that the tide was still rising.

Very early next morning we decided to go and say good-by to our favorite places in Paris. My wife drove her little white car. The weather was glorious and a sunny, golden mist enveloped the city. In the empty streets traffic policemen, faithful to their duty, stopped the infrequent cars with touching conscientiousness. I needed a raincoat and a suitcase. We went into several stores. The saleswomen were attending to their duties carefully and courteously as usual. Many of them had red eyes from having wept all night, but with one accord they kept silent about what was in the minds of all. Then we went to the Invalides, and from there along the quais as far as Notre Dame and the Ile Sainte-Louis. We returned by the Place des Vosges. Since the roads were filled with refugees it was high time to start for Buc. From the balcony of the apartment in Neuilly, which we had loved so much, we looked for a last time together at the trees of the Bois de Boulogne, the Arc de Triomphe and Mont Valérien crowned with its Italian cypresses. Then we embraced. We did not know whether we should ever see each other again.

"These fifteen years have been wonderful," my wife said.

She remained standing beneath the horsechestnut trees of the Boulevard Maurice Barrès until my car had disappeared.

. . . .

To my great surprise I reached the Buc Airdrome without difficulty. The myriads of cars that were leaving Paris that day were heading toward the south, not toward the west. At the entrance to the field a sergeant of the military police painstakingly verified my identity.

"The Germans are within thirty kilometers, *mon Capitaine*," he said.

That wasn't far, but he was calm and, like the little saleswomen in Paris, he was performing his duty to the last moment. The airplane which was to take me had not yet arrived. I sat down on the grass and waited. The heat was stormy and oppressive. I went to sleep and dreamed of my childhood, of the forked lilacs of Elbeuf and of the white and pink anemones that faded in my hands. A noise awakened me. It was a big Flamingo plane landing. Lord Lloyd got out. I knew him and went up to shake hands.

"I've come to see Reynaud," he said. "Is he still in Paris?"

"Yes, I think so . . ."

It was his fine plane in which I was to fly; but when the pilot tried to start it one of the motors refused to run. After twenty attempts the young flier said angrily:

"And that's how we're winning the war!"

At that moment another Flamingo arrived—a much less elegant machine, but it ran—and I was told to get in.

CHAPTER XXIV

The Tarpeian Rock

But break, my heart, for I must hold my tongue.
SHAKESPEARE

IN THE plane that was taking me to England, seated on the metal hull and watching the clouds and waves flee by below me, I summed up the situation. It was frightful. France had been defeated and it seemed impossible, unless America and England were in a position to furnish her with aid in immense quantities immediately, that she would be able to continue fighting. A foreign army then was going to occupy our country. My wife and children were still there; I was going to find myself separated from those I loved. All the ideas and all the sentiments that were dear to me: liberty, honesty of judgment, impartiality, generosity and charity were going into a period of eclipse and the defeat, interpreted by enemy propaganda, could not fail to set loose evil passions. A world was coming, in which I no longer saw any place for myself. "If this airplane," I thought, "were to fall into the Channel it would do me a proud service."

This moral depression was brief, and as soon as I saw a way in which I could be useful I recovered my will to live. From the Hendon Airport, where I had landed, I had myself driven to the French Military Mission which was under the command of General Lelong. He received me cordially, inspected my traveling commission and sent me to Captain Brett who took me to the Ministry of Information. There I found Charles Peake of the Foreign Office whom I knew.

"You want to explain the situation of France to the English public?" he said to me. "You come at exactly the right moment. There is a press conference beginning in five minutes. You will talk to all our correspondents."

I protested: taken unaware I had nothing prepared and to improvise on such a subject . . . But Brett, Peake and Sir Walter Monckton who had joined us dragged me onto the platform, and in torn, breathless and burning phrases I described the martyrdom of France:

"It is not in 1941 that you must help us, it is not next month, it is not tomorrow, it is today, it is this hour, it is this minute . . ."

When I had finished, to my great surprise the three hundred journalists stood up and applauded for a long time.

"You should be pleased," said Harold Nicolson, who was Duff Cooper's assistant at the Ministry. "You stirred up those hard-boiled boys of the press."

"But why? . . . I only said, very badly, what everyone knows."

"Don't you believe it," he told me. "Our people are far from understanding the gravity of the situation. You must repeat these things on the radio for the whole English public, then for the Dominions, then for America . . ."

Thus began a week during which I talked on the B.B.C. two or three times a day and sometimes in the night until two A.M. I was dead tired, but I received hundreds of touching letters and visits. Hence there rose in my mind natural but naïve illusions about the efficacy of my mission. As a matter of fact, though the masses of the people were filled with good will, the means of helping us were nil. The divisions that had returned from Dunkirk had left their equipment in Flanders. Not only tanks, but artillery and even rifles, were lacking. "There was not a single division," Lord Gort was to write later, "in condition to fight." It was pitiful and terrifying.

One morning Sir Walter Monckton called me on the telephone and told me the Queen wished to see me at Buckingham Palace. I presented myself there immediately and Sir Alexander Hardinge introduced me into the private apartments. The Queen was infinitely gracious and compassionate. She told me that she intended, that very evening, to address by radio the women of France and to tell them, not as a

Queen, but as a woman speaking to other women, the share she took in their sufferings. In that interview with her at that moment and in a setting I had so often described apropos of Queen Victoria and of King Edward VII, there was something unreal and enchanting that moved me profoundly.

However at the moment when the footmen, dressed in red livery embroidered in gold, showed me into the drawing-rooms of Buckingham Palace, my entire wardrobe consisted of a uniform and two shirts; my entire fortune of a few francs. At the beginning of the war I had had all the money due me in England and America sent to France so that I no longer had any credits abroad. The news from France became worse and worse. From the fifteenth to the seventeenth of June I went to spend the weekend at Marlborough, the home of my friends the Phipps. There I found, as always, the most affectionate loyalty, but when on Monday the seventeenth the radio announced that an armistice had been asked for I shut myself in my room, threw myself on my bed and wept like a child.

At this moment the British reaction was far from hostile to unhappy France. The Phipps expressed their heartfelt sympathy. When I returned to London Lord Winterton, Lady Diana Duff Cooper, Harold Nicolson, the Amerys, Desmond MacCarthy and Raymond Mortimer all were admirable in their kindness and tact. Since I was still wearing uniform, strangers would stop me on the street to express their sympathy. But doubt gave birth to constraint.

"And the fleet?" people would ask me anxiously.

What could I reply? I knew nothing. Then began an exchange of bitter and hostile communications between London and Bordeaux. I was deeply disturbed by that war of words, which seemed to me devoid both of dignity and discretion. There was nothing vainer or more dangerous for the two countries than recrimination after a defeat for which they had been jointly responsible. To whom could their discussions be helpful except to those whose whole propaganda had been calculated to produce just such a break? I understood very well that England had been painfully surprised by some of the clauses of the Armistice. So was I. But did not France too have numerous causes of resentment? Was it not, therefore, the part of wisdom to cancel out these equal and opposite grievances? The only attitudes that seemed to me proper in our sweeping and common misfortunes were, on the part of England, the affectionate deference of a warrior for the wounded comrade he must leave behind; and, on the part of France, the sorrow of a soldier disarmed, the mute despair and the silent exhortation to his happier fellows who can continue the strife.

Charles Corbin, the French Ambassador to London, and Roger Cambon, Counsellor of the Embassy, both tried and true friends of Great Britain, shared my feelings on this subject. But the passions on either side carried the day against justice and common sense. For me the situation was agonizing. I have written elsewhere that I was at that time "like a child whose parents are getting a divorce"; it would be more exact to say: like a victim of torture who is torn apart by horses. At no other moment in my life have I suffered such conflict and torment of mind. For twenty-five years I had been studying England and I had grown attached to its traditions. I was not unaware of its political mistakes; I had frankly spoken of them in time of peace; but I knew its courage, its tenacity; I believed that its victory would assure the future freedom of France. I still ardently hoped that the two peoples would one day find themselves united, but I had, alas, an agonizing presentiment that before this came about there might be—and that before long—distressing and perhaps sanguinary quarrels.

I had promised in the preceding year to deliver the Lowell Lectures in Boston in October 1940. And it had been agreed in Paris with the Ministry of Foreign Affairs that even if the war were not over, I was not on any account to miss this important engagement. And so I had among my papers a letter giving me permission to go to Boston, but it did not provide for my departure until the month of September. Did I have the legal right, on the strength of this official letter, to go to America in July? I consulted the Marquis de Castellane, Chargé d'Affaires at the French Embassy since the resignations of Corbin and Cambon. He said:

"There is no reason at all to hesitate . . . Since you have permission to go to the United States, go there . . . And go at once."

He gave me a French diplomatic visa. With the letters from the Lowell Institute I had no difficulty with my American visa.

Before leaving I went to say good-by to Maurice Baring, who was living at Rottingdean near Brighton, and who was very ill. Lady Phipps and her son Allan, a naval officer temporarily on sick leave, accompanied me. Maurice, suffering from paralysis agitans, trembled so violently that his whole bed was shaken. On his shoulder perched a bright-feathered parrakeet. The trembling, which shook the bird, blended the colors and produced a confused and iridescent image. Like Alain and Bergson, Baring's mind was intact. As was his custom, he talked on graceful, poetic and frivolous themes and ended suddenly on a profound, religious thought. We left him after a short time in order not to tire him, and while waiting for train time all three of us went for a walk on the seashore. Everywhere soldiers were at work erecting barbed wire entanglements and constructing casemates. A few more weeks of respite and England would be ready to repel an invasion. The monotonous sound of the pebbles rolled by the waves calmed me. How many men and women would still come to this beach to the end of the centuries, and for them our frightful adventure would be only a cold page of history!

. . . .

My boat, the *Monarch of Bermuda*, left from Glasgow. In *Tragedy in France* I have described that sunny crossing, the deck covered with children, the destroyers that accompanied us and my small cabin-mate Adrian Van Millingen. He was only seven or eight years old but he had the courage and the deportment of a man. In my book I described him without giving his name or that of the boat. Nevertheless his family recognized him and wrote to me. At the end of ten days we arrived in Halifax. There I learned first from a Canadian newspaper man, and later from a telegram, that my wife was waiting for me in Montreal. Since our separation in Neuilly we had had no letters from each other. Nevertheless we had written, and it is a curious fact that two letters written on the same day (the fourteenth of June 1940), one by me in London, the other by Simone in Périgord, reached us on the same day in New York, three months late. Mine recounted what I have told at the beginning of this chapter. Here is a fragment of my wife's:

My dearest, I am addressing this letter to the French Embassy and I hope that they will forward it to you. Where are you? What has become of you? When shall I see you again? . . . Since our separation on Monday I have been ceaselessly posing these questions.

I left Neuilly at the wheel of the car, with the cook in tears beside me. By the end of the day I had received my baptism of fire, for the procession of refugees crawling south from Paris at twenty miles an hour was flown over by slow planes coming very low. The section where I was received no bombs; there was simply machine gun fire on the road near Dourdan. After that I went through the forest of Vierzon without headlights with my little "passive defense" lamps, through pitch blackness to the rhythm of the cook's sobs. By a miracle I found Gerald in Vierzon. There we waited in the street for dawn and got under way again between three and four o'clock in the morning. I mustn't complain since I have saved my life, our son and the family archives, and since I have taken only two days and one night to get to Essendiéras.

Excideuil, Saint-Médard and Hautefort are overflowing with refugees; the house is full. There are friends here and a crowd of strangers. Maman and Madame Menicot have succeeded in lodging 127 people, making the most of both houses, the stables and even the sheep folds. To feed these poor exhausted people we have had to kill all the chickens in the poultry yard.

André, my dear, we are very unhappy. But there remains one steadfast hope; our country cannot die. France is immortal and she has a persevering and unshakeable ally. . . . We too have something that even defeat cannot take from us: an immense love, beautiful memories, a long past of affection and trust. If the war reduces us to poverty, we will start again from zero. We will attempt to remake our lives. You will be a professor of literature somewhere in the United States and I will be a stenographer . . .

A few days later she wrote me again, this time from Madrid. The Armistice was about to be signed. Rightly thinking that I would be demobilized and would then go to Boston to give the Lowell Lectures as I had promised, my wife was determined to try, she wrote, to make her way to the United States in order to rejoin me there or to wait for me. I had not received either of these letters, but happily our decisions coincided. It is easy to imagine my joy in finding her on the station platform at Montreal. From Canada we went at once to the United States. During the trip Simone gave me a surprise. I had some notes to prepare in English. She said to me:

"You can dictate them to me."

"But you don't know English shorthand."

"Yes, I do . . . I have learned it during the war."

This new accomplishment was to be of great service to us in the United States.

To find ourselves once more in New York sadly evoked the shining memories of the preceding year. To our personal suffering was added the distress of finding public opinion in large part hostile to France. Not only was our unhappy country occupied, despoiled and humiliated, but it was slandered as well. With sorrow and surprise we became aware of the development of a campaign, highly suspect in origin, that charged our soldiers with not having defended themselves. I, however, had seen our armies and our leaders; I knew their faults, but also their virtues; I knew the fault had been not a lack of courage but a lack of preparation, and if one were looking for those responsible they were to be found in England and in America as well as in France.

Hence came the idea that I ought to write with as much exactitude as possible what I had seen in this war and reveal what, in my opinion, had been the causes of the disaster. In haste I wrote a number of articles which were subsequently collected in a volume under the title of *Tragedy in France*. It was the month of August 1940. New York was submerged beneath a wave of humid heat and in order to work I had to stay between two electric fans. When the articles were published I received many moving letters.

"At last we can hold our heads up," wrote the sailors from a French boat interned in the harbor of New York.

"I wept a great deal while reading your book," said a little French dressmaker, "but you have restored my pride."

As for the British readers, all those who knew the facts considered that I had been fair in what I said about the relations between the two countries. One of the English writers, for whom I have the highest esteem, wrote me: "What a good book, if I may say so! . . . A fair minded, fine minded, charitable and essentially healing book . . ." I take the liberty of quoting this one from among many letters because later on an attempt was made, for unworthy reasons, to distort the meaning of the book. General Gort's report a year later should serve to prove both the exactitude and moderation of my account.

Following this publication the Dutch Treat Club, an important group of journalists and editors, asked me to come and talk to them about the lessons of the war. Frank Crowninshield introduced me and I gave a brief address that ended thus:

> France, today, is stunned by the blow. But her soul has not changed. How could France change? Do you believe that a conqueror could deprive French men of their culture? How could he do it? Even if he burnt all the books, the French women, who know by heart the most beautiful texts of French literature, would teach them to their children. Do you believe that a conqueror can deprive our young men of their patriotism and military virtues? No. We had been spoiled and softened by victory. They shall be braced and hardened by disaster. These young lieutenants of the Maginot Line, these young pilots of the French Air Force, so brave so keen, and who were never given a chance to show their mettle you will see what a generation they will build for France. You will see that the old tree will, one day, blossom again.
>
> Sometimes, in the cellar of a French château, one finds a French masterpiece that the centuries have covered with dust and smoke It is so black that you can hardly tell what it represents. But clear it, restore it, and you will discover soft, clear tones, a witty smile a lovely eighteenth century face. France, to me, is such a master piece. At present we cannot very well see her. She is covered with

the smoke of bitterness and the dust of misery. You do not understand what she does, why she does it. Very often, I do not understand it myself. But I do not need to understand. I *know* that, one day, we shall clean this beloved canvas and gaze once more, with loving hearts and glad hearts, on the beauty, on the glory, and the wisdom, that was, and will be France.

After that I was asked to talk at the Harvard Club, at Columbia University, at Town Hall, at twenty other places. This activity was useful in helping me to bear the anguish we suffered over the news from France. Oh, but it was hard to substitute for the picture of the proud, rich country we knew this picture of misery and weakness! Soon under pressure from the invader racial laws were promulgated. They struck Frenchmen of long standing, excellent citizens, combatants in two wars. For me they posed a painful problem of conscience.

"Don't go on," the cynics advised me, "being the champion of France. What has she to offer you in the future? A life of humiliation and poverty. Make a conspicuous break. That will earn you profitable popularity here. And there's no risk at all! If the war turns out well you will return home in triumph; if it turns out badly, you still have America and the Dominions which are practically invulnerable. A child could see where your interests lie."

Unfortunately one's duty is rarely to be found in the same camp with one's interest. My duty, it seemed to me, was to serve unhappy France to the extreme limit of possibility without asking anything in return. I determined in my speeches to defend, not of course what seemed to me indefensible, but French culture, the memory of our dead, the honor of our army and above all the French children and the French prisoners who had such great need of aid from America.

Then for several weeks I lived in a state of despair and exultation. France bound in chains became for me the captive Andromeda whom as a boy I had so often longed to love and to rescue. Alas! the opportunity to prove that personal grievances would not weaken my fidelity was not long in coming. A despatch published in the American newspapers informed me that our old mill in Elbeuf was to be taken away from us. My first thought on reading this news was: "And so, if my father were still alive they would have dared to say to him, to the man who together with his family had *made* this firm and had run the greatest risks to keep it French, that he was unworthy to direct it!" Then I asked myself in bitter sadness if the new management would pull down from the wall beside the gate the black marble tablet:

DIED FOR FRANCE:

CAPTAIN PIERRE HERZOG

Chevalier of the Legion of Honor, Croix de Guerre.

LIEUTENANT ANDRÉ FRAENCKEL

Chevalier of the Legion of Honor, Croix de Guerre.

That evening an American newspaper man asked me for an interview about this spoliation:

"It will do you good!" he said. "You can tell me what's in your heart."

"I have something in my heart," I told him, "but it is not anything against France . . . I know that as soon as she can she will recognize her own."

CHAPTER XXV

Amica America

T HE object of my trip to America was, as I have said, to deliver the Lowell Lectures at Boston. Perhaps some of my readers may not know what this institution is. John Lowell, Jr., a member of the illustrious Lowell family, died in 1836 leaving a large sum to endow the Lowell Institute, an organization for liberal higher education. Each year writers and scholars are invited to give free public lectures. Lawrence Lowell, then president of the Institute, had asked me to speak there in French. When he wrote me in 1939 he had in mind a series of literary lectures, but when I arrived in New York he advised me to tell of my experiences in the war. In Boston I found to my great surprise a loyal audience, for these lectures in a foreign language, of from four to five hundred people. Some were Frenchmen, professors or musicians from the Boston Symphony Orchestra; others were students from Harvard, others again Canadians, Belgians, Swiss and also numerous English people.

My host, Mr. Lowell, former president of Harvard University, was eighty-five years old and possessed of amazing youthfulness of spirit. One day when I had said that the United States was slow in preparing and that it ought to make a total effort, not tomorrow, but today:

"I don't agree with you," he said.

I asked in surprise:

"And when do you think the United States should make this effort?"

"Yesterday," said Mr. Lowell.

He took me to the Saturday Luncheon Club to which Oliver Wendell Holmes and other illustrious Bostonians had belonged. On the day I was invited the members were celebrating the eightieth birthday of Bliss Perry, former professor at Princeton, Harvard and the Sorbonne; and one of those present, Professor Rand, at the time when the toasts were proposed, improvised a fine speech in Latin, which showed me that the city of Boston was unlike any other in the United States.

Just as it was, I loved it. I loved its narrow streets, its houses, its English squares, the ancient rooms where American liberty was born, the beautiful Capitol with its gilded dome, and the snow-covered Commons. I loved to argue with certain of the Harvard students who were intelligent but partisan; and who, when I preached national unity in time of danger, would reply with asperity:

"Isn't it always the poor people, and the poor people alone, who are asked to sacrifice their rights in the interests of the nation?"

I loved the schools around Boston; Andover, where I found leading the French Club the daughter and son-in-law of my old friend Alma Clayburgh; St. Paul's, Exeter, Groton, close relatives to Eton and Harrow. I loved the Bostonians who were modest in their way of life and proud in their way of thought, thrifty and very rich; they reminded me both of John Marquand's characters and of the manufacturers of Lyons. Thus mingling work and social life, I spent two useful and stimulating months.

I returned to New York at the time of the presidential election. I was anxious to observe the reactions of the crowd at the moment when a decision was being made on which depended the policy of the country during a crucial period. I was surprised by everybody's calmness. As soon as the first returns raced around the cornice of the Times Building the final result was certain. But the people around us, whatever their party, joked gaily. Next morning I took a taxi and the chauffeur turned around toward me:

"You have seen this election," he said . . . "Fifty-five per cent of the country is for Roosevelt; forty-five per cent for Willkie . . . What does that prove? That we are about evenly divided, that it is not possible to govern against the will of forty-five per cent of the population and that we shall have to meet each other half way."

His good sense impressed me. When I saw that this attitude was fairly general I realized that American Democracy was healthier than French Democracy had been. I was confirmed in this belief when I heard Willkie's speech on the role of the loyal opposition.

Simone and I spent New Year's 1941 alone in a hotel room. American friends had invited us to a supper party, but the news we received from France was so sad that any gaiety distressed us. When the twelve strokes of midnight sounded the radio brought us the joyous uproar of Broadway. We thought of Essendiéras and of what sadness must be there on this first New Year's after the defeat. Where now were the little Alsatians who had sung the *Marseillaise* on New Year's Day 1940? . . . A little later renewed cheering came over the radio; a jazz band joined in; it was midnight in St. Louis, Missouri . . . What were they thinking about France in St. Louis, Missouri? . . . I was soon to know, for I had promised to go there to give a lecture. It seemed that the relations between the two countries were a little better. An Ambassador, Admiral Leahy, had just been sent to France by the President, and *Life* had asked me to write an article to explain this decision . . . We talked about our children, our friends and my mother for whom life must be so hard . . . Finally a new burst of laughter and songs announced that the twelve strokes of midnight were ringing out in San Francisco. All America had now entered upon the year 1941.

. . . .

My lecture tour took me to the four corners of the United States. I traveled a great deal by air. In my childhood I had enthusiastically read and reread a book by Robida, *The Electric Life*, in which aerial liners were described. At that time this seemed to be the maddest and most extreme of dreams. Now the classic waiting rooms at the airports with their baggage scales, loud speakers, flood lights in front and recreation rooms for the pilots seemed to me as familiar and matter-of-fact as the station at Elbeuf had been. I flew mostly at night above a black abyss which was brightened from time to time by enchanted cities and the blue and red jewels of signal lights.

I spoke at Charlotte, at Palm Beach, at Atlanta where I had luncheon beside a modest young woman with eyeglasses, who said to me toward the end of the meal:

"You know, I write too . . ."

"And what have you written?" I asked with polite condescension.

"I have written a novel."

"Oh, indeed . . . And what is the title?"

"Gone with the Wind," she said softly.

I spoke in Texas at Houston, Austin and Fort Worth; then in Louisiana at New Orleans. I spoke in Los Angeles and in San Francisco, in Omaha (Nebraska) and in Denver (Colorado), in Cincinnati and in Baltimore. Sometimes after a lecture the French people of the city would ask me to say a few words to them. I preached unity:

"You tell me that you are divided by your opinions and nevertheless when I talk to each of you separately I find that all of you have only one opinion: that is, love of France. What France? *The* France. There is only one. The physical, spiritual, living France; the France of the villages and the cities; the France of Chartres and Amiens; the France of Fleurus and of Valmy, of Verdun and of the Marne; the France of Voltaire and of Péguy, of Pascal and of Valéry. Do not forget that if this France at present is defeated and in bondage, it is because of our past quarrels. Do not compromise her deliverance by our present quarrels. You may be of divided opinion about the means of obtaining your objective, but you are agreed upon the objective, which is the liberation of our country. Strive then to be united and do not hate any Frenchman who is of good faith; in our mother's house there are many mansions."

I spent the month of February at Knox College in Illinois and returned full of esteem for the good sense of the students and professors in the Middle West. In the traditions and customs of Knox there was something robust and healthy that seemed to me invaluable for America.

"Where do you get your ideas about life, death, morals and what you may and may not do?" I asked twenty members of a fraternity who were sitting around me on the floor or on the arms of easy chairs . . . "Do they come from books, from the courses you take, or from the sermons of some minister?"

"No," one of them said. "They come from our families."

"Do your father and mother talk to you about these things?"

"Very seldom, but without talking about them they give us their example."

"Yes," another broke in, "we are all formed by our homes."

In the Eastern universities I had noticed in the case of certain young people an attitude of rebellion toward their family backgrounds. At Knox there was nothing of the sort. They said:

"I am a little more liberal than my parents or a little more radical but our fundamental beliefs are the same."

Then came the questions about the war:

"Briefly, what was the cause of the French disaster?"

"Lack of preparation, lack of troops, lack of national unity. Our soldiers had neither the necessary planes, nor tanks, nor artillery. We realized the danger too late. But one must add that the responsibility of England and of America is equal to that of France."

"Equal, sir? After all, England and America are going on fighting, while France ——"

"England is going on fighting with a courage I admire, but all the same she is protected by the Channel and America by the ocean. Imagine Illinois or Sussex lying between Loire and Garonne; they would have been occupied in July 1940."

"When you talk about American responsibility, just what do you mean?"

"I mean that America, by refusing to ratify the guarantee of the League of Nations, rendered this new war possible, even probable. The Treaty of Versailles was not a very pretty baby, but it was a baby that your country presented to Europe. You laid it on the door-step and resumed your bachelor life. Today the abandoned child has grown up and since it was badly raised it is giving you trouble. That's natural: after all the poor boy never knew his father . . ."

My young students at Knox had honest minds. They admitted the facts:

"Agreed . . . Our refusal to enter the League of Nations was a dreadful mistake . . ."

"And also your refusal a few months before this war to abrogate the Neutrality Act . . ."

"Agreed . . ."

.   .   .   .

In March and April I lived in Buffalo where I had been invited to give a course in French Literature at the University. In New York people said to me:

"You won't like Buffalo. The climate is very harsh. They have only two seasons there: winter and the month of August . . . And it is principally a manufacturing city."

As a matter of fact I did like Buffalo. No city in the world has more beautiful trees. Along the wide avenues they form leafy Gothic vaults. The sea of foliage I saw from my window reminded me of our house in Neuilly and the green waves of the Bois. Even the cemetery had the charm of a park. The graves were arranged in judicious disorder on the sides of wooded hills that were decorated here and there by beds of pink or pale yellow flowers. On the pond haughty swans tacked nonchalantly on white wings. Wandering through this beautiful scene amid the shadows with some fair stranger, I sometimes felt that I myself was a shade or, as Lord Beaconsfield said, "dead but in the Elysian Fields."

But it was not only the city that delighted me. Among its inhabitants I found friends after my own heart. Dean Julian Park, many of the professors, the French people of the neighborhood, and of course the students, formed an audience for my lectures which to my great joy grew larger day by day. What culture there was in this little group and what good will! When the accounts of cruelty in the letters from Europe made me despair for the future of humanity, I used to think with hope of these numerous American communities where true values are still honored and which in a world gone mad still cherish Christian civilization.

Unhappily during all this spring of 1941 the relations between

France and the United States were once more growing worse. Our
unfortunate country was accused of a thousand faults. Ill-informed as
I was, I could hardly distinguish the true from the false. But when
facts are lacking, "loyalty is the light of the spirit." I determined not
to judge a case in which I did not have the essential evidence, and to
continue to talk to Americans about the enduring virtues of France
rather than about her ephemeral errors. The Red Cross and the
Quakers needed money for our prisoners and our children. I gave
lectures for their benefit in Buffalo, then in Baltimore, Washington,
San Francisco and New York. All life is a surprise. However en-
venomed the political atmosphere might be, our meetings were stirring, our halls full, our prisoners and our children received aid.

.   .   .   .

The time had come to fulfill another engagement I had undertaken: to participate in the summer session at Mills College in California. We crossed the continent by plane. There is nothing more
astonishing than the immense desert that separates the Middle West
from the Far West. Seeing these stretches of arid ground, gray and
cracked like the hide of an old elephant, stretching as far as the eye
could reach, we admired the pioneers who had crossed this country
on foot or in their poor covered wagons. The ascent to 12,000 feet in
order to cross the Rocky Mountains made us gasp for breath but the
descent at Reno, the rich and verdant oasis of divorce, and that over
San Francisco Bay, the most beautiful of landscapes with its globular
islands bald and volcanic that rose from the blue water, repaid us
for our mountain sickness.

"Here," I said to my wife, "is the Promised Land . . ."

It was even more true than I had thought. To me California remains the land of happiness. It is not overpopulated; it is fertile; it
has the most constant and most healthful climate on the planet. It has
beauty like that of Greece, sweetness like that of France, picturesque-
ness like that of Spain and vastness like that of Africa. Perhaps the
East is more lively; the Middle West more energetic; but California is
wiser. The citizen there is still not far removed from the pioneer.

I spent two days near San Francisco at Bohemian Grove, a part of a forest of giant trees where 1,500 business men, artists and professors from San Francisco and elsewhere spend two weeks in the open air, sleeping in tents and eating together. I was enchanted by the beauty of the spectacle which evoked the youth of the world. In the central clearing a huge log fire blazed and the flames rose to half the height of the great trees. On a platform on the side of a fern-covered hill Lauritz Melchior sang and Irvin Cobb told stories. I was thrust under the spotlights:

"Tell us about France!"

I did my best. The trees that surrounded me, I was told, were standing there when Christopher Columbus landed.

.   .   .   .

At the beginning of this book I described Mills College. I had men and women students many of whom were teachers of French. In their company, for the space of two months, I lived in a beautiful dream. Together we read great books; the Budapest Quartet played Beethoven for us in the evenings; Darius Milhaud taught music, Fernand Léger taught painting; Madeleine Milhaud phonetics; René Bellé poetry, all with ardor and ability. This "Maison Française" was an old tradition at Mills College and, together with Middlebury, it was one of the centers of French studies in the United States. At the time of the disaster it was feared that it might be swept away by the debacle. Then President Reinhardt and Mademoiselle Cécile Réau had the courage to retain the session. We knew that upon our success depended the future of the institution. And so the teachers worked with an enthusiasm that attested their common desire to inspire, in these bad times more than ever, a love for our culture.

More even than at Princeton I felt the joy of following one of the callings for which I was born: that of teacher. Often I would take my seat on the benches and send a girl to the blackboard and we would together construct the outline of a thesis. It seemed to me that this work of construction was one of the most urgent needs of these American minds, full of freshness and poetry, but unaccustomed to an orderly discipline of ideas.

On the evening of July Fourteenth the students met in the hall and asked me to say a few words to them. I chose as text a beautiful passage from Romain Rolland which one of them had quoted to me the day before: "How is it permissible to slander a people who for more than ten centuries have been active and creative? . . . A people who have passed twenty times through the ordeal of fire and have emerged tempered by it . . . A people who without ever dying have been restored to life twenty times . . ." Madeleine Milhaud read poems by writers who had died in one or the other of the wars. There was a few minutes' silence and then we parted.

The heart accustoms itself too quickly to peace. I had already grown used to thinking happily, when I awoke in the morning, of the pretty, attentive faces I was about to see and of the emotions that would be communicated to them by this sentence of Stendhal or that letter by Flaubert. When the day of "the last class" arrived I remembered the time in my childhood when Kittel had wept as he read us Daudet's story. If I had not lectured myself, I might well have wept too as I reflected that this little group, now united by so much affection and so many common enthusiasms, was about to dissolve forever.

CHAPTER XXVI

The Kingdom of God

The Kingdom of God is within you.
LUKE xvii : 20

I AM finishing this book high up in a tower overlooking Manhattan. This morning in the violet haze of dawn I seem to see an Italian city at my feet, bristling with churches and fortresses. In the distance the blue lake in Central Park, surrounded by pale foliage and wrapped in mist, recalls those tiny scenes almost lost in luminous confusion in the background of the paintings of the Primitives. Innumerable cars, yellow, gray and black, glide by even at this early hour, obediently following, on the checker board of the streets, their precise ballet to the rhythm of the red and green lights. The pedestrians, seen from above, are no more than dark or brighter spots. Isolated on this peak I sometimes have the illusion of escaping like a lonely hermit on his column from the vanity and uproar of the city. These heights are favorable to contemplation. Let us take our bearings.

"Here below we are like spectators in a theater," wrote Chateaubriand, "if we turn our heads away for a moment, a whistle shrills, the enchanted palaces vanish and when we bring our eyes back to the stage we find nothing but deserts and unfamiliar actors . . ." For a long time on the stage of my own life I had seen a familiar setting which I thought was permanent. "A view that cannot be taken away," the architect had said when I bought my house in Neuilly. In this setting of the Bois, of Paris, of France, players whose lines and ability I knew had been enacting for twenty years a drama whose vicissitudes and dénouement I believed I had foreseen. The whistle of Destiny shrills. The view that "could not be taken away" disappears. The Bois de Boulogne ascends into the flies; the Arc de Triomphe fades; the scene shifters bestir themselves in the shadows. When the footlights come up again the spectator discovers a backdrop that represents Rockefeller Center, the Empire State building, and on the stage are characters that had no part in the preceding scene and who do not even speak the same language.

"My life is like a story from *The Thousand and One Nights,*" I said to myself during my days of good fortune, "in which the magician comes to seek a cobbler in his workshop and make him a caliph. My life," I said, "is a fairy tale. One morning I am living in a sorry province admiring from a distance great men whom I despair of ever meeting; that evening I have left my sorry province and those whom I idolized without hope have become my friends." I forgot that often in *The Thousand and One Nights,* on the last page, the magician turns the caliph back into a cobbler again. This also is the ending of the strange story that I call my life . . . Friends, fortune, honors, home, I have had them all, lost them all, and now nothing remains except my workshop of public scrivener. More than ever my life is a fairy tale, but one in which the bad fairies have had the last word.

Let us take our bearings. As in the photograph of an infant we find, to our surprise, the outlines of an old man's face, so in the heart of the man still burn the passions of the boy. The desperate need of devotion that I felt at eight when seated in the forked lilac tree in Normandy I read *The Young Russian Soldiers,* is the need which today still dictates for me a course of conduct that is so far from easy. The happiness I found in a well-turned phrase at the time when I was discovering the classics at college, remains one of my greatest pleasures, and the first dollars I earned in this country went to collect around me once more Pascal and Bossuet, Retz and Saint-Simon. These scholarly virtues, this thirst for knowledge, this desire to teach, they were what made possible last summer those delightful weeks at Mills College.

Among the characters of fiction I find brothers who help me to understand myself. One is Tolstoy's Prince André; the other is the Dr. Antoine Thibault of Roger Martin du Gard, both curiously moral without knowing why, through simple need of personal integrity. The Ethic of Loyalty, I believe that is the definition of the personal code that controls my actions. It seems to me that in an indifferent universe man cannot rely either on nature, whose laws ignore our feelings, nor on the masses of humanity, whose actions are still natural phenomena, but that he must be able to rely on himself and on like-minded companions. The Kingdom of God can only be in the hearts of the "faithful." I have attempted all my life, by instinct rather than by deliberate choice, to be faithful to agreements, to the persons I love, to my country. Sometimes contradictory loyalties have made the choice difficult, almost impossible. I have done my best, not without anguish, awkwardness and mistakes.

I say: "faithful to my country, to persons," not to a doctrine nor to a sect. Few men are less partisan in spirit than I. I do not like systems and I do not believe in them. I do not concern myself with factional disputes except, as Montesquieu said, "to bewail them." I will accept tomorrow any form of government the French freely choose for themselves provided it assures their union, their independence and their security. But if in effort and in action I conform to the most exact disciplines, I cling tenaciously to liberty of mind. The scrupulous scholars who taught me physics, chemistry and history made me singularly exacting when it comes to determining facts. It is not enough for me that an event should support my thesis for me to believe in its reality. I listen to an adversary with the dangerous desire to understand him. I have difficulty in imagining bad faith, deliberate ill will, Machiavelianism. Hence a naïve trust, countless imprudent actions, and the vain hope of converting fanatics by proving to them that they are wrong. That is to forget that they want to be wrong.

Are the fanatics mistaken? I believe so. But I know that others whom I admire hold the contrary view that these bitter and furious minds are the salt of the earth. "You lack aggressiveness," Lucien Romier used to say to me; and it is true that the moderation which is natural to me robs the mind of its mordancy. "Truth is excessive," our Alain used to teach, "and one must go beyond, well beyond, the point of moderation if one wishes to understand even the simplest thing." And Blake: "The road of excess leads to the palace of wisdom." I see clearly what they all mean by this, but excess is a climate in which I cannot live and in which I do not think wounded France has any chance of regaining her strength. Perhaps all sorts are necessary to make a world: the fanatics to shake the masses out of their lethargy and impartial minds devoid of bitterness, to appease, when dawn appears, the Furies, daughters of the Night.

Misfortune which throws some souls into revolt has cured me of certain prejudices. Because I began life in the camp of those who command, for a long time I had difficulty in understanding the grievances of those who are commanded. I would gladly have said with Goethe: "I prefer an injustice to disorder." Through my misfortunes I was to acquire, I hope, more tolerance, patience and pity. For a long time I believed, too, that every woman whose beauty enchanted me was intelligent, modest and good. Experience has not confirmed this agreeable belief and the cure has been painful. But another fundamental truth that misfortune has taught me is that sacrifice, when it is unmixed with pride, gives man incomparable joys. In fact, the greatest happiness of my life, the brief moments of ecstasy and rapture, have been those when I was delivered through love or charity from vain consideration of myself. To forget oneself is wonderful and in humility, if it be complete and freely accepted, there is immense security. According to the beautiful words of Sygne in Claudel's *Hostage*: "I am then seated in the lowest place, I can no longer be deposed."

Night is falling. Shadows envelop the city while myriads of lights spring up. A long string of rubies mark out Park Avenue; then suddenly they are replaced by a long string of emeralds. In the direction of the East River the earth is more thickly sown with lights than the sky of Périgord was with stars. The nearest ones are fixed; those on the horizon twinkle in the trembling mist, outlining unknown constellations. To the south towers and steeples glow. Illuminated by the white radiance of flood lights, pitted with dark holes, the giant figure of Radio City resembles a Brobdingnagian honeycomb raised against a stormy sky. The lines of the other buildings retreat and are lost in the night, but their bright windows rising skyward to the stars are like the stained glass of an immense cathedral, huge as the city. From these millions of faithful what prayer ascends?

Ah, I know very well what they would ask if they were wise, or rather what they would swear to keep. It is what they have. It is this liberty, this tolerance, these relatively gentle ways. Happy America, remember our mistakes and our anguish; do not believe that the future can be founded upon contempt for the past; reform and preserve; work, do not destroy. What have these many catastrophes taught us? That there is no justice without discipline. I was and I remain a liberal; that is to say, I believe men are happier and better if they enjoy the essential liberties. But I know today that there is no liberty without security, no security without unity. I know that if France wishes to remain a great country after this war she must fill in "the bloody ditch" and reconcile the French.

Last summer when my students at Mills College brought to life some of my heroes I was struck by the predominance in my books of the theme of Reconciliation. *Colonel Bramble* was an effort to make the French understand the English soul; the English the French soul; *Bernard Quesnay* was an effort to show that good faith is to be found on the employers' side as well as on that of the workers; *Atmosphere* was an effort to present fairly the woman's point of view and the man's point of view in a marriage; *The Family Circle* was an effort to reconcile the generations. Always I have believed that words rather than facts pit men against one another and that in silence or in action understanding becomes easier. Even today in this chaos in which a civilization is dying I search anxiously for opportunities of conciliation, and frequent failures have not killed in me the persistent and perhaps absurd hope of seeing love triumph over hate.

Lack of realism? Not entirely, for love is a reality. But no one can bring it about that men shall be devoid of passions. The problem is to have them live under such institutions that these passions themselves will unite and reinforce society. I do not think this is impossible. More than once in the course of history a happy equilibrium has obtained. Never doubt that after this war a new equilibrium will be found. For a decade or a century it will seem stable. Then once more the fragile edifice will begin to tremble. "What are the best laws?" Solon was asked. "For what people and at what period?" he replied. Nations, like individuals, through all their lives ascend a steep slope, flanked by precipices, on which they are never permitted to rest. Each minute is a departure, each day a battle. Life is a game from which no one can withdraw with his winnings at any time.

· · · · · · ·

News of the world still comes to me in my tower. A young man asks to see me. He has arrived from Elbeuf and shows me little photographs in which one can see, reduced to powder, the houses that were the setting of my first years and the ruin of the fine quais of Rouen that I used to admire each morning with never-failing pleasure as I crossed the Boïeldieu Bridge. I question him and discover he is the great nephew of the fire chief with the copper helmet and the red plume who is my earliest memory.

"And what became of the Captain?"

"I only knew him," he says, "as an old family legend . . . His son, my uncle, became a Colonel and died several years ago."

A telephone message informs me that the former headmaster of the Lycée of Rouen has come as a refugee to his daughter's home in New York. I go to see him and am pleased to find an old and charming French scholar who in the time of disaster still wisely quotes the classics.

"How fine it was," he says, "that Court of Honor, the Corneille of David d'Angers and the noble chapel of the Jesuits in front of which I was going to restore the statue of Loyola. . . ."

The mail brings me a letter from Gabriel Hanotaux. Despite his eighty-eight years he remains courageous and brilliant. "Everything," he writes, "is going as well as anything can when all goes ill." A letter from Louis Gillet, excellent and heroic as befits that great-hearted man. A letter from André Gide, grave and affectionate; one from Anne Desjardins who is in Algeria and is bravely trying to supply my children with food, for France is famished and food occupies a pathetically large place in our correspondence. Gérald has found a position and is at work; he has lost twenty pounds. Olivier is in a school in the mountains. Of my daughter and my mother I have no news except through the Family Journal which my mother-in-law edits for us at Essendiéras and which will be for our great grandchildren a precious chronicle of this frightful epoch. From these wounded envelopes, bandaged by the censor's stickers, there escapes an air of sadness. One dreams, one longs to see again those whom one loves and to say to them those things which letters must omit.

But it is time to get back to work. Already in the neighboring room can be heard the clicking of my wife's typewriter. Occupied simultaneously by this book, by the lectures that must be prepared, by the war charities that are at present so difficult to support, we live almost alone and never have a moment's boredom. A happy marriage is a long conversation that always seems too short. Sometimes in the evening when the news from France has been better, when we have been satisfied by the day's work, when the lights of the city in the calm of night afford a sublime spectacle, we experience a fugitive, a culpable, a foolhardy feeling of assurance.

"Alas!" Simone says shivering . . . "What more is going to happen?" She knows now, as I do, that happiness like the pink and white anemones of my childhood is a flower that must not be picked.

Is she right? Will the whistle blast of Destiny in a few seconds put an end to this setting as it once caused the trees of the Bois to vanish? Will Rockefeller Center and the Empire State ascend into the flies? Will the fragile and precarious existence that we have so painfully constructed during this year collapse like the one that formerly seemed to us so substantial? And what shall we see when the footlights come up again, if ever they do come up? No one knows. But timidly, anxiously, ardently we hope that it may be noble and lovely Périgord, a long valley lined with poplars, the red roofs of the farm at Brouillac lighted by the setting sun, and when the night shall come, in a French sky above the plane trees and the cedars, familiar constellations which French voices will call by name in the most beautiful of languages.

New York City.
8 October, 1941.

* * *
* *
*

Circumstances have decreed that this book should not be published until a year after its completion. During that year, the enormous wheels of Time have turned, the United States has entered the war, the lights of New York have been extinguished, following those of Paris and London. The large shadow which envelops the earth has united us across the oceans. But now, on the fringes of this night, it is possible to perceive the light of dawn. The giant forces of America are made up, not only of plants, planes and tanks, but of courage and of faith. In hoc signo vinces.

A. M.

Index

Index